THE PEACE CORPS:

THE EARLY YEARS

Historical Analysis of Development of a New Government Agency Organization and Management of Policy for Public Administration

By

Charles Clyde Jones, Ph.D.

and

Keith Allan Jones, Ph.D.

(Second Edition)

1

The Peace Corps: The Early Years / Historical Analysis of the Development of a New Government Agency Organization and Management of Policy as a Case Study in Public Administration / Second Edition

By Jones, Charles Clyde (1926-1983)/ with edits and additional original material by Jones, Keith Allan (1953-)

A Qualimatics Press imprint of CreateSpace and Amazon.

Based on W.V.U. dissertation (1967) as originally published by University Microfilms as document # 67-11,787.

ASIN: B00NVQR4YU
ISBN-10: 1502795078
ISBN-13: 978-1502795076

1. Political Science 2. Public Administration / I. Title: The Peace Corps: The Early Years. II. Title: Historical Analysis of the Development of a New Government Agency Organization and Management of Policy for Public Administration (2nd Ed.) / Bibliography / Index

DEDICATION

This book is dedicated to Frances E. Jones, Ph.D.,
the wife of Charles Clyde Jones, Ph.D., the author;
who typed and edited the original dissertation of her
husband upon which this book is based, before she was
later to receive her own doctorate several years later.

TABLE OF CONTENTS

FORWARD

The second edition of this book reflects many changes that were recommended by readers of the first edition, as well as focus more directly to readers as was first intended.

This is not a book with footnotes for academic research, as the original doctoral dissertation upon which it is based from 1967 can be obtained at libraries, online, or from the original Univ. Microfilms site as previously cited.

This is also not a book of anecdotal stories by returning Peace Corps volunteers (RPCV). A multitude of such books already exist and there are already many websites to blog and share their stories on internet and social media.

The purpose of this book is simply to provide a case study for Civics and Social Studies classes in Advanced Placement secondary education, and undergraduate college courses, which involve a wide range of political diversity. Most of data upon which this book is based were from the Federal Register, letters or surveys from Peace Corps staff.

Overall, this book demonstrates a high level overview of what is involved when a new Federal agency such as the Peace Corps is created, rapidly organized in the same ways as military organizations prepare for a new war threat, or a new private corporation is built quickly to a secure financial entity; as well as the special considerations that reflect the ongoing back-and-forth of political representations of the Executive Branch and Congress to 're-fund or de-fund' all such governmental organizations and agencies over time.

This book is thus an introduction into the harsh politics Peace Corps faced, as well as many 'Best Practices' of management it demonstrated, to bridge ideals to reality of the goals and best intentions of the American people.

CHAPTER I

EARLY HISTORY OF THE PEACE CORPS

On March 1, 1961 the U.S. Peace Corps fully progressed from an idea to reality. Yet, the idea of the Corps was not so novel when it is seen from developmental and historical perspectives. In a most basic sense, it represented a fundamental secularization of many deeply-rooted and humanitarian non-secular volunteer traditions of our American views, beliefs, and sincere desires to share freedom and prosperity for all peoples.

The first Peace Corps volunteers of the Sixties were actually doing, without religious connotation, what Christian missionaries had done for many years. At a time when people looked increasingly to the government to provide leadership for freedom and security, and when the same needs in underdeveloped nations was great – and when number of U.S. people for volunteer work was so large – the appearance of the U.S. Peace Corps as an American humanitarian innovation was not surprising.

The U.S. Peace Corps also appeared as a natural development in another historical perspective. Nearly twenty years of experience with U.S. Foreign Aid assistance programs had demonstrated that funds and expertise were not always sufficient to bring about economic and social modernization in many underdeveloped countries that had received such Foreign Aid for many decades. Most well-conceived and well-financed programs were most often

9

ineffective due to lack of "effective middle-level manpower and expertise".

The success of non-secular religious missionaries in many under-developed nations for decades and centuries prior to WW II, and most especially Christian Catholic and Protestant missions, were in total very successful in humanitarian efforts that were appreciated and respected by the local people that they helped, as they lived alongside the people of such under-developed nations, and shared their challenges, pain, poverty, and their living conditions. Yet, the people of these same nations were not as positive in their views toward those that came as representatives of U.S. and western European governments, who lived in relative affluence in the capitol cities of such underdeveloped nations, and were regarded as 'Corrupt Colonial' rather than humanitarian, and by 1960 commonly referred to in the of the pro-leftist or even pro-communist local press as altogether to be 'Ugly Americans'.

Thus, the ordinary people in such countries most often saw themselves as 'outsiders', and not likely to benefit from any of the vast great development schemes that were funded with best intentions by U.S. Foreign Aid to their countries. Yet, in the U.S., as the many books and movies that made well-intentioned good people, most of whom fully supported and helped to fund such Christian missionaries through their local churches, it was a very shocking and disturbing that the efforts of our government and business abroad were so badly perceived. Therefore, it was a great hope of all Americans of Good Will that a U.S. Peace Corps could provide a better way for Government and Big Business, to help the ordinary people find ways to work together to improve their local way of life, in a model that was largely built upon Christian missionaries.

In this regard, the Peace Corps was to be a further step in the history of American assistance programs. The Peace Corps was conceived as a 'helping-hand' program to be carried out at the humblest levels of a Rousseau social contact, and to help build personal relationships between Americans of Good Will, in a manner to advance Freedom and Democracy for the entire world.

Pragmatic Origins of the Call for an American Peace Corps

The original Peace Corps volunteers were first directed to teach basic agriculture, industrial techniques, and other secondary school subjects, as were most often requested by potential host nations. The first Peace Corps volunteers were thus intended to help increase practical and mutual understanding as an aid to world peace.

For most Americans, it was difficult to realize that over two-thirds of the people of the world are actually underfed, and hungry each day. At the same time, barely eighteen per cent of the world's current population controlled over two-thirds of the industrial capacity.

The fundamental purpose of the Peace Corps was thus to aid world peace by assisting "poor workers to overcome illiteracy, hunger and disease, and thus to create a bond of friendship." The American foreign assistance experience indicated that nations in the elementary stages of development are "insulated from massive infusions of capital or sophisticated aid." In its most basic sense, the main limits on financial investment in underdeveloped nations were not only security, but infrastructure to support basic human needs to be productive.

Significant basis for origins of the Peace Corps concept were thus largely due to American realization that many billions of dollars spent on foreign aid "had failed to make much of an impression on the ordinary people in the recipient countries." It was recognized by 1960 that a multitude of young Americans with skills, education, and good will could potentially help make a unique contribution "by living with local people, working with them, and imparting some of their knowledge."

Although Foreign Aid had become a solidly established part of the United States foreign policy for almost a century – it was commonly accepted by most Americans that our basic shortcoming had been a failure to comprehend the simple and clear distinction between the needs faced in the underdeveloped countries, and needs faced by post WWII Europe. Although Re-Construction Foreign Aid to European countries after WWII was largely successful, despite in many cases was not partially or fully repaid; yet this was not yet permitted regarding Foreign Aid to under-developed nations, such as in the Third World.

Yet an additional growing concern of the American people was that such Foreign Aid in the third world nations was increasingly to involve payments to dictators and corrupt politicians in such third world countries, which was never to benefit or reach the oppressed people of such countries – and was to instead add 'fuel to the flames' in the message of pro-communist agitators in those countries, and to further spread their convenient myth of the 'Ugly Americans'. Thus, it became a growing hope for all good American people that there could be an effective alternative to better apply American tax dollars for not only secret clandestine operations, but to balance that with much more transparent humanitarian operations of a U.S. Peace Corps Agency.

The foundation of the flourishing industrial economies existed in Europe before World War. In underdeveloped countries, the political and social foundations of flourishing economies had to be re-created.

While assistance to rebuild the many developed nations after WWII had substantial concrete and potential trade benefits, the assistance to underdeveloped nations had limited payback potential.

In simple frank terms, support to the European nations that had formerly been enemies of America were more favorable to bankers, as they most often had very significant collateral to justify Aid, just like loans.

But the Third World had no such collateral; all they had was their underdeveloped mineral resources, which all of the world's bankers and industrialist wanted – yet could not overcome the risk and costs to get to those resources without to eventually have to address the compromises of a traditional colonial business model – which no longer fit into the world in a generation after WWII that was already increasingly independent and to throw off the bonds of colonial abuses of past centuries.

So in 1960, at the time of President Kennedy to be elected, already it was a very different and volatile dangerous world compared to the past decades and centuries – yet, it was also a point of cross-roads – as there were many astute observers at the time who saw many both positive and negative influences.

Yet most were aligning to see benefits of a U.S. Peace Corps, including both the 'power-elite' of both the Left and Right, of the entire American people.

Thus, the lack of basic human needs of the general population needed to support healthy economies in underdeveloped nations seemed to be increasingly recognized as one of the primary reasons for the reduced effectiveness of our foreign-aid programs.

Such foreign aid programs gave funds directly to leaders of such underdeveloped nations without any stipulations other than to assure security around military bases that were regarded as critical to strategic worldwide military deployments.

Despite this was in fact very important to world trade and our international security, it was increasingly apparent that we also needed another layer of U.S. Foreign Policy, which also included direct contact between Americans and people of nations that were strategically important to the U.S.

Accordingly, President John F. Kennedy stated, in March, 1961, that any discussion of foreign aid must begin by recognizing that "existing foreign-aid programs and concepts are largely unsatisfactory and unsuited for our needs and for the needs of the underdeveloped world as we enter the Sixties." This view led to the U.S. Peace Corps.

In the face of such weaknesses and inadequacies, President Kennedy felt that the United States should revise its foreign-aid organizations, and our basic operational concepts to meet the problems then faced, by the creation of a two-tier Foreign Policy.

President Kennedy also stated in the same speech that "no objective supporter of foreign aid can be satisfied with the existing Foreign Aid programs."

William James Proposal for an American Peace Army

The original concept of an American Peace Corp can be largely attributed to American psychologist and philosopher William James. Dr. James published and spoke widely in the 1890's about his concept that a peaceful, constructive work organization for young men should be an alternative to compulsory military service.

This was to be more critical to James after the Boxer Rebellion in China, when thousands of humanitarian

Christian missionaries and their converts were slaughtered by anti-Western Chinese dissidents in the late 1890's.

The concept gained wide support after a speech which William James made before the Universal Peace Conference at Boston in 1900. James was a leading advocate of many American sentiments against drafting young men into compulsory military service even in time of war, and proposed many exemptions from such mandatory conscription – including the origins of what later became 'Conscientious Objector' draft exemptions that were first implemented during WWI in U.S. by many of his students.

This early proposal by American psychologist and philosopher William James was based upon many of his revolutionary but simple theories about development of human beings – which were to involve many pragmatic psychological theories that are widely today to be regarded as more significant and far-reaching than what Sigmund Freud was publishing from Austria at the same time.

William James had an intuitive sense of the impact of biology upon the mind, and postulated that all young men were like young of most animals – including bulls and other wild animals – to have a 'natural need' to 'butt heads'. James regarded such aggression was a 'direct consequence' of very primal needs to engage other males in often violent and ultimately very counter-productive expressions of normal mating drive mechanisms which are increasingly confused in our modern world.

Thus, in line with many of his American Pragmatist philosophies it was the opinion of William James that it was "both possible and necessary to channel young men's aggressive nature away from military drills, and into a more constructive direction; to fight against poverty, ignorance, and disease, instead of to help their fellow humankind".

15

Again, this was in the year 1900 – over a decade before anyone in the world was yet to anticipate World War I; and was instead to be based upon the research of Dr. James upon U.S. Army conscription veterans of the Civil War, who were permanently disturbed after what could called 'Post Traumatic Stress Syndrome' (or PTSD – yet not yet defined in 1900 or even 1918 – but a century later).

William James called for a "counter-conscription' to form an army against nature". What Dr. James called for was to simply organize an 'army of war veterans' – to help them find 'peace with purpose' – and to help others as 'traveling soldiers for peace', across a U.S. homeland.

These ideas were initially related only toward the domestic American sphere – and were notably directed to help a far smaller number of Spanish-American War veterans than were two decades later to return from WWI .

At the time, William James expressed no desire for his army to help indigent people of developing countries. The proposal never became a reality, as the idea of conscription and drafting young men to 'forced labor', for military or charitable services, was repugnant to most Americans; so initial positive reaction quickly evaporated.

Later, James further developed the idea in an essay that was published in 1911 entitled "The Moral Equivalent of War", in which he discussed the need for an outlet for the aggressive impulses that he considered to characterize dangerous violence in modern societies. Dr. James believed that assigning American youth into disciplined peaceful service would endow them with "more healthy progressive sympathies and sober ideas."

By 1911, several leading American religious organizations had adopted many of ideas from William James into voluntary service abroad, as Catholic and

Protestant Christian inter-faith missions, which become increasingly popular in first decade of the 1900's.

Prior to that time, most Christian missions established in foreign countries were very aggressive and highly competitive, and built mostly only churches; but by the first decade of the new century, many inter-faith Christian missions were to increasingly focus on health, education and agriculture infrastructure and buildings.

Thus, despite a general negative reaction by Americans to the concept that U.S. Government would draft young men into any kind of forced service – similar to still recent memories of conscription in the American Civil War – the concept of voluntary service as Christian church sponsored missionaries became increasingly popular with most Americans. Thus, America began in the early 1900's to sponsor many charitable non-secular foreign voluntary missionary programs which contained most aspects of the William James so-called "American Peace Army".

Despite William James first publicly expressed and formulated the concept of an official government sponsored 'alternative young men conscription program' of youth labor service – for which Dr. James was the first to propose also 'equal year of paid college education for first two years of Peace Army voluntary or conscription service', in reality, the precedents of more than a century and a half of toil and effort by "American missionaries was probably even more important as a source of plans and methods for the present Peace Corps."

Since 1809, American churches have been sending missionaries abroad to work in underdeveloped areas. Although all American missionaries had religious teachings as the main focus of their activities, some performed, and are still performing, many tasks in addition to preaching the Christian religious gospels and building churches.

Many American missionaries by 1900 had not only built churches, but also built schools and hospitals to train teachers, doctors, nurses, and technicians.

However, this trend was to increase dramatically following the proposals of William James, the Philippines Teaching Project, and the global sympathies of Americans after WWI, as was advocated by President Wilson in creation of the League of Nations.

Notably, after the Chinese Boxer Rebellion in 1898, many multi-faith and humanitarian organizations were to partner with more traditional Christian missionary organizations for projects that were more often to include building of schools and clinics than churches.

The foreign missions by American churches built upon all of these concepts to create independent volunteer organizations that embodied much the future Peace Corps efforts. Both were to focus more on humanitarian goals.

By 1960, American missionaries had become a very potent force to build good will between America and its allies overseas.

The statistics are very revealing to the American people "400 separate religious agencies, maintain 34,000 missionaries abroad; 27,000 Protestant and 7,000 Catholic."

The extent of the missionary overseas coverage was significant, as a number of missionary programs were similar to the original U.S. Peace Corps. By 1960, emphasis had been placed less on religion and more on humanitarian charity missions to assure material well-being of all people with more non-denominational Judeo-Christian charitable coordination – and more often to coordinate with the League of Nations, and later the United Nations.

Experience of Thomasites in the Philippines

One such program was already being organized at the time of William James's Universal Peace Congress address. In 1901, following the end of the Spanish-American War, American Army soldiers in the Philippines were asked by public relations branches of the U.S. Army to stay on, to teach English and help to gain support of the native populations – and a great number of them accepted the challenge.

There are many conflicting historical accounts for the source of the origin of this movement. Equally many attribute the idea to have originated by U.S. Army Public Relations; early Philippine democratic government; existing Christian Catholic and Protestant missionaries, and even a group of soldiers onboard the U.S.S. Thomas transport ship awaiting return of all Army veterans to the U.S.

Most likely it was all of the above, as a growing grass-roots movement at the end of the Spanish-American War, who were all excited at prospect of making the Philippines a 'protectorate' of the United States and to advance the ideals of freedom and democracy.

But the most important point was that press across the U.S. inspired Americans to secure the funding support of Congress, and was thus also part of the Republican platform that helped to elect Spanish-American War hero, Teddy Roosevelt, as the next President.

In philosophy, in numbers, and in motivation – this experiment in government-sponsored humanitarian Foreign Aid was very similar to our present-day Peace Corps – starting as a simple civilian teaching program by Army soldier veterans in a foreign country. Later in 1901, "a Philippines teaching program was transferred to civilian authority, and a fully volunteer program was organized by the U.S. Army to build, furnish and support local schools as young English speaking teachers."

Six hundred U.S. Army soldier veterans were selected for the first group. During the thirty-year life of this program, between 1901 and 1933, a total of over twelve thousand men and women, with preference for retired Army volunteers, were to serve alongside active military public relations organizations. They were taught local language and got the same as basic U.S. Army pay.

The first group "arrived in the Philippines on the Army transport U.S.S. Thomas – and as a result acquired a lasting name – the Thomasites." These volunteers regularly joined the original 600 American soldiers who had been given the choice of being remobilized in the Philippines to be civilian teachers working for the Army, as 'Good Will US Army Operation' – to 'win friendly hearts and minds'.

Many soldiers who had no family connections volunteered to work as English teachers. Thus, many American soldiers from the Spanish-American War stayed on in the Philippines, and lived in small one-room schoolhouses, built by the Army Corps of Engineers – where they taught English in elementary and secondary education similar to one-room schools in rural America.

Thousands of Filipinos, including Ambassador Romulo, had their first education from such Army built one-room schoolhouses by American civilian and former soldier teachers. Their work was performed under serious handicaps and security risks, as they lacked official government sanction by the U.S. government – so as an independent volunteer organization, despite they worked closely with the U.S. Army, they often labored with no military protection and inadequate health facilities.

The Thomasites endured the same hardships as the local people, which greatly increased the respect and trust of the Filipino people, and continued to be one of the most important factors behind the close bond between the Philippines and United States of America.

After three decades of this program, this volunteer service had helped to establish a strong bond between the two people's loyalty and friendship that were critical to defeat of Japanese invaders during World War II.

Origins of the American Civilian Conservation Corps

In addition to the first public programs that can be traced directly to William James proposals were the youth work organizations initiated by administrations of President Franklin D. Roosevelt.

Although no conscription was involved, the purpose was to employ young people for constructive work, and give them their first employment opportunities.

Notably, many of the 'public work' programs that were to be developed and implemented under President Roosevelt in the 1930's had roots in many of the proposals fully 3 decades earlier by Dr. William James.

However, there was also considerable evidence that many of these programs were also proposed directly to President Franklin Roosevelt by his Vice President Wallace, and related to their common beliefs as Free Masons, and in alignment with writings of President Thomas Jefferson as well as U.S. founding father Benjamin Franklin.

It was also notable Vice President Wallace had been a Republican, and first to serve a president to come from a different party.

The work of the Civilian Conservation Corps as was designed by Vice President Wallace and first implemented by President Franklin Roosevelt greatly resembled the Peace organizations William James had first described – except that members of the Roosevelt C.C.C. were chosen only from indigent and displaced families.

They wore uniforms and lived in field camps performing conservation work. This early organization was to be first implemented under a Presidential Executive Order by FDR. To many during the same time as much turmoil in Europe, this was painfully similar to Nazi youth.

Two years later, the U.S. National Youth Administration was established, and came even closer to the ideals and purposes of the modern Peace Corps.

The members of the National Youth Administration did not live in camps or wear uniforms. Yet, only a few years later, NYA was dissolved and folded into full military US Army WWII service commissions, after attack on Pearl Harbor – and did wear uniforms.

British International Voluntary Services (IVS)

After WWII, the voluntary service organization, that many had pointed to as a related prototype of the U.S. Peace Corps, was the International Voluntary Services (IVS), which was first organized as a British nonprofit organization in 1953. This organization was committed to the idea that American youth could make a valuable contribution to American "foreign policy by establishing contacts with people of other countries, through a service program which the people of the host countries would want and in which they would participate."

The International Voluntary Services (IVS) grew out of a fear that British and U.S. foreign-aid programs were not succeeding because the International Cooperation Administration (ICA) agreements were forced to operate on an impersonal government-to-government basis.

Most people in underdeveloped countries resided in villages seldom serviced by British, or even American, local volunteer services representatives.

The British ICA, as well as the AID in U.S., were aware that something needed to be done at the grass roots, and decided to send young people just out of college to a foreign country under a two-year contract program.

In order that the U.K International Voluntary Services as founded in 1953 would not outbid the military services for talented people, it was decided to give IVS volunteers the same pay they would get in military service, and to provide all necessary expenses at the same level afforded to their nation's military personnel.

The British International Voluntary Services started work mainly in remote rural areas. The projects were at first paid for by private foundations, but by 1960 most were either under contract with International Cooperation Administration, or Agency for International Development, with supervision by the World Bank.

The volunteers worked under the general supervision of IVS technicians overseas. Their primary goal was to create good will and understanding through being good neighbors and showing local people how to benefit more efficiently from the assistance they received from various English-speaking foreign-aid programs up to 1966.

From 1956 to 1964, the International Voluntary Services, initially a quasi-religious organization, conducted eleven projects in nine countries, mostly in Africa and the Middle East, but also in Asia as well.

Eight of these projects had been operated by a contract with the International Cooperation Administration and others by contracts or grants from exclusively secular private foundations, which increasingly funded IVS.

The volunteers had been mainly assigned to projects for agriculture and village development. The functions and purposes of this organization were similar to idea of U.S. Peace Corps and provided a proven prototype.

It should thus be noted that the Peace Corps was not solely an American idea. This also included some similar programs that had been operated by other nations, including the United Nations, and other non-religious secular organizations, with funding by private foundations and corporate sponsors, as well as Christian church groups.

British Voluntary Service Organizations (VSO)

Several countries had organizations similar to private voluntary charitable organizations and agencies in U.S. and Britain. According to the United Nations Educational, Scientific, end Cultural Organization (UESCO), more than 300,000 volunteers from forty-one countries went abroad by 1960 for varying periods of time to work in technical-assistance programs.

The foreign organization that came closest to embodying the U.S. Peace Corps concept was the Voluntary Service Overseas (VSO) program of Great Britain. This program was very similar to the International Voluntary Services (IVS), but without allowing for religious or charitable foundation sponsorship. In effect, VSO was a new non-government standard for humanitarian aid.

The Voluntary Service Overseas program was an independent organization, organized within Great Britain – but it was gradually becoming more officially government sponsored, as it requested and received more funding from U.K. government than private foundations.

It was started barely 2 years before the U.S. Peace Corps in 1958, to give young British men and women the opportunity to serve for a year or more in developing countries, most often with parallel corporate sponsorship.

Voluntary Service Overseas sent carefully selected volunteers to needy underdeveloped countries to serve in many fields of endeavor. The volunteers had to be at least eighteen to go overseas, and are usually recruited either before or soon after their university educations.

Others had been recruited for VSO from industrial apprenticeships, and had been fully sponsored financially as employees of British or U.S. firms.

The VSO volunteers were sent overseas to specific locations deemed useful to build international business partnerships that were regarded as valuable to western corporations and people – in order to "bridge the gap until a sufficient number of indigenous people could be trained to meet the needs of their own country."

The established reputation and prestige of the British VSO was as the first independent non-religious technical organization, and resulted in a steady flow of application for their services by third world nations.

The 1960 cost of administration, selection procedures, briefing courses, the transport of volunteers to and from their assignments, insurance, and other expenses overseas average from $900 to $1800 for each VSO volunteer per year (thus between $9,000 to $18,000 USD per year compared to 2010).

Notably, this was only between 10-20% of the costs of each American Peace Corps volunteer when it first started in 1961, but the difference was supported by American taxpayers, as budgeted by the U.S. Congress.

The differences between the U.S. Peace Corps costs versus the VSO volunteers were explained to Congress as due to the fact that VSO was an essentially an independent organization that relied heavily upon subsidies from private foundations and private corporations for up to 80% or more of actual costs to support each volunteer.

The costs of the Voluntary Service Overseas volunteers had to be met by generous assistance provided by various trusts, foundations, and sponsorship of public and private industry.

For example, shipping firms have provided free passes for unlimited personal travel of VSO volunteers. The VSO continued during the same years as the early days of the U.S. Peace Corps to propose solutions by British Government, which competed for host nation projects.

The British Government had demonstrated its confidence in the Voluntary Service Overseas by making a grant to cover three fourths of the cost of the program. VSO also required that the host country must provide all board and lodging, medical care, and cost of any necessary local travel. The Peace Corps, as an official agency of the U.S. government, paid all costs out of U.S. tax revenues.

Training for the British VSO was very simple compared to the elaborate U.S. Peace Corps training program. The VSO orientation program lasted only one week, and mostly informed the volunteers of problems they were likely to encounter -- and suggested solutions.

VSO provided some information about the type of work they would be performing, and advised volunteers how to prepare themselves to tackle their projects successfully on their own, with whatever level of assistance was available from their corporate or foundation sponsors.

The British VSO originally was conceived as sending "young people from United Kingdom to do voluntary work in developing countries of the British Commonwealth." Yet, between its inception in 1958 and 1965, the program expanded all non-Communist countries.

The VSO program was originally very modest in size, starting with only eighteen volunteers in 1958. By 1961, it had expanded to one hundred and sixty volunteers sent to thirty-eight countries.

The original VSO volunteers in 1958 included many skilled workers from British corporate sponsors, and was more practical that academic.

The first VSO pilot program specifically for college graduates was launched in 1962, when thirty-six volunteers from leading British academic institutions were assigned to third world teaching posts in their leading English-speaking 'world-class' universities.

By 1964, three hundred and thirty graduates were recruited to fill teaching, agricultural, and social welfare posts in various countries. Then the number was leveled off at three hundred and fifty per year forward by 1966.

The British Voluntary Service Overseas was by 1966 drifting more toward the American Peace Corps model. However, the American Peace Corps model had a far wider presence and visibility, and as a fully U.S. government funded agency, supported far more volunteers.

As in the U.S. Peace Corps, most of the British VSO volunteers served as teachers; but many more than in U.S. Peace Corps served in local government services administration, than in engineering or in agriculture, and were more like British 'Foreign Service' adjutants.

The VSO usual length of service was one year; but many decided to stay on for an additional year, often at their own expense – or with a negotiation of extension with their corporate or foundation sponsors.

The British volunteers give their service freely to VSO, and were paid only by their private corporate and foundation sponsors; and despite the host country bore the cost and responsibility for all supervision and administration, host nations often preferred to pay these costs versus no cost to them to request our Peace Corp volunteers – fearing complications of U.S. involvements..

This was confusing, as many VSO volunteers were not only sponsored by British corporations, but often paid full salaries as employees on-loan from those corporations, often at 5 to 10 times more than U.S. Peace Corp volunteers. Eventually, it began to concern U.S. State Department officials as well as Congress there was fear of retaliation from the enemies of U.S. and western governments, to introduce even more dire complications.

Proposals of Heinz Rollman and Eleanor Roosevelt

In the United States political arena, the idea for a "Peace Corps" type of worldwide organization was first widely and openly proposed by a WWII refugee from Germany named Heinz Rollman. His ideas were warmly received and promoted by Eleanor Roosevelt as a tribute to her late husband President Franklin D. Roosevelt after the end of WWII.

Heinz Rollman believed that organizations such as the League of Nation, and United Nations, had their place in diplomacy and managing impending outbreaks of war; yet were too bureaucratic and detached from the people to be able to "build from grass roots for future world peace".

During the first five years after World War II, Heinz Rollman took on an avid letter-writing campaign. As a naturalized American citizen, his letters were directed to top U.S. government officials, emphasizing that "the best way to win peace is to solve problems to help elevate underdeveloped nations, to better leverage availability of their natural resources, and in the process help to finance elevation of their education, health and prosperity".

Throughout the 1950's Heinz Rollman continued his campaign for support of an American Peace Army Plan, writing letters and discussing personally with leading U.S. government officials, including President Eisenhower, who responded with usual form letters from his WH staff. However, his letters to Eleanor Roosevelt got more personal responses, and several personal introductions.

The direct activity of Mr. Rollman was totally unable to attain much response, as he lacked wide awareness of the American public.

Then Rollman approached Eleanor Roosevelt regarding his many proposals to the U.S. government for programs to apply U.S Civilian Conservation Corp projects with American volunteers to assist local workers in European WWII Reconstruction efforts, with funding that was already committed and budgeted by U.S. government as part of several post-WWII agreements that were negotiated by U.S. and its Allies, as the Marshall Plan.

Eleanor Roosevelt encouraged Heinz Rollman, and it was at her suggestion that he print and send his concepts of a world Peace Army in his book titled 'World Re-Construction", which he self-published in 1954.

Although self-published, Mr. Rollman gave wide distribution of his printed book among congressional leaders and government officials, and delivered copies personally at their offices, along with letters of introduction from Mrs. Roosevelt.

Although copies of his book have not been preserved in its entirety, Rollman made a great impression on many emerging leaders in American politics of the 1950's, many of whom referenced Rollman's book in their own writings and speeches.

Eleanor Roosevelt was also so moved by the letters from Heinz Rollman that she wrote personal letters and made phone calls in which she indicated that Rollman seemed to have the "same inspiration and sentiments" as her late husband, President Franklin D. Roosevelt.

She made many personal contacts to arrange direct meetings for Rollman. However despite an introduction from Mrs. Roosevelt, Rollman received a tacit cool reception from Eisenhower and his White House.

Part of this reaction may have been partisan, as Vice President Nixon was openly against any 'Peace Army'.

Yet President Eisenhower was reported to have commented that the concept was 'interesting – but naive at a time when we face military aggression from communism around the world'.

Therefore, Eisenhower was to accept several meetings and calls to discuss with Rollman and Eleanor Roosevelt, despite V.P. Nixon opposed their ideas.

Mr. Rollman had proposed an all-embracing 'Future Peace Allies' movement among the countries of the world, beginning in the United Nations. Rollman wrote:

"The nations of the world can organize as effectively and efficiently for peace as for war".

One his ideas that he proposed to the United Nations was for World Re-Construction that called for the U.N.to "establish a Peace Army consisting of Three Million men and women, who would be sent to the world underprivileged and underdeveloped countries."

Despite many nations of the early United Nations were very sympathetic to proposals by Heinz Rollman and Eleanor Roosevelt – the immediate reaction was commonly that 'maybe if he had proposed 300 or 3,000 – but to request even a so-called Peace Army of 3 Million just a decade after WWII seems dangerous and perilous'.

In response, Rollman alone without further support from Eleanor Roosevelt that "a United Nations Peace Army will end imbalances between countries'.

After this, very little was heard from Rollman or Eleanor Roosevelt about the concept after it was first introduced in the mid 1950's.

However, despite missteps of Rollman to introduce this concept, the idea was to remain in American memory of press for the next decade, and to rise again.

Point Four Proposals of Cong. Reuss and Sen. Neuberger

Of much more tangible value in the original political movement to establish a U.S. Peace Corps involved the efforts by Democratic Congressman Henry Reuss from Wisconsin.

Although Congressman Reuss had said that he was only indirectly aware of proposals from Rollman as personally promoted by Eleanor Roosevelt – due to discussions with other Congressman – he contended his own passion to establish an American Peace Corps was a direct result of his own very personal experience while on a Congressional mission to Southeast Asia in 1957.

Congressman Reuss was among many who were concerned about the influence of the power vacuum that was created by the withdrawal of French, Dutch and other European nations from Southeast Asia in the 1950's, and the rising influence of communism as it could impact American influence on Philippines and other Pacific allies.

Reuss was also aware after attending over a dozen conferences on American foreign-aid programs that many already agreed that U.S. must find ways to improve its impact abroad – as foreign-aid funding alone was being matched by communists – and there was growing consensus direct contact at a personal level was critical.

While Reuss was on a Congressional visit to Cambodia in 1957, he was made aware he was riding on a thirty million dollar highway built with American funds.

The driver informed him that the highway was based on same engineering used by Eisenhower to build Interstates in the U.S., yet had very little traffic – as there were very few automobiles in all of Cambodia.

This was to lead Reuss was to comment later that "these funds could have been better used in the U.S.".

Reuss was told that the highway was mainly used by Cambodians leading their buffalo along the shoulder of the highway – which he was able to confirm after seeing no other automobiles all morning, yet dozens of buffalo led by local farmers walked barefoot on concrete pavement.

A little later that day, in the remote jungles of Cambodia, he saw and talked to a team of four idealistic American graduate school student volunteers working with a grant for UNESCO, who were "going from village to village repairing schools that the French had neglected and abandoned after a hundred years of colonialism."

This experience was credited by Reuss as the critical moment when he came to understand the need for an American Peace Corps as a way to build for peace – just as Rollman and Eleanor Roosevelt had advocated – and he dedicated himself to do all he could to make this happen to show to the the world that "We are not Ugly Americans – We are your Best Last Hope of Freedom!".

The four Americans Congressman Reuss met that day were all working for the United Nations Educational, Scientific, and Cultural Organization (UNESCO).

What made the deepest impression on Congressman Reuss was that – although all of the four

American volunteers had greatest respect for the United Nations, they all indicated that they felt limited by the fact, just as Rollman had observed, that the United Nations was mostly an organization to respond to threats of war and respond with diplomacy and threat of military action – and although there were divisions within UN such as UNESCO and WHO to provide humanitarian assistance – there was as yet no formal commitment by any nation including U.S. to simply "help people help each other" at a local level – and despite millions of dollars in U.S. Foreign Aid, very little was actually reaching the local communities.

The very simple but honest expert opinions expressed by these four young American UNESCO volunteers were what became known as the "Point Four", or "Four Point" priorities of emerging nation needs for assistance from developed nations.

"The Top Four Priorities are: 1) Education; 2) Community Services; 3) Healthcare; and 4) Sanitation."

Congressman Reuss often commented that 'the order might change but these are the four most important things underdeveloped nations need first – not highways, not banking, not international trade, not even military weapons or training – these four points must be first simply achieved before these underdeveloped nations are ready for anything more'. This simple movement of "Four Points First" has since been the basis of all of the most practical measures of humanitarian success since 1958.

When he first returned to the United States, Reuss decided to see what could be done to fix U.S. foreign-aid programs. As a result, Congressman Reuss proposed what he called the "Point Four Youth Corps" as a solution that fit in within all of the issues he experienced in Cambodia, and in his chance encounter with the four American UNESCO volunteers -- whom he credited with the origins of "Four Points" that first brought them to his attention. American UNESCO volunteers. His proposed solution was first announced in a speech at Cornell University in 1958, and widely republished in the world press. It is also notable that Cornell University was to take special interest in this proposal, and was critical in both the creation of the U.S. Peace Corps, as well as its evaluation for decades.

Congressman Reuss found the response to his proposal overwhelming, and he continued to discuss the idea and to promote a "Point Four Youth Corps". The proposal was refined "through meetings and conversations with government officials, religious and welfare leaders, and university teachers", and was widely accepted worldwide.

By the end of 1959, Reuss had prepared legislation which he submitted to Congress early in 1960, calling for a study of his proposal.

At the same time, his colleague Richard Neuberger, Senator from Oregon, submitted similar legislation in the Senate.

Neuberger commented that he was co-sponsoring the passage of the House bill by Congressman Reuss; however he also commented that the concept behind the bill was already widely discussed, and had been growing in support in the Congress and Senate for over a decade.

The authorization for the study became law in June, 1960, and appropriation made in September, 1960. The Mutual Security Act of 1960 made available by amendment $10,000 for study of a "Point Four Youth Corps". This was a small sum even in 1960; however it was a very unusual budget commitment to be passed across bipartisan Senate and Congress so quickly at that time.

The contract for this particular study was awarded to the Colorado Research Foundation, and placed under supervision of Dr. Maurice Albertson. This Colorado State

University research report was fully completed in May, 1961, yet a preliminary copy of the report was given to the new President John F. Kennedy in February, 1961. Notably, much of the original U.S. Peace Corps organization and policy were based on this study.

The active support and public discussion of Congressman Reuss proposals for a youth corps were significant for a number of reasons.

His proposal specifically tied the idea to United States foreign-aid programs and specified it should be organized and administered by the United States government aid agencies.

The proposal was immediately adopted by the Organization of Young Democrat Clubs on college campuses, known widely as "Young Democrats".

These clubs began promoting the idea throughout the country, especially in cities with universities, as a reason for young people to vote Democratic.

Notably, the organization known as the "Young Republicans" also widely promoted acceptance of the concept of a U.S. Peace Corps a few months later – however, only after results of the 1960 Presidential election.

The National College Student Association also became active in the early popularization of the idea of a U.S. Peace Corps.

The activities of these student organizations were responsible, to a considerable extent, for the "spontaneous" enthusiasm which greeted John F. Kennedy's proposal for a Peace Corps in Presidential campaign of 1960.

Their enthusiasm, as well as continued efforts by Congressman Henry S. Reuss, also led to the first specific plan for a U.S. Peace Corps, which was submitted to the Senate by Hubert Humphrey on June 15, 1960.

American Peace Corps Proposal by Sen. Hubert Humphrey

Senator Hubert Humphrey was yet another Congressional leader in the front rank in the development and eventual establishment of the American Peace Corps.

Humphrey said he first came upon the idea when he observed the work of the American Friends Services Committee. The Senator was impressed with their work, and also proposed the idea to college groups during the late 1950's, where he made many speeches – and spoke directly to college students about their concerns and opinions about future needs of American Foreign Policy.

The American college groups Senator Humphrey spoke to were very enthusiastic; yet at the time in the early 1950's the concept was not taken seriously in official U.S. government circles. Yet, members of his staff were assigned to research the idea for him, and the results of these studies increased his fervor for the program.

On June 15, 1960, Senator Humphrey formally introduced legislation in the U.S. Senate calling for the establishment of an American Peace Corps -- which was the first time that this name was officially used. Bill S3675 was introduced "to establish a Peace Corps of young men to assist the peoples of underdeveloped areas of the world to combat poverty, disease, illiteracy, and hunger."

Senator Humphrey realized that the introduction of the bill was very late in the session, but he wanted the bill to be printed and appropriately referred so that it could be the subject of discussion and intensive study during the coming months approaching the Presidential election.

There were last minute changes submitted to include young women as well as young men however most did not get approved in time to quickly pass the bill; this slight was later unfortunately to hurt Sen. Humphrey with women voters in his own future political campaigns.

The purpose of the bill, according to Senator Humphrey, was to develop a genuine people-to-people program in which "talented and dedicated young American men will teach agricultural and industrial techniques, literacy, English language, other school subjects, sanitation and health procedures in Asia, Africa, and Latin America."

This Senate bill was not meant primarily to be an anti-communist measure; however, even in 1960, that was a critical issue to help get any bill passed quickly with bipartisan support, and Humphrey was quick to respond.

When asked by the press if an American Peace Corps as an alternative to military action against communist aggression, Senator Humphrey was to say: "even if Communism did not exist, there still would be just as much need for action to develop the potential of the underdeveloped nations."

As Senator Humphrey also commented at the same time regarding the growing impending threat of communism: "Events that formerly took centuries are now taking place in a few years, and we have to catch up".

Senator Humphrey, as well as a solid bipartisan majority of both houses of Congress, felt there was sufficient evidence in hand to justify moving directly to the formation of an American Peace Corps, rather than waiting for additional studies, such as "Point Four Youth Corp" study at Colorado State Univ., still as yet to be completed.

Thus, the overall concept of an American Peace Corps was widely accepted within the bipartisan Congress and U.S. government to be a people-to-people approach, which they believed was more often missing in U.S. foreign aid programs, which were widely regarded as mostly payments to heads of foreign political regimes that rarely resulted in any real benefits to people in those countries.

According to Senator Humphrey, a 'tidal wave' of mail praised the Peace Corps idea. The Senator was also heartened by the fact that there was little Congressional opposition to the legislation.

Yet another observation should be made about the timing of the efforts by Senator Humphrey to push through this Bill so quickly during a presidential election campaign – since it was already clear Kennedy would be Democrat presidential nominee; yet many political analysts believed Humphrey was being considered Vice President.

However, in many was felt his legislation was 'grand standing', and would have been more appropriately introduced after the Colorado State University research report was completed and published.

But in response, Humphrey claimed that he desired the bill to be the subject of discussion and study within broad awareness of the American people, without waiting for several years to get recommendations from the Colorado State University study as requested by Congress.

Shortly thereafter the idea was projected into the public consciousness to a greater extent than Senator Humphrey or any previous advocates of an American Peace Corp could have hoped. The Peace Corps concept became a major issue in the 1960 Presidential campaign.

Peace Corps Movement Impact on 1960 Pres. Campaign

There was no evidence that at the start of the campaign either candidate possessed the idea that a U.S. youth peace corps would rank highly with American voters.

However, there was substantial historical evidence that Democrat Candidate Senator John F. Kennedy was made critically aware of the idea by Democrat party strategists as early as February, 1960.

Kennedy was first asked about the American Peace Corp proposal at the College News Conference that month, where he seemed extremely well prepared to make an impassioned and rational argument to support an American Peace Corps as an alternative to elevating military threats by communist super-powers in the Cold War.

His responses did seem very close to the press releases issued by Senator Humphrey's office. Regardless, Kennedy opposition was blind-sided, and largely frustrated that this balanced approach resonated with voters.

Although the platforms of both political parties expressed in general terms an aim to help improve the security and living standards in underdeveloped countries, during the campaign up until that time, neither political party proposed a specific suggestion to channel the energies of young men and women into such an international goodwill technical-assistance program.

Yet, despite Kennedy continued to push the concept of an American Peace Corps, and despite Humphrey had spear-headed to get a specific bill passed to support it, Kennedy did not give any specific details about how he would implement such an American Peace Corps.

But during the summer and fall of the 1960 Presidential campaign, both political parties leaked anonymous descriptions of an American Peace Corps organization that were floated and proposed without official confirmation on either front.

Meanwhile, Heinz Rollman in North Carolina was running for Congress on his World Peace Army Plan as a Republican. With virtually no support for Rollman by even Eleanor Roosevelt (who was reportedly offended that

Rollman was to run for Congress as a Republican), Rollman was to receive less that 2% of the popular vote.

Yet, Heinz Rollman was reportedly to have had direct contact to influenced journalist and Democrat speech writer Bill Moyers – later appointed Deputy Director of the Peace Corps – who also supervised the campaign activity for Vice-Presidential candidate Lyndon Johnson – and wrote at least two campaign speeches proposing the American Peace Corps as a program that was touted as a primary responsibility of Johnson if Kennedy was elected president – despite no such official confirmation or related statements were ever issued by Kennedy; and both parties continued to ' float' the idea.

Meanwhile, Chester Bowles, Presidential Candidate John P. Kennedy's foreign-relations adviser during the Presidential campaign, also used the Peace Corps idea as speech material.

Yet Bowles only raised the Peace Corps issue in speeches for other Democrat candidates to bring to a general public awareness, and made no statements either way about how Kennedy felt about the issue. Instead, most Democrat Congressional candidates made vague blanket statements that they would help Kennedy to enact the views of the people on such issues if elected.

Meanwhile, Victor Reuther, of the United Auto Workers, expressed favorable opinions on the Peace Corps concept in speeches and union articles, and asked for feedback on the concept of an American Peace Corps; after which he reported to the press that UAW workers were very much in favor of an American Peace Corps.

At the working level of the Democrat Party, the American youth peace corps concept was discussed as way to excite and assure high turn-out of Young Democrats in the 1960 presidential election.

Thus, the first official mention of a Peace Corps by Democratic candidates in 1960 came only in the form of quoted endorsements by Young Democrats chapters at college campuses in state elections, and their publications.

In a message to young first-time voters on October 5, 1960, just weeks before the election, Kennedy proposed a specific plan for young people that would not only include opportunities for college students, but also equally all young people with skills and willingness to serve America in a peaceful way, as a potential alternative to a draft (as the War in Viet Nam was already being feared).

This was also an issue that was increasingly to be presented by American TV and newspapers to influence young men approaching draft age and their families, as the prospects of a war (or wars) seemed increasingly likely.

The mail response began immediately after the message, and increased steadily throughout the campaign.

The first time that Presidential candidate Kennedy proposed the Peace Corps idea was on October 14, 1960, in an extemporaneous speech delivered at the University of Michigan. Within two hours there were over 9,000 students and more than double that two hours later, who cheered Kennedy and delayed his departure till the next day.

This was within the final days before the Presidential Election, and it is also notable Kennedy surged far ahead in the polls to predict him to be election.

The first major speech directed specifically on the topic of an American Peace Corps was delivered two weeks later at San Francisco on November 2, 1960 after the election of Kennedy as next President was assured.

The material in this first specific speech to propose an American Peace Corps was based upon interviews of students at the University of Michigan by speech writer Samuel P. Hayes, which he documented in several academic articles to describe origins for the speech.

Concurrently, as the topic of an American Peace Corps grew to resonate with young American voters, more extensive speech material for the Kennedy campaign had been developed by writer Archibald Cox, an experienced speech writer for the Democrat party.

This speech built upon the proposals of Rollman, Reuss and others up to include Senator Humphrey; but Archibald Cox greatly expanded all previous proposals for an American Peace Corp to focus more to include women, and the age requirement was relaxed to include seniors – who were for the very first time mentioned as potential Peace Corps volunteers.

This speech material written by Cox, and others, were customized for Kennedy as well as other Democrat candidates in the 1960 election, and touched off a great wave of enthusiasm to lift the idea to a higher level.

John F. Kennedy thus officially adopted the concept of an American Peace Corps, as an alternative as singular military action in response to the threat of world communism in the Cold War, as one of his primary campaign promises.

If elected, Kennedy committed to make an American Peace Corps an issue of national policy.

Letters and telegrams, as well as a flood of new campaign contributions, flowed into the Kennedy campaign offices at an ever increasing rate. The political process was at work, and the foundations for an American Peace Corp were politically assured.

Although the Nixon campaign strategists tried to also adopt it, they were increasingly unable to hold on to voter groups who were increasingly excited about issues such as a new American Peace Corp, without risking to lose part of a more politically conservative Republican base.

Peace Corps Memo in 1961 by Dr. Max Millikan of MIT

Dr. Max P. Millikan, Director of the Center for International Studies, Massachusetts Institute of Technology, published a report in January, 1961, regarding an "International Youth Service" (which was easily known at the time it was published to be to mean an 'American Peace Corp). The report had originally been requested by Chester Bowles for an undisclosed Democrat candidate in December, 1960.

The problem, as stated in the study, was to create a new government agency which could match the needs of the underdeveloped countries for trained manpower with the increasing supply of dedicated and highly educated young people in U.S. willing to participate in constructive activity to help people in underdeveloped countries.

The Millikan MIT memorandum contained clear-cut statements as to the need for independent person-to-person contact as well as foreign aid to governments that rarely benefit their individual citizens.

This MIT memorandum set forth the following recommendations: "1) the program should be launched on a small pilot basis; 2) the standards of selection should be maintained at a high level; and 3) volunteers should serve in operational capacity and not simply advisory consultants". The recommendations were accepted by Congress.

These recommendations became the 3 Prime Directives the fundamental basis for all future American Peace Corps policy, despite the Millikan Report did not specifically address and American Peace Corps.

Millikan was to view that such a U.S. International Youth Service should include all youth, regardless of education, and anticipated a worldwide youth movement of all democratic nations.

Dr. Millikan recommended that such programs be established as a practical way of matching the enthusiasm and dedication of all American young people for International Service with the equally great manpower needs of the underdeveloped countries.

Memo by Prof. Hayes in 1961 to Kennedy White House

Professor Samuel P. Hayes of the University of Michigan also prepared a memorandum published early in 1961 that outlined an idea for international youth service. This memorandum was also requested personally by Kennedy speech writer Archibald Cox in September, 1960.

Dr. Hayes's memo was one of the first to express the "middle manpower theory".

This theory proposed that ratio of unskilled labor in underdeveloped countries was most often in direct proportion to the number of top leadership in developing countries who personally benefit from foreign aid in exchange for political stability, yet the lack of parity to local citizens eventually results in reduction of political stability.

Hayes provided evidence that the more that top leadership of nation receiving U.S. foreign aid keep for their own personal benefits, rather than distributing to their citizens, the more likely that the citizens of such nations will feel oppressed – often to the point of revolt.

In order to prevent this, Hayes concluded that there are only two options: either abruptly cut off the foreign aid directly to such leaders, or gradually phase out such payments to corrupt leaders – and instead build up programs for local assistance such as in the proposed concept for a U.S. Peace Corps.

This report by Dr. Hayes also stressed that a critical gap existed at the lower and middle unskilled labor levels for people in such nations to develop their own skilled labor without help from developed nations.

But also more important Hayes stressed that most important for successful assistance was middle level where skilled technical managers and professionals can best help to direct and mentor even unskilled workers to be most productive in rapid progress in underdeveloped societies.

Dr. Hayes observed such mid-level skills could be mentored and taught by volunteers from developed nations to local unskilled and semi-skilled workers to take on these roles, he concluded that this was a critical first step – which could be quickly addressed by the mass mobilization of recent American college graduates as 'advisors'.

This study thus recommended an American Peace Corps should seek as its greatest priority to fill this gap.

The central purpose of an International Peace Corps, according to Professor Hayes, was to help provide the missing element in the socioeconomic structure of those nations that desire to speed up their development:

"The additional middle manpower to leverage both their internal unskilled and semi-skilled resources with American college graduates for middle technical and business management would best supplement American Peace Corps technical assistance, aid, and investment.

This added element would have a more significant impact on the social and psychological changes in underdeveloped countries."

The report was well received and taken into account to organize the U.S. Peace Corp.

Preliminary Peace Corps Report by Colorado State in 1961

On February 27, 1961, Dr. Maurice Albertson, Director of the Research Foundation of Colorado State University submitted a draft for the preliminary report on the "Point Four Youth Corps" feasibility study as authorized by Congress.

With two associates he had traveled in search of information in ten countries of Asia, Africa, and South America, essentially to confirm the "Four Points" were identified to Congressman Reuss by the four UNESCO volunteers he met in 1957.

The result was a report that was extremely positive to the concept of a "Youth Corps", and to give strong approval to the advisability and practicability of an American Peace Corps. It set objectives to follow and recommend an organizational structure.

The report proposed selection and training methods for volunteers. The study suggested terms and conditions for the proposed agency, including pay and training. The report indicated programs that would be most successful: education, community development, and health and sanitation.

Notably, these were many of the same as the original "Four Point" needs proposed by Congressman Reuss and the four American UNESCO volunteers.

Except for its recommendation that the Peace Corps should become a part of the U.S. Agency for International Development, all policy and organizational recommendations set forth in the report were later followed in their entirety by Peace Corps administrators and approved by Congress for funding of the new agency.

Generally, the study was enthusiastic about the prospects of the proposed agency of an 'American Peace

Corps', although the study only used the generic name that had been in its charter from Congress.

The study concluded that "it has become increasingly apparent that if there was to be permanent peace and freedom, the developed nations must assist the underdeveloped nations to achieve a life of dignity and economic well-being for their people."

The report concluded that an "American Peace Corps is practical because it can work easily within the resource capabilities of our nation and existing instruments of American Foreign Aid".

Their report estimated more than enough qualified men and women graduating annually from universities to recruit approximately ten thousand volunteers costing approximately $90 million per year.

The preliminary study by Colorado State University concluded it was also advisable to help create mutual understanding between the American and foreign people of potential for shared benefits from education and culture of the more developed nations, to promote the economic and social progress of the less developed countries by providing an essential ingredient now lacking moderately skilled manpower.

The study also expressed the belief that the American Peace Corps volunteers "could best further the goal of building mutual understanding if they lived under conditions similar to their counterparts in their host country."

This conclusion implied that such conditions would gain respect from the local host population as well as help the volunteers to better understand needs of the local population they could not otherwise assist to overcome.

President Kennedy State of the Union Message in 1961

The combined activities of these many individuals and groups made it evident that the enthusiasm surrounding an American Peace Corps was not limited to the political campaign. A Gallup poll released in mid-January, 1961, revealed that an overwhelming majority of seventy-one per cent of the American people favored the idea and only a very small minority of eighteen per cent opposed it.

In his first State of the Union message to Congress on January 30, 1961, President Kennedy made a further commitment to the Peace Corps by promising its establishment. Similar ideas for government programs had been proposed for sixty years. Private agencies had a long and successful record of activities of this type.

Yet, never before had a President supported the idea of an official American Peace Corp agency, and made it an important corner stone of his administration. This was at the same time as President Kennedy was to also announce the 'Mission to the Moon', which resulted in creation of NASA and 'Space Race' versus the USSR, as well the U.S. Peace Corps.

Soon after taking office in January, 1961, President Kennedy set up a study committee under Mr. Sargent Shriver to develop and round out the American Peace Corps idea, and prepare a comprehensive report and plan for its implementation. The report was to be completed by March 1, 1961.

It was well known but not mentioned previously, that Sargent Shriver was married to the sister of President Kennedy, and father of Maria Shriver, future respected TV journalist and wife of a future governor of the state of

California; so this was only noted to how personally important the Peace Corps was to President Kennedy.

Mr. Shriver initially set up temporary headquarters in a two-room suite in the Washington, DC's Mayflower Hotel, and began immediately to hosted a series of conferences to invite specialists from business, government agencies, and volunteer organizations.

It was also reported from many sources that Shriver would go for breakfast at the Congress cafeteria every morning, and would make a point to introduce himself to every Senator and Representative and their staff, in order to take every opportunity to plead the case for a U.S. Peace Corps.

On February 28, 1961, Sargent Shriver, drawing from all of these diverse sources and others, completed his report for President Kennedy.

Mr. Shriver referred specifically to the Millikan report, the study of Professor Hayes, the proposals of Congressman Reuss and Senator Humphrey, the report of Dr. Albertson, and the suggestions of his own task force.

The task force had concluded that the agency could begin in low gear with only preparatory work undertaken until Congress finally appropriated special funds for it; or it could be launched without delay by executive action making sufficient funds available from existing Mutual Security appropriations to permit a number of substantial projects to start immediately.

However, Mr. Shriver felt strongly that the Peace Corps should be launched immediately, in order that the opportunity to recruit the most qualified people from that year's graduating classes would not be lost.

President Kennedy agreed and signed an Executive Order for the creation of the U.S. Peace Corps on the same day as his meeting with Mr. Shriver, which was to be funded initially by temporary budget just as Shriver had recommended.

President Kennedy 1961 Executive Order For Peace Corps

On March 1, 1961, President Kennedy signed executive order No. 10924, establishing the Peace Corps on a temporary pilot basis pending formal organization and funding of a permanent Peace Corps by the U.S. Congress.

The executive order announced that the new agency would be responsible for training and service abroad of American volunteers for new programs of assistance to foreign nations. The agency was to be financed entirely by temporary authorization to expend budgeted funds already authorized under the Mutual Security Act of 1954.

The executive order from President Kennedy stressed that at this stage the Peace Corps was to be strictly experimental in nature. Though it sought only to get the agency started, the executive order raised the ire of some Congressmen who felt legislative power was being usurped, and that Kennedy should have waited for the Congress to first schedule hearings, and then introduce a bill later.

Notably, in the five decades since this, Presidential Executive Orders have become increasingly common — but this action by President Kennedy was one of the first examples of use of an Executive Order to immediately start an executive agency on a temporary and experimental basis, in order to address an immediate national issue or problem, by very limited and restricted funding under existing budget allocations, and then allow Congress time for hearings and public commentary in order for bipartisan Congressional coordinated House and

Senate effort to co-write an effective Bill to replace the Executive Order with Law.

It was also important to point out that this original prototype for the process of using Executive Orders to use currently approved budget funds for temporary organization of new Executive Agencies, and at the same time initiate Congressional bi-partisan efforts to hammer out a permanent Bill to enact into Law – was actually not an innovation that was first conceived by President Kennedy – this approach was actually conceived, advocated and implemented by Vice President Lyndon Johnson. So despite Executive Orders have become increasingly partisan in the decades since, creation of U.S. Peace Corps was a bi-partisan effort.

After discussions with Congressional leaders of both parties, Kennedy followed his Executive Order only two days later by announcing that he was requesting Congress to approve a new agency, U.S. Peace Corps, and to formally approve his nomination for head of that agency, subject to appropriate Congressional hearings for their approval.

In order to implement the establishment of the agency, on March 4, 1961, Kennedy formally announced his brother-in-law, Sargent Shriver, to be first Director of the U.S. Peace Corps, subject to traditional and constitutional law with approval and consent of the U.S. Congress.

The temporary Peace Corps creation on March 1, 1961 was to be a source of 'new ground' in the establishment of presidential executive orders for initial funding of a U.S. executive branch agency. Many in Congress and Judiciary in 1961 were concerned it was illegal expansion of Executive Powers of a president.

Even Vice President Johnson was reported to have expressed private concerns to President Kennedy, yet he also was reported to have widely urged others in government to overlook it as 'a well-intentioned and practical action that could easily fit into traditional procedures'. Thus, in the first of many potentially difficult dealings with Congress, Vice President Johnson was able to advise President Kennedy to help him be more effective.

Kennedy quickly contacted members of Congress in both houses and parties to explain and build bipartisan support for his executive order for a U.S. Peace Corps.

He reportedly expressed to all that he contacted directly that he personally believed there was already substantial and overwhelming information and experience to permit the immediate creation of an American Peace Corps with effective and actionable plans for a permanent Peace Corp organization, and that any delay would miss a great opportunity to counter communist enemies in the Cold War. Reportedly, without exception all that he called were convinced by President Kennedy about need to create U.S. Peace Corps.

There was after that time both support for the executive order to begin training of Peace Corp volunteers with the objective of placing them overseas by late fall, as well as bipartisan support of Congress for the new agency of a Peace Corps with Sargent Shriver as the first Director. The reaction of the American public to press releases regarding the new Peace Corps agency was also overwhelming, as applications of volunteers flooded the Kennedy White House.

President Kennedy then also took the unprecedented action to address both houses of U.S. Congress to asked permission to authorize "a permanent Peace Corps, as a pool of trained American men and women sent overseas by the United States Government or through private organizations and institutions to help foreign countries meet their urgent needs for skilled manpower."

In his message to Congress, President John F. Kennedy gave his reasons for the establishment of a Peace Corps: "Throughout the world the people of the newly developing nations are struggling for economic and social progress which reflects their deepest desires. Our own freedom, and the future of freedom around the world, depend on this.

In a very real sense, their ability to build growing and independent nations where men can live in dignity, liberated from the bonds of hunger, ignorance, and poverty. One of the greatest obstacles to the achievement of this goal was the lack of trained men and women with the skill to teach the young and assist in the operation and development projects of emerging nations."

President Kennedy went on to emphasize that the volunteers would offer skills needed in the country to which they are sent. Their work would supplement that of technical advisers but would not compete with it.

Early volunteers would not only go abroad as technical experts and advisers, but would be undertaking operational tasks as workers at the level of local people, and work with them 'shoulder to shoulder'.

By putting their advanced technical skills directly to work in the 'real world' development of countries 'struggling to advance out of poverty, volunteers would contribute to economic growth and understanding among nations – and at the same time provide a patriotic service to both America, and humanitarian service to humankind'. This was based on a view from many presidents to use Executive Actions to protect America and World Peace.

President Kennedy 1961 Bill for a Permanent Peace Corps

On May 31, 1961, President Kennedy sent to Congress the administration's bill "to provide for a Peace Corps to help the peoples of interested countries and areas in meeting their needs for skilled manpower." The following day the proposed Peace Corps Act was introduced as Senate Bill 2000 by Senator Hubert Humphrey, with the co-sponsorship of several other Senators. Senator Humphrey described the bill to establish a Peace Corps of American volunteers as a means to carry America's skills and talents and idealism abroad to help other peoples help themselves. Humphrey indicated that the Peace Corps was designed to provide a framework for expression of America's Idealism, humanitarianism, and generosity to help build a better world for mankind.

President Kennedy concurrently announced to the world his intention to encourage and to foster the social, economic, and political reforms that would mean a better livelihood for the ordinary people of Asia, Africa, and Latin America. The Administration's Bill (H.E. 7500) was introduced in the House of Representatives by Thomas E. Morgan of Pennsylvania, Chairman of the House Foreign Affairs Committee. This was an important and critical political statement that there was official support to begin to balance the direct payment of U.S. Foreign Aid to leaders of nations, with other alternatives, including to begin to link such payments to cooperation of such leaders to accept and encourage Peace Corps volunteers as well.

Some other nearly identical bills also were introduced the same week in the House, including one by Congressman Reuss, which was largely intended to include the "Four Points" back into the central focus of the formal creation of an American Peace Corps.

The bills were all discussed and debated in their respective chambers. Some opposition was expressed relative to creating a Peace Corps without waiting for an opportunity to study the results of the pilot program and to get public comments back from the recently released Colorado State University, yet the interim results and draft of that study were already widely distributed and even regarded as fully to support the consensus to move forward quickly to pass the Peace Corp Act.

Despite many partisan expressions of concern, the Peace Corps Act was approved by a vote of fifty-nine to thirty-two in the Senate, and by 288 to ninety-seven in the House. Notably, Shriver reported his personal lobby efforts involved meeting over 360 Senators and Representative, over breakfast in Congress cafeterias.

The bipartisan support for the Corps was unusual, but was evidenced by the bipartisan vote in the Foreign Relations Committee, which had approved the bill by a vote of fourteen to zero. The final legislation providing for a permanent Peace Corps was signed by the President on September 22, 1961.

This Act authorized $40 million to be appropriated to enable the Corps to have 2,700 men and women in service by the end of fiscal year 1962. Notably, this was over 10 times greater than the total number of British IVS volunteers during the same time period.

The estimated average annual cost per volunteer was $9,000. This was only about 10% of the average costs of British VSO volunteers, who are often subsidized by large British corporations and usually resided in corporate hotel suites, compared to more modest living conditions among the local people by Peace Corp volunteers. Most important, the U.S. Peace Corps idea was now a reality.

Summary of Early Development of the Peace Corps

The development of the U.S. Peace Corps has been placed into a historical perspective. The practical aspects of utilizing the skills and idealism of Americans in programs of peaceful service — the essence of the Peace Corps concept — had deep roots in American desires to help others. Few other nations ever attempted the same.

The practices of the Thomasites, the Christian missionaries, peace movements, federal programs, private organizations, and individual proposals, all contributed to the development of the Peace Corps. Next this book will examine more operational aspects and considerations of Peace Corps in its first five years, as a historical foundation.

All past historical, traditional and fundamental views, beliefs and commitments to freedom, democracy and American way of life – based on fairness, hard work, and the desire to share all of their health, happiness and prosperity with the rest of the world – were to be the hope and desire of good Americans throughout the 1960's.

This was to be manifested, and nobly attempted to be realized in formation of U.S. Peace Corps and NASA, as first established under presidency of John F. Kennedy, and continued under Lyndon B. Johnson going forward.

Historical Significance of Kennedy Era Executive Orders

Among the most significant American political innovations of the second century of American history must include the use of Executive Orders by President Kennedy to create the U.S. Peace Corps and NASA. Historical evidence indicates Vice President Johnson was the first to present this concept to President Kennedy.

Their concept of establishing new executive agencies by Presidential Executive Order was unique; and similar to many throughout U.S. history of presidents, including actions by Jackson, Wilson, FDR and others, including Lincoln, during time of war – with objectives to protect the U.S. government and people. But Executive Orders by President Kennedy to create the U.S. Peace Corps and NASA during a time of peace, with objectives of peace, were a new innovation, which Americans applauded.

These Executive Actions by Kennedy were, by aggressive support of Johnson, to be implemented as 'temporary re-allocation of Congressional budgeted funds to short term funding to create new agencies within timeframes of current budget pending Congress approval'. In this case, for U.S. Peace Corps and NASA, the Kennedy White House directed Johnson to lead the efforts to secure the bipartisan approval of Congress and American people to pass bills, legislation and budget funding for these newly proposed agencies, the very next year. This new innovation was not only approved by the American people, but also by U.S. Federal Justice Dept.; as well as our Supreme Court.

This book is primarily about the consequences of the original and seminal 1961 Executive Orders to create the U.S. Peace Corps – which was fully supported by American people and a bipartisan Congress – and yet was still a very difficult, and complicated, process. In the next chapters the many successes and challenges to create and improve these processes for creation of such agencies are presented and analyzed in detail.

CHAPTER II

EARLY OPERATIONS OF THE PEACE CORPS

An examination was made in the previous chapter of the historical and early development of the U.S. Peace Corps from an idea to reality up until the early 1960's.

In implementing the early ideas to reality, substantial organization, programs, and policies had to be established in order to transition a temporary Executive Order by President Kennedy into a fully independent agency enacted into Law.

With the establishment the Peace Corps as a new independent agency by Congress it effectively became a permanent reality.

From then on, its strategic and tactical organizational dynamics became a more necessary integral foundation for early Peace Corps operations.

As such it is useful to understand the early organization and operations of the Peace Corps, as it developed from concept to reality by implementation to real operations, and changes within the early years.

59

Early Organization of the Peace Corps by Kennedy

Early discussions within the 'inner circle' of the Kennedy Administration (including Bobby Kennedy and Vice President Lyndon Johnson) concurred with the decision that the Peace Corps should be an autonomous agency within the Department of State. This decision followed very strong arguments by several initial Peace Corps officials (including Sargent Shriver) that status as a autonomous agency within the State Department was necessary to effectively recruit, train and deploy U.S. Peace Corps volunteers as quickly as possible.

Others in the Kennedy Administration argued just as strongly that the Peace Corps should be organized under in the new Agency for International Development, which was established within the State Department to absorb several existing foreign-aid agencies (as was the first recommendation of the Colorado State University report).

Yet, at that time (and arguably since), the credibility and past track record of the Agency for International Development (AID) had been 'mostly aligned' to Big Business interests; and their 'behind closed door partners' in the bureaucracies of Third World nations – so were less trusted by the people of the same nations who receive such AID – which led to the need for an alternative to AID, which could be more responsive to the diplomatic needs of State Dept. and the American people.

This opinion was at the fore-front of the Colorado State University report funded by Congress as it resonated to traditional views, based on the idea that a more coordinated country-by-country approach was needed to determine the overall types of foreign aid which would best serve a nation – and thus many officials in both

Congress and Executive branch strongly believed the Peace Corps ought to be an integrated part of this approach.

This view was founded upon a wide-spread view by both some Congress and many career Executive branch staff, who felt only the State Department was able to make critical strategic decisions – of which countries should receive exclusively Foreign Aid payments only to the leaders of such countries, and to restrict alternative funds by people-to -people programs such as the Peace Corps.

This view was usually based upon top secret analysis of the state department (with help of CIA as well as top military), for directives regarding potential stability challenges in such nations that were regarded as 'hot spots'.

Their sincere concern was that even a very slight reduction to the past payments of such Foreign Aid to humanitarian projects, or even to keep such Foreign Aid payments as the same level with even a very modest request to supplement with people-to-people humanitarian aid, might likely turn many such governments to instead seek out communist alternatives, and oppress their own people.

Several bills were proposed to committees of both the House and Senate to enact a process with strict Congressional oversight, as military 'black operations' might be necessary for any deployment by the Peace Corps in any nation – as well as routine control over 'messaging' in activities to teach, and reach out, between America and underdeveloped nations. But President Kennedy disagreed, and he supported an independent American Peace Corp agency that was to answer directly to White House staff.

This view by Kennedy and his White House staff were related to many initiatives related to the concept of a U.S. Peace Corps which were all stubbornly idealistic, and often difficult for political establishment of both parties of Congress to understand or easily accept.

These idealistic beliefs resulted in an early characterization by the press as a new 'Camelot'; which was eagerly embraced by both 'Young Democrat' and 'Young Republicans' on college campuses, while at the same time to alienate powerful politician of both parties in Congress.

Arguments for a Peace Corps Reporting to White House

Sargent Shriver in a letter to Senator Humphrey set forth his reasons for suggesting that the Peace Corps be created as an independent agency. This letter was intended to help give additional support to Humphrey who was regarded to be leaning to support for a new agency.

According to Acting Director Sargent Shriver in his letter to Senator Humphrey:

"First, the agency was described in all past Bills as a program of international service, relying on people who are volunteers and not employees earning salaries.

Secondly, it was necessary for the U.S. Peace Corps to reach people with a special motivation to join a unique program designed as fully independent of military or even political considerations.

Third, many nations would welcome the volunteers because they would not be a part of traditional forms of foreign aid.

Fourth, the separateness from the aid program had created enthusiastic response from colleges and agencies which have not found it practical to work in partnership with existing aid programs.

Fifth, the status as an agency within the Department of State presents an opportunity to work directly with Congress in a way to reflect its will."

These 5 points were difficult for any opposition to the support of an independent Peace Corps as presented by Senator Humphrey and his colleagues at several Congressional oversight committees to counter.

Thus the consensus grew in Washington to support the idea of an independent Peace Corps agency. Several Bills in the first year of President Kennedy's new administration were overwhelmingly passed to create a new independent U.S. Peace Corps agency, as well as to provide substantial independent funding for it.

This was first of many bi-partisan Bills that were passed by both houses of Congress with wide public support, not only related to the Peace Corps, but creation of NASA and other new independent agencies as well.

It was also important to note that in every such case, Vice President Lyndon Johnson was involved in personally steering such legislation though both houses of Congress, in support of the idealistic agendas of President Kennedy and his White House. This was despite the official role of Vice President Johnson was first and foremost to focus on Poverty and Civil Rights.

As a result of these bi-partisan Bills, the U.S. Peace Corps was to report only indirectly to the Secretary of State, and would deal directly with Congress for its funding.

All hearings by Congress to consider budget requests by the Peace Corps were widely publicized, and uniquely 'politicized' in a bi-partisan manner, as both parties courted the Peace Corps and its reporting by press.

The New U.S. Peace Corps Inspires American Idealism

As a result, the Peace Corps became a favorite topic of the American public; yet this visibility and popularity led to a lot of very serious underlying resentment by the rank and file in State Department.

Despite widely reported 'anonymous' opinions, on an official level, State Department leaders reported to the U.S. Congress Foreign Relations Committee in 1961 that "the Peace Corps is so unquestionably different that there is no organizational reason why it should be a part of the existing Agency for International Development".

This was a very convoluted and seminal example of political 'double speak' as it had been used from days of Rome till today, and will probably continue to be attempted in the future.

The simple truth was that the U.S. Peace Corps had never been 'officially' proposed as part of any bill of Congress to be part of AID – despite this was in fact what many in the U.S. State Department actually wanted.

In fact, one bill had U.S. Peace Corps had been proposed to be part of the Dept. of State – but always to be independent from AID, due to growing data of opinions that many third world nation's peoples that did not trust AID due "to perceptions that so many Millions of U.S. Dollars spent do not have any impact on average people".

This was a perception that was understandable to both the U.S. Congress and American people, who together were not always able to see any direct benefits of such aid to the people of such countries, or citizens of U.S. who paid for it with their taxes – and wanted a more transparent and idealistic way to both show to the average people of third world countries that: 'We the People of the United States feel your pain – and want to help".

This was a dramatic turn-around from all previous assumptions and documents that had been presented up until that time by the U.S. State Department before

Congress regarding the potential role of an American Peace Corps versus traditional U.S. foreign aid.

Pragmatically, it was also a reflection of a point in time that new Kennedy appointees to high level positions within the U.S. State Department first clashed with existing career State Department civil servants, and pushed to support the agenda of the new President that appointed them. This was no different than practical realities of the American system that faced any new administration.

The new U.S. Peace Corps was expected to carry out functions which had not previously been performed the U.S Government.

This was confirmed by many polls of U.S. voters, who regarded the Peace Corps as a promising new hope for peace and freedoms led by Americans.

Also, despite that most U.S. voters of all ages and across both parties were overwhelmingly positive about the concept, it was the young people who were the most likely to want to volunteer.

As with most of the idealistic movements across history of human civilization, it was the young people who are most inspired to take risks for humanitarian causes, and in this case, the U.S. Peace Corps was like a New Crusade.

The large scale recruitment of civilians by the U.S. Government for service overseas on a voluntary basis had no precedent. Their responses were overwhelmingly positive, and idealistically hopeful.

In short, there was no identical, or even nearly identical, event in history of the U.S. government to embark on such a vast, totally humanitarian and benevolent commitment to help other people outside of the U.S.

Yet, despite it was a secular movement, the main support was largely based upon American foundations of

Christian mission organizations, which were by this time becoming increasingly interfaith and non-denominational.

President Kennedy Establishes Independent Peace Corps

The final decision of President Kennedy followed a two-month tug of war within the early days of his new Administration. For early Peace Corps officials and the American People this was a monumental development.

These officials had argued that without a special identity of its own, the early Peace Corps would attract few recruits, get hopelessly snarled in red tape, and reduce its overall effectiveness abroad.

More importantly, they argued that a large base of support for the election of Kennedy had been based on idealism of young people, students, as well as many pluralist groups who had enthusiastically voted for Kennedy because of his message of 'Hope and Change'; and they might have become disillusioned and cynical if Kennedy were to 'cave in' to conventional politics.

Reportedly, President Kennedy made his final decision after consulting with Vice President Johnson, who had advocated the concept of an American Peace Corps even during the early days of the 1960 presidential election.

Johnson had even lobbied widely up to that time, that as Vice President his main task should be to head up such an American Peace Corps.

However, Johnson reportedly told Kennedy that night that he had come to believe that an American Peace Corps deserved to be a unique new agency rather than a suitable project for the office of a Vice President. Reportedly the same night Johnson advocated the same about the creation of National Aeronautic Space Agency, later to be known as NASA; and instead Johnson asked to work primarily to on Poverty and Civil Rights.

Coordination of Peace Corps With Existing Foreign-Aid

The establishment of the Corps as a separate agency in the Kennedy administration should not be construed as evidence that they did not believe it was closely related to, and should not be closely coordinated with the existing foreign-aid program, such as Agency for International Development and World Bank.

As each new Peace Corps project was being explored and developed, it was to be coordinated closely with the State Department, Agency for International Development, and United States Information Agency.

Yet, the critical new innovation was that should 'coordinate with', rather than 'answer to' the existing State Department, and to the U.S. military establishment.

This status based on equal and independent footing was a true innovation with significant implications.

The Peace Corps – as well as NASA as another idealistic and independent new agencies – reported directly to the Kennedy White House.

Although the activities of the Peace Corp were reported directly to the White House for approval or 'redirection', all their activities were also reported – as a matter of 'formality' – to the U.S. State Department, the Department of Defense, and the Justice Department, and also included both the FBI, and well as the CIA.

All activities and decisions by Peace Corps (and also similarly NASA) were subject to elevation by these executive branch departments.

In such cases (which were rare), there could be vigorous debate – but in all such cases, the President would make all final decisions.

Yet, in terms of budget and headcount within the government in the early years of the Peace Corps, only a small number of high-level, or even mid-level, staff at the independent Peace Corps agency had any direct or indirect contact with either the staff or even the leadership of the Secretary of State, Department of Defense, or Department of Justice, or either FBI or CIA.

However, all plans by the Peace Corps were instead to be submitted directly to Congress and its oversight committees.

Yet, even substantial modifications to budget and operations in early days were only shared informally with the Secretary of State, Defense Department, Justice Department, FBI and CIA as routine notifications rather than to request their approval.

This was most important as the U.S. Peace Corps represented an innovation to the Executive branch as a smaller sub-department that was also an alternative to large bureaucratic cabinet departments, which were of special or emerging interest, and thus significance appropriate to direct 'dotted-line' reporting to the President.

This innovation by the Kennedy administration, with respect to both Peace Corps and NASA (among others) was thus very historically significant.

Early Peace Corps Administration in U.S. and Overseas

The major responsibility for placement, support, and guidance in the early Peace Corps was performed by the Office of Program Development and Operations.

This office had five divisions in Washington, plus: Latin America Regional Office; North Africa, Near East, South Asia Regional Office; Far East Regional Office; Africa Regional Office; and Program Development and Coordination Staff.

It had been widely observed that much of the original organization of the Peace Corps was somewhat similar to the organization of emerging newly created humanitarian divisions of the United Nations.

This had also been suggested by many historical analysts as an additional factor in growing support for the U.S. Peace Corps by other previous and existing U.S. government agencies.

It was widely to be observed at the time, and even more so in retrospect, to include the history of United Nations in the next decades, as powerful communist nations exerted their influence within the U.N to attempt to counter and confuse the impact of the independent U.S. Peace Corps for their own personal agendas.

Although within the first two decades of the Peace Corps, such communist and other oppressive nation's strategies largely failed.

It can be easily argued that within that time, the immediate impact and resulting threat of the a humanitarian alternative at a person to person level greatly complicated and hurt the spread of communism.

Notably, this created a need for communist and oppressive totalitarian governments to try to counter the U.S. Peace Corp with 'knock-off' communist equivalent projects that were promoted to the leaders of third world nations who received more direct 'Foreign Aid' from U.S., and effectively created an aggressive 'bidding war', which became a new front for the Cold War, which was raged primarily between the CIA and KGB.

If all else failed, the communist super-power nations resorted to arming of mercenaries, extortion, and even violence to include mass murder in order to subjugate local people in third world nations that accepted either U.S. foreign aid or U.S. Peace Corps humanitarian aid.

This was a very desperate and weak 'last ditch' effort response of communism to simple humanitarian person-to-person Peace Corps aid based on goodwill.

Starting in the early 1960's, there was a very great increase in the 'divide and distance' between the foreign policies of both American and the communist super powers. This was to coincide with the creation of the Peace Corps and NASA by President Kennedy.

Although it is impossible to say to what degree the creation of new humanitarian and benevolent agencies such as NASA and the Peace Corps were have had direct impact to speed up the growing polarization of democratic versus communist super-power nations, the violent tactics and atrocities by the communist super-powers began to increase at an alarming rate after creating these agencies.

Despite the original objectives of the Peace Corps were to counter exactly these kinds of communist abuses to third world nations, it was noted by many in the press that there seemed to be an increase in such violence and atrocities at an accelerating rate that matched the actual deployment of Peace Corps volunteers to these nations.

Early Organization of Peace Corps as an Agency of U.S.

The early Peace Corps as it was first founded in 1961 had a well-defined organizational structure.

The new Peace Corps organization was to be headed by a Director, and aided by an Executive Secretariat staff, with and five organizational staff support divisions.

Notably, much of the original Peace Corps organization was based loosely on new United Nations humanitarian divisions, which had progressed and expanded greatly during the time between when Congressman Reuss met the 4 American UNESCO volunteers and the actual creation of the U.S. Peace Corps.

Also notably, from the very first month of the establishment of the Peace Corps, in every critical vote by Communist China and Soviet Russia in the UN Security Council repeatedly attempted to hindered nonpolitical humanitarian aid efforts – while at the same time, the U.S. Peace Corps acted on its own for nonpolitical good will, which was backed up by American government.

The organization of the early U.S. Peace Corps was further divided into five functional offices, which were similar to several humanitarian organizations that had been added to the United Nations within the previous decade.

These included divisions for: Public Affairs, Program Development and Operations, Peace Corps Volunteers, Planning and Evaluation, and Management.

Overseas, the overseas operations in each local host country was managed by a Peace Corps representative with his supporting staff.

The overseas support staff in a country usually consisted of a medical doctor, a secretary, and one or more administrative and communications officials, depending on the number and type of local host Peace Corps projects.

Foreign nationals were employed to the extent necessary for an efficient staff operation. This normally included translators, receptionists, and drivers.

Yet, from office to office, and nation to nation, the details of how the individual Peace Corps offices were administered became increasingly confidential, and were not made widely public outside of the U.S. government.

This reflected the growing coordination and sharing of information between the Peace Corps and the U.S. intelligence agencies – despite this had been a matter of White House debate early after creation of the Corps.

However, sharing of 'high-level intelligence' between the Peace Corps and U.S. intelligence agencies was demonstrated to have significant mutual benefits.

This information led to much greater success by U.S. Peace Corps local insights about local community power structure and preliminary needs assessments for planning its humanitarian missions.

As a result communism lost its power grip and much confidence of the people in undeveloped nations.

The communist super-power propaganda machines, and local pro-communist press in the nations served by the Peace Corps, tried desperately to attempt to link the Peace Corps to CIA and 'American Imperialism'.

Yet, in fact, the policy of the White House was, from the very beginning, that the Peace Corps should not 'either give or receive' confidential intelligence information that involved any operations of military significance.

This was actually a critical pillar of the original U.S Peace Corps charter as written by the Kennedy White House staff, and has continued to be the case to this day.

Peace Corps Volunteers and Supervision

According to the manner in which the U.S. Peace Corps initially carried out its overseas administration was explained in a 1962 Congressional presentation to the Congressional Committee on Foreign Affairs:

"On matters concerning his job, the volunteer is responsible directly to his host country supervisor. The Peace Corps representative in each country is responsible for the general performance, behavior, and welfare of all the volunteers there. Accordingly, he maintains contact directly or through staff or volunteers."

Despite the executive leadership of the early U.S. Peace Corps reported directly to the President and White House, the individual Peace Corps volunteers reported directly under a hierarchy network that led to the U.S. Ambassador for their country, and were thus to be ultimately accountable to the U.S. State Department.

This included all program development and operations, field negotiation, and thus the coordination of all operational aspects of the Peace Corps program.

In effect, this meant that the U.S. State Department, by virtue of the decisions of the U.S. Ambassador for the host nation, could in fact change the details of plans or current status of any Peace Corps project or activity on short notice – including to evacuate U.S. Peace Corps in the event of any new U.S. State Department advisories related to any new host nation developments that could endanger American lives.

This was a very serious responsibility recognized from the beginning of the Peace Corps, as a critical safety mechanism to protect all Volunteers serving overseas.

The Peace Corps representative in each host nation reported directly to the U.S. Ambassador, and was responsible for providing the "imagination and ingenuity necessary to retain the freshness and uniqueness of the Peace Corps and keep its objectives clear and its organization appropriately modest".

However, it was also their responsibility to maintain constant and close contact with the U.S. embassy and ambassador, but also as well as the AID mission office.

The local host nation Peace Corps representative thus utilized, as appropriate, services and facilities of the embassy and other United States agencies, but "without too closely identifying the Peace Corps with those agencies". Notably, this was often a very difficult task to bear.

These Peace Corps representatives were assisted, in many instances, by deputy Peace Corps representatives in the programs for large countries, or by an associate or assistant Peace Corps representatives.

Again, the actual number and organizational structures for each host nation were not to be circulated outside of the U.S. government, as this was regarded to be a 'risk exposure' that could invite their targeting by local pro-communist press in order to disrupt U.S. operations.

When there was a deputy or associate Peace Corps representative in a country, the officers divided the responsibilities according to their abilities and experience.

In a few countries where the size and complexity of a country requires additional staff, the work was normally divided both functionally and geographically.

Peace Corps representatives are also assisted, in many instances, by volunteers with special expertise.

In most cases, these 'special advisory' volunteer leaders for a project were selected from outstanding volunteers in planning for that project.

Such volunteer leaders were expected to provide on-the-job supervision of volunteers, handle logistic support for the projects, provide counsel and guidance, and be on the lookout for difficulties in job relations or personal adjustment.

In order to give Peace Corps representatives and volunteer leaders more time in the field, both Peace Corps staff, and local host nation, secretaries were used.

It should be clear that as early as two years after the creation of the Peace Corps, initial funding was already running short, largely due administrative delays that were to be common in the transfer of fully budgeted and allocated U.S. funds to the foreign local host nations.

Because the program was new, at the beginning most funds transferred to the Peace Corps host nations were sent through the same financial channels and international banks as traditional U.S. foreign aid payments.

This resulted for several years in a vast number of misdirected and even 'missing' payments involving large sums of USD funds, which had to be tracked down by U.S. government treasury officials and auditors.

In most cases, there were simple and honest mistakes by low-level bureaucratic employees in both the U.S. as well as the host nations, who erroneously sent or received such Peace Corps payments, putting them into accounts already set up for U.S. foreign aid payments, often directly to local host government officials.

In the vast majority of such cases, the mistakes were easily corrected, despite it often took a year or more to fully track down, explain, and resolve.

This was an unexpected, but unfortunately typical, for all new U.S. government agency program operations.

Meanwhile, many early Peace Corps projects in the third world were 'strapped for cash', and had to 'get creative' for such 'bridge funding' – which usually was to involve some combination of soliciting large U.S. companies operating in the local host nation, as well as to recruit more local host nation workers, who were willing to accept 'I.O.U.' writs for their services until the new flow of funds directly to the Peace Corps were fully established.

This was unfortunately not to account for all of the missing payments. In many cases, early Peace Corps funds that were to be erroneously transferred into the accounts previously established for U.S. foreign aid payments proved to be very difficult to recover.

Although specific details of such 'situations' in these nations were never fully released to the U.S. press or American public, there were rumors as well as 'off the record' comments by 'anonymous U.S. government sources' that many such payments were never recovered.

Reportedly, in some cases, the mistaken transfer of funds was tracked down to a 'dead end' – whereby the funds were evidenced to have been transferred quickly to an 'anonymous series of accounts' into Swiss banks. Often in such cases, local host nation officials, or local national bankers that they usually dealt with – simply disappeared.

In other anonymously reported cases, some leaders of the local host nations who were already also receiving U.S. foreign aid openly admitted that they had actually received the funds intended for transfer to the Peace Corps, and brazenly announced that they were keeping them, as a kick-back or even 'bonus' for agreeing to allow the Peace Corps to operate in their country to begin with.

This was to unfortunately to begin a long and totally unexpected complication that confounded the early years of the Peace Corps – and had unfortunate far reaching consequences to many other U.S. agencies that were to already have an existing presence in these nations.

It was an unfortunate reality that many of the very third world nations that the U.S. Peace Corps was created to give person-to-person humanitarian goodwill aid to, which had actually previously received foreign aid from the United State – were in fact totalitarian dictatorships..

This was a fact that was known to both the U.S. Congress and American people, and had been part of the argument for the Peace Corps to begin with, in order to counter such U.S. foreign aid payments to dictator nations.

The critical problem was that the fast deployment of the U.S. Peace Corps to so many third world nations quickly played easily into the self-serving schemes of such greedy dictators who could not care less about helping their own people with help of humanitarian organizations such as the U.S. Peace Corps.

Notably, many officials of the U.S. government, including the State Department, who had originally expressed concerns about U.S. Peace Corps were first to leak these situations – and even talk openly about them 'off the record' or quoted as 'anonymous government sources'.

One such official was quoted as saying: "We tried to warn them. By moving too quickly to put these new humanitarian goodwill aid projects in same countries where we have invested a lot of traditional foreign aid to prop up Banana Republics to be friendly to U.S. should have been easily seen in advance to rock a lot of boats to capsize. This is going to be a rough ride from now on".

Thus, the decision to create an independent U.S. Peace Corps to report directly to the President and White House began to be challenged more frequently by the U.S. State Department, Defense Department, and others on a regular basis starting in early 1963, when the Kennedy administration was already overwhelmed by such critical military issues as the Cuban Missile Crisis, Berlin embargo, and many other 'end game' situations of growing Cold War.

As one anonymous White House staffer was to also comment off the record: "Kennedy is getting tired of Peace Corps issues getting brought up at same meetings that discuss potential end of the world. He seems to be wondering why he set it up independently to begin with".

So barely two years after the creation of the new independent Peace Corps, there were at least two very critical complications that confounded its original charter. These were beyond normal problems to start a new agency.

One, the fact that the U.S. Peace Corps had been set up as an independent agency to provide 'temporary contractors' to third world nations created a problem since the volunteers as well as their local host nation managers were not 'officially' part of the U.S. government.

They all signed contracts that deferred to the local host government as 'final arbitrators' in mediation of any disputes. This was intended to help build trust with such governments in order to encourage them to request more Peace Corps projects.

The 'fatal flaw' in this strategy was simple, as was also quoted by another 'anonymous government source': "The real problem was simply to try to 'gain trust' of third world nation leaders who were 'not trustworthy'. They were to immediately see opportunities for advantage and personal gain – and course many were to take it".

Thus, in many cases, such corrupt dictators were to basically say to the U.S. government: 'If you do not like it, then sue me – but as your own contracts say – you will have to sue me in my own courts in my own country. So good luck with that!'.

Notably, no actual litigation of any kind was ever filed to attempt to recover Peace Corps funds mistakenly transferred to existing U.S. foreign aid accounts to any of the corrupt leaders of such nations.

Yet, even though the GAO was prohibited from to publically announce the total U.S. losses that were 'written off for convenience of the government' – Congressional oversight committee members were altogether furious – and although they could do nothing about it, there was also a growing consensus of both Congress and U.S. executive branch agencies to 'systematically degrade and oust' such dictators – in 'black operation' projects funded by Congress that were also to become more common for many decades.

Two, there was growing consensus, even with the Kennedy administration White House, that these situations would not have occurred if the Peace Corps had been originally chartered to have been required to work under a 'veto power' relationship under both the State Department and Defense Department with regard to the risks of projects in host nations that might not be totally safe to deal with due to possible concerns about the real risks regarding long-term U.S. interests.

Kennedy was reportedly to have decided to 'draw the line' on decisions by Peace Corp for projects in any host nation without consensus approvals of the cabinet agencies in mid-1963, with the comment:

'It all boils down to the fact you simply cannot trust untrustworthy leaders of any foreign nations. Peace Corps and all of us here have been too trusting of too many dangerous leaders of nations that oppress their citizens. We have to learn from all this. We all thought these third world leaders wanted help but only wanted graft. This is a dangerous world in very dangerous times.'

This was in fact to have been documented in both the Kennedy and Johnson presidential libraries as a turning point to make them both to realize the complexities of trying to fight communism and totalitarian dictatorships by humanitarian means – which they had both learned as a result of their experience with the early response of such nations to the Peace Corps. There were also rumors that both Kennedy and Johnson were to record this experience of the Peace Corps in the reputed journal of advice to each departing president to his successor that was legendary to have started with President Truman to all presidents since.

Meanwhile, even in mid-1963 when this was first to come to the attention of the Kennedy administration, most of the corrupt leaders in third world nations who had used such tactics were to directed by Kennedy to each of the U.S. intelligence agencies to begin to closely monitor such leaders in order to determine if they were also courting the communist super-powers for greater 'foreign aid' payments in a 'bidding war' that included to accept only communist technical advisors instead of the U.S. Peace Corps.

Although their results were 'classified', there were several 'anonymous government sources' that were to report to the U.S. press that 100% of the leaders of nations that were already accepting U.S. foreign aid payments directly to themselves, their families, or their cohorts were in fact to already be actively negotiating with the communist super-powers to expel U.S. government and humanitarian volunteers, and instead turn to communism.

Host Nation Volunteer Secretaries for Peace Corps

During this same time that policy changes were being made at the highest levels of the U.S. government, the Peace Corps in many nations were running out of cash.

After considerable pressure from State Department and other cabinet departments, as well as key Congress committees, the U.S Peace Corps administration publically agreed that a substantial saving could be realized by temporarily using local host nation staff rather than using regularly compensated secretaries in other nations, who were in effect 'volunteers' in other host countries.

Such 'volunteer' host nation secretaries and other office staff administration were thus allowed to be accepted by the Peace Corps at recommendation by the State Department – under its new oversight to approve or disprove local host nation administrative policies, as was decided by President Kennedy in mid-1963.

This was despite there was originally no effective means or procedural guidelines to investigate such local host nation secretaries and office staff, as the resources of both the local host nation Peace Corps offices, as well as the office administration at most volunteer project sites. The results were very predictable in retrospect.

For at least the next year to even beyond two years, it was also to be later confirmed by 'anonymous government sources' to the press that:

"Fully 100% of the Peace Corps host nations that had been involved in early diversions of Peace Corps funds to their existing U.S. foreign aid accounts were also determined to have place host nation secretaries and support staff who agreed to work for delayed pay vouchers. In nearly all cases, these workers were determine to also being paid high compensation to report back to the same local government officials that already under suspicion".

In effect, this was not only a severe breach of trust, but also a serious security issue. Fortunately for once, the fact that the Peace Corps had been strictly separated from receiving any confidential military information was to turn out to have been a 'blessing in disguise'.

Several intensive security audits by U.S. intelligence agencies were to confirm to the Kennedy White House and Congressional oversight committees behind closed doors that the only information in Peace Corps files related to data about local economies and local community leaders who were sympathetic to working with the Peace Corps, as well as local needs assessments for possible projects.

This was to make many in the Kennedy White House administration and 'closed door' Congressional committee members 'more comfortable'. However, within the next two years, it was brought to the attention of both the Congressional closed door oversight committees, as well as the new Johnson administration White House that an increasing number of the same local community leaders listed in Peace Corps files were to be victims of assassinations, or to simply have 'disappeared'.

As a result of this very disturbing but growing trend, there was a 'scrambling' to accelerate the capabilities to both screen and monitor all foreign nationals that were to work with the Peace Corps, notably similar to the same level of screenings of non-U.S. citizen local nation staff that were approved to work at U.S. embassies and consulates. This was also notably to involve similar methods that were under prevue of the FBI, rather than the CIA. But the situation was perceived so dire that Johnson ordered both.

The new President Johnson was to order for the first time that joint task force involving both CIA and FBI personnel should work together to share methods for the investigation of foreign national backgrounds before they were to be approved to work with the Peace Corps, or with any organization or project within U.S. interests; and even after such approval to closely monitor such foreign nationals, but only within the scope of their activities and actions while communicating with, or on U.S. interest sites.

This was to be a very controversial new directive that President Johnson was to initiate; however, it was fully supported across both U.S. government agencies as well as 'black operations' Congressional oversight committees, as they were to be made aware of evidence that the KGB and communist super-powers were already to be monitoring to spy on not only activities at USSR embassies and work sites at nations that agreed to accept USSR advisors and foreign aid – but were also to aggressively spy upon the internal operation of U.S. embassies and U.S. companies doing business abroad, but also even private residence of U.S. citizens in their personal lives, for various nefarious goals.

Despite all of this going on 'behind the scenes' at the same time as such major events as the Cuban Missile Crisis and other communist military threats, the Kennedy as well as Johnson administration had to try to limit the awareness of the growing complexity of new technology to enhance the abilities of the KGB to spy on Americans in order to damage U.S. international interests (and was also instead to need to begin to develop many necessary counter-measures that might be equally offensive to many U.S. citizens).

So all of these issues had to be 'hidden' from the U.S. public, and emphasis of more open Congressional hearings needed to be focused on issues like 'need for more secretaries in foreign nations, and volunteer pay rates.

It was officially pointed out in Congressional hearings by the Peace Corps in mid-1963 that it was difficult to get American volunteers to accept assignments overseas at low pay, yet U.S. press seemed unconcerned.

Despite a considerable number of Peace Corps applicants also had secretarial skills, there was scarcely any consideration Peace Corp volunteers could fill part time demand for secretaries, or any proposals to provide such volunteers as direct staff to work with local host nations in dual roles, even if they had advanced language skills and cultural skills useful to coordinate across nations.

This was to be a first serious time that Peace Corps advocates among American pubic began to be concerned.

Meanwhile, the Peace Corps administration sought, and obtained, a change in legislation which permitted use of a maximum of one hundred volunteer secretaries from other host nations (with all proper screening), was recommended officially by the U.S. State Department.

The Peace Corps announced that the change was in keeping with their belief that "as much opportunity as possible should be provided for foreign host nation administrative personnel to serve on a voluntary basis, and that opportunities for Americans to serve overseas as volunteers should be expanded whenever possible, with maximum support by host nations."

These local host secretaries received most of their training in regularly scheduled volunteer training programs, with expenses paid in full under U.S. Foreign Aid budgets.

They were given the same allowances as U.S. volunteers, and are expected to conduct themselves in all respects alongside U.S. Peace Corps volunteers. These host nation volunteer secretaries were widely publicized to bring to the Peace Corps in a host country the same spirit as U.S. volunteers. Also reported 'anonymously by government official sources': "Most of these fully investigated local host nation secretaries were offered future visas for U.S. citizenship for both themselves and their extended families if there were able to serve U.S. interests at least 5 years".

Justification for New U.S. Peace Corps Super-grades

The Peace Corps staff next was, at the recommendation of State Department, to request to Congress and receive approval to include up to thirty super-grade positions – which included two statutory positions with the salary $500 above super-grade top level of all previous U.S. executive branch Federal workers.

This was very highly unusual, but very quickly approved within budget of the Peace Corps with consent of Congress, as an emergency measure. This was reported by the U.S. press to have been related to 'some kind of stop gap situation that was not fully disclosed in hearings'.

This included "ten non super-grade positions compensated without regard to the Classification Act, but not higher than the top of the GS-15." This number of super-grades was higher than any government agency.

The U.S. Congress Committee on Foreign Affairs supported the Peace Corps to justify this high number of super-grades. Director Shriver presented to the Committee on Foreign Affairs his purpose in requesting them as follows (which had since become a familiar mantra):

"In order to enlist top flight men and women whose experience and abilities are necessary for success of the Peace Corps program, a program which can contribute substantially to manpower needs of underdeveloped nations, and perhaps even more important, can increase the effectiveness of American efforts in interest of freedom, we must pay higher salaries beyond what private sector pays."

As a result, the Committee on Foreign Relations expressed approval in its report: "To be successful, the Peace Corps must be staffed, from top to bottom, with first rate personnel. The Committee therefore strongly recommends to the Senate that it authorize the full number of high-level positions the Peace Corps requests".

Congress fully accepted these recommendations. However, volunteers for the Peace Corps as well as the American people began to suspect that many things were starting to happen beyond what they signed on for.

Early Peace Corps Reliance on Highly Paid Consultants

The new Peace Corps agency, like all government agencies, increasingly engaged the services of experts and consultants or organizations for the performance and support of high-level administrative functions.

Individuals employed by the Peace Corps could only be compensated at rates at standard government rates not in excess of $75 per day, and while away from their home may be paid actual travel expenses and per diem.

However, increasing investigative journalist reporting was to begin to focus upon 'matching' payments to Peace Corps consultants by lobby organizations, including foreign governments receiving U.S. Foreign Aid; which were mostly stopped quickly after initial publication, and after that often to not be printed. Within first two years of Peace Corps, polls of American support were eroding.

First National Advisory Council for the Peace Corps

President Kennedy and future presidents were granted by Peace Corps Act to appoint twenty-five persons annually to a National Advisory Council for the Peace Corps. This Council was a new innovation followed by many future independent agencies to report to the President on activities, for Presidential Approval of their actions. Such was initially also the case for the Peace Corps.

This Peace Corps Advisory Council was by statute composed of persons who were representatives of educational institutions, voluntary agencies, farm organizations, labor unions, and other groups who are interested in the programs and objectives of the agency.

The Council advised the President as well the Peace Corps with regard to strategic policies and programs designed to promote the agency's purposes.

The distinguished people selected from various categories of life give advice on what they felt day-to-day operations should be, and where activities might be channeled in another direction or improved. These members served without compensation.

The President got most names from current Congressmen, White House Assistants, the Vice President, and the Peace Corps Director. The interest, background, and experience of the National Advisory Council were intended to qualify them to assist in developing policies for the effective conduct of Peace Corps operations.

The Peace Corps Advisory Council met approximately twice a year, but individual members were frequently called upon for advice and counsel by mail and telephone by White House staff.

This was the primary political body to direct and control the U.S. Peace Corps from its first year, across the time of President Kennedy assassination, and even more within the early years of the presidency of Lyndon Johnson as he put his own stamp on Peace Corps.

Peace Corps Under President Lyndon Johnson

For over two years after the President Lyndon Johnson was sworn in after the assassination of President Kennedy, the U.S. Peace Corps was not a major focus of White House interest, and was mostly left to be under continuing and growing influence of U.S. State Department, for which the new President Johnson was to have reportedly declared he would take a 'hands-off' policy, and try not to intervene despite his 'personal interests'.

President Johnson had more serious interests to further NASA as an independent agency, and also was increasingly drawn into the complexities of the growing prospect of War in Vietnam (which was after 'War on Poverty' and 'Civil Rights', was one of his most serious grave responsibilities); yet he attempted to build support across all of these, hoping to use same support Kennedy had mobilized on college campuses – with partial success.

After Lyndon Johnson won his first election as U.S. President in a very difficult campaign versus Barry

Goldwater in 1964, many more critical issues dominated his attention. However, he eventually the next year got back to his personal interest and belief in U.S. Peace Corps, as he had always felt it was a great opportunity for world peace.

President Johnson in January, 1965, named Vice President Hubert Humphrey to be chairman of the U.S. Peace Corps National Advisory Council.

In January, 1965, members of the first U.S. Peace Corps National Advisory Council included:

"Joseph Beirne, Communications Workers of America; Janet Leigh, actress; Arthur Fleming, president of University of Oregon; Peter Grace, president of W.R. Grace; C.J. Haggerty, president of AFL-CIO; Rabbi Benjamin Kahn; Mrs. Robert Kintner, UNICEF Hospitality Committee; Mrs. Lee Ozbirn, Federation of Women's Clubs; Donald Petrle, CEO of Avis; Dr. David Rubinstein, head of Preventive Medicine of Harvard; Mrs. Harvey Schechter, Council on Mexican-American Affairs; Harry Belafonte, entertainer; Palmer Hoyt, publisher of The Denver Post; Ralph Lazarus, CEO Federated Department Stores; Murray Lincoln, Nationwide Mutual Insurance Company; Benjamin Mays, president of Morehouse College; James A. McCain, president of Kansas State University; Franklin Murphy, chancellor University of California at Los Angeles; Reverend Clarence E. Pickett, executive secretary of American Friends Service Committee; Reverend James Robinson, director of Operations Crossroads Africa Inc."; and many more.

There had never been any more political body to be organized either before or since that time. This observation was made by many in the U.S. press, but some dared to make two more critical observations.

One, all of those that President Johnson had appointed to this committee had been minor contributors to his election campaign.

Two, in addition, almost none of them admitted to U.S. press they knew anything about the Peace Corps.

This was widely regarded by the a major core of original support by American college students, in both 'Young Democrat' and 'Young Republican' clubs, as an insult and betrayal, despite anything else that was good about the initiatives of President Johnson.

The same college students and recent college graduates who had supported to elect Kennedy, came to regard Johnson as a 'sell-out' to the establishment – who they all mostly felt would easily send American youth in a draft to die in the Viet Nam war (which they felt was in complete opposition of the idealism of the Peace Corps).

In short, despite young Americans continued to love the concept of an American Peace Corps, they began to begin to feel betrayed by an American political system that treated them like 'pawns' on a chess board between U.S. and communism; which seemed to them to be easily willing to sacrifice them for political goals that did not seem to be within what they regarded as 'American'.

As a result, many rebelled by to go 'full-circle' to embrace again the original teachings and philosophy of William James, and to claim 'Conscientious Objector' status; or to run away to Canada, to avoid the Draft into War in Viet Nam. This was reported to 'sadden' Johnson.

When asked about these issues at a White House Press Conference in 1965, Director Shriver response was:

"The National Advisory Council advises the President and the Peace Corps on how to meet the agency's objectives."

Notably, by that time there were already even more security issues raised due to events that were highly publicized in U.S. press related to increasingly dangerous and complex considerations to protect U.S. Peace Corps volunteers in missions that were located near conflicts.

These were all to even more divert and distract President Johnson from his top priorities of Civil Rights and War on Poverty, as international crises were to erupt.

Revised Objectives of Peace Corps in the Johnson Era

President Johnson White House released many statements related to the Peace Corps Act during his administration, such as:

"In the language of Congressional legislation the purpose of the Peace Corps was to promote world peace and friendship through Good Will – which shall make available to interested countries and areas men and women of the United States qualified for service abroad and willing to serve, under conditions of hardship if necessary – to help the peoples of such countries and areas in meeting their needs for trained manpower, and to help promote a better understanding of the American people on the part of the peoples served and a better understanding of other peoples on the part of the American people."

Among other similar statements by the Johnson administration included:

"The objectives of the Peace Corps are much broader than any other form of U.S. Foreign Aid. The Peace Corps is an American response to suffering and human hardship of the less fortunate peoples of the world.

The Marshall Plan was intended primarily to rebuild a war-torn Europe, and it involved mostly money. The people of the underdeveloped countries indeed need financial assistance, but they also need technically trained people. The primary purpose of the Peace Corps is to provide the opportunity and organization for Americans to help. Our Peace Corps was designed to provide a framework for individual Americans to help other nations."

According to a statement issued by Senator Humphrey at the same time: "The Peace Corps is the full expression of America's idealism, her humanitarianism, and her generosity, that can find no greater expression than by helping to build a better world for mankind."

Yet, these statements were only moderately effective to satisfy most Americans to continue support of the Peace Corps through presidency of Lyndon Johnson.

Growing Complications of Reality to Early Peace Corps

In all honesty, the fundamental motives of the United States in establishing the Peace Corps were not entirely or strictly humanitarian.

The United States and even the new President Johnson had some arguably selfish reasons for the establishment and continuation of the Peace Corps.

The Peace Corps volunteers made possible a new level of international and intercultural understanding; but they also had the potential to open doors to make personal connections to the citizens of other nations in ways that traditional Foreign Aid could not.

This included to collect information and intelligence of vital importance to United States missions of the State Department, foreign aid, and business interests.

In the Johnson Era, U.S. State Department began to utilize Peace Corps volunteers to understand the 'hopes and dreams' of host country 'common people'.

For example, during that time in the Dominican Republic, the U.S. Peace Corps volunteers were the only official contact between the United States and that country.

Peace Corps volunteers personalized a new humanitarian dimension of American foreign aid, which was often so well received by the people of such nations that even initially resistant leaders of such nations began to openly embrace it, and to ask for more from Peace Corps.

According to one of the many official press releases by the Peace Corps during the Johnson era:

"The Peace Corps volunteer converts modest material aid into powerful social and economic reform to help people. Such service in the Peace Corps stimulates volunteers to pursue a career in foreign services, to travel abroad, or to work for private industry or foreign governments. This additional contact will aid both in the formulation and execution of American foreign policy. The Peace Corps is a new emerging and successful part of the total foreign policy of the United States."

Originally, President Kennedy had announced to the many underdeveloped countries of the world that the U.S. intention was: "to encourage and to foster the social, economic, and political reforms that will mean better lives for the common people" of the world.

By mid-1963 President Kennedy also was reported to have said:

"The emphasis of the Peace was originally to focus on programs that could directly benefit local people in underdeveloped third world nations, regardless of their political situation.

The Peace Corps was thus designed primarily as a way to deliver progressive humanitarian aid using a more people-oriented concept of American assistance.

To work in a highly personal way for peace, to labor for eradication of disease, for the reduction of illiteracy, and for the elimination of poverty was an original and lasting challenge to the Peace Corps."

In this sense, the Peace Corps in the Johnson Era was completely in line with the original concept as expressed by President Kennedy, and President Johnson repeatedly reconfirmed his commitment to that same vision. Yet, one more 'anonymous government official' from the Johnson White House was reported to have said: "The Peace Corps will always be close to the President Johnson's heart – but only rarely now close to his mind".

The Need for the Peace Corps Affirmed by Johnson

Among other official releases by the Peace Corps under the Johnson Era were such statements as:

"The Peace Corps is a bold new dimension in American assistance programs. Other programs provide capital and technical assistance to developing nations. Most developing countries have a surplus of unskilled labor. But the key to Peace Corps assistance is trained manpower.

The desperate shortage in the underdeveloped two thirds of the world was middle manpower – somewhere between the highly trained experts and the untrained or unskilled majority.

Without this middle level, the advice of the experts cannot be properly utilized. It was this missing link which the volunteer seeks to supply. Rather than to simply advise the local people, the Peace Corps will help to do the work, and in the process teach the local people to perform the same tasks themselves in the future".

Also another official press release from the Johnson White House was to say:

"The Peace Corps has a multitude of goals – to help give a new dimension to our foreign-aid programs; to be an important factor in the ideological struggle with communism; to help Americans communicate with and understand millions of people who have little in common with us; to help identify America with the revolution of rising expectations taking place in the underdeveloped countries; to provide opportunities for personal fulfillment; to demonstrate dignity of labor; and help the citizens of the United States understand world affairs."

One of the great strengths of the Corps was the multiplicity of its purposes. This theme was mirrored in many internal Peace Corps memos related to as increasing coordination with State Department agencies, including the newly reorganized agency for Aid to Economic and Social Development.

By the 'mid-years' of the Johnson Era, the State Department and AID were to begin to see great value in the Peace Corps as an independent agency that could help to provide information and intelligence directly from interpersonal relationships built by Peace Corps volunteers to local host citizens.

According to internal memos of Peace Corps administrators that were circulated as 'talking points' when meeting with Congress and State Department officials:

"There are three ways Peace Corpsmen can aid host nations in local economic and social development.

First, the Peace Corps volunteer can demonstrate the techniques of getting a skilled job done, and transfers their skills to their host nation counterparts.

Second, he teaches the skills of the organization for effective action.

Finally, he demonstrates the dignity of labor. In many underdeveloped countries, there is no significant shortage of technicians, yet they lack the dignity of fair pay.

The lacking element is the willingness of the educated technician to perform the less glamorous tasks that a sound lasting development program requires.

By demonstrating such willingness, the Peace Corps volunteers can inspire and activate local technicians."

This was noted by one journalist as seeming to be 'similar to speech by an American union labor leader'.

Promotion of Understanding and Trust by Peace Corps

During the Johnson Era, the Peace Corps did more than serve as an operational resource in oversea development programs.

The Peace Corps originally provided only trained technical manpower, but under Johnson, the mandate shifted more to good will rather than merely technical advice and assistance.

Congress gave the Peace Corps the purpose of promoting mutual understanding between host and American peoples.

Congress had expected better understanding from the people-to-people approach of the volunteers, as 'local ambassadors', to 'win the hearts and minds of peoples'.

As Peace Corps Director Sargent Shriver had written in an article published in mid-1965:

"The opportunity for developing a growing understanding between peoples was perhaps the greatest potential the Peace Corps can offer.

Volunteers are meeting the people of foreign countries on an individual basis at a different level than most Americans abroad, and can serve to overcome many of the stereotypes about America that are cast by enemies of Freedom".

Mr. Shriver commented that the contribution of the Peace Corps had been "less in direct economic development and more in social development – health, education, construction, and community organization."

However, Shriver was also convinced economic development was directly related to social development. As Shriver also commented:

"The Peace Corps is not primarily a foreign-aid agency. Two of the three purposes as defined by Congress in the Peace Corps Act deal with understanding issues, not simply economic assistance.

The individual Peace Corps volunteers challenge was to triumph over the idea that man was incapable of shaping his destiny."

Thus, Shriver believed that the Peace Corps volunteers make possible a new level of international and intercultural understanding:

"To achieve the objectives of the Corps, to increase mutual understanding, and to supply the middle level manpower to the less developed countries, the Corps requires fundamental policies, programs, and projects."

Johnson Era Peace Corps International Objectives

The overseas operations of the early Peace Corps under President Johnson were divided geographically into four major areas.

The largest, making up thirty-nine per cent of all volunteers, was the Latin-America program. Seventeen countries in Latin America had programs, with Colombia having the greatest number of volunteers.

Next was Africa (South of the Sahara) with volunteers in seventeen countries comprising thirty-two per cent of all volunteers.

Thirdly, the program embraced eight countries in the Near East, South Asia, and North Africa made up eighteen per cent of the total volunteers.

Finally, the program of six countries in the Far East entailed eleven per cent of the total volunteers.

The type of program assigned to a particular country was a reflection of the socio economic structure of that nation. As official Peace Corps recruiting documents pointed out:

"The critical needs of the developing countries for middle manpower such as those supplied by the volunteers cover a wide variety of subject areas.

For example, in Latin America, where poverty and disease are so common as to be regarded with indifference, program emphasis is on rural and urban community action.

In Africa, where new nations seek the intellectual stimulus so necessary for the responsibilities of self-government, the emphasis was on education at all levels."

With regard to Peace Corps project planning, one of the most fundamental aspects of Corps policy, according to Sargent Shriver, was that: "volunteers will not serve in any country where they are not wanted or needed."

Also according to Shriver: "indications as to countries and the type of programs in which volunteers might usefully serve may come to the Corps from the American Embassy, the Agency for International Development, or a private source. Project proposals may also come from personal contacts between representatives of host governments and Corps officials that visit the country to explain the aims and objectives of the Corps."

Also according to Shriver: "Once these Peace Corps proposals, regardless of internal or external origin, have been judged by the Peace Corps as to the feasibility of volunteer participation, the projects can be quickly evaluated as to the genuine need of the potential host country for Peace Corps resources – as well as potential to share resources for a project with the Agency for International Development mission in the host country, the American Embassy there, or directly with the United States State Department.

All coordinated projects must be approved across all of these agencies before they can be carried out. This can include projects simple as to build a pump for a water well into a holding tank for purification, up to a medical center or more."

The selection and careful development of individual projects were regarded from the start as essential to the success of the Peace Corps.

In their presentation to Congress for fiscal year 1963, while Kennedy was still president, the Peace Corps had listed five basic criteria for determining eligibility of a potential project:

"First, the project must make a contribution to the economic, social, cultural, or the political development of the host country. The host country must have requested the project and given evidence of its willingness to cooperate.

Second, the project must require primarily volunteers who are workers with skills not sufficiently available in the recipient country.

Third, maintenance must be in accordance with Peace Corps standards.

Fourth, the host country must be able to utilize volunteers for a minimum of two years.

Fifth, sectarian religious propagandizing or proselytizing was officially prohibited."

The early Peace Corps thus stressed programs which aided in the pragmatic development of the host country. It favored projects that involve maximum contact between the volunteers and the people of the host country.

Whenever possible, citizens of the host country participated in the work of every project with the goal for them to eventually take over the jobs of the volunteers.

Contributions by the host government to the projects were encouraged. For example, Ghana paid the entire living allowances of the volunteers.

This was notably similar to many host nations past experience with the British VSO program, which required such matching. This was in fact a common matter of honor for African nations, in order to agree to accept the help from VSO or U.S. Peace Corps.

Many nations would not accept Peace Corps projects if they could not provide 'respectable' furnishings at host government hotels, rather than to live in same humble circumstance as their local people.

In some cases, the leaders of these countries just could not understand why Americans would want to live among the poor. In many cases there was suspicion that the Americans might try to indoctrinate or alienate the poor against their leaders (which was already being done by pro-communist agitators in many such underdeveloped nations), and many demanded that no Peace Corps volunteers would be allowed to have direct contact with the local people without supervision by representatives of the government of the host country present. These kinds of cultural differences had to be managed on a country by country basis by Peace Corps administrators in each nation.

A working project agreement was usually signed by the Peace Corps representative and a government official of the host-country being served. This agreement described in detail the working, living, and support arrangements for the volunteers and described the respective responsibilities of the two countries.

In effect, such agreements were in fact legally binding contracts subject to the laws of each individual country, which had been recommended by early advisors to both President Kennedy and President Johnson.

In most countries, such agreements were honored in good faith by both parties – however, in some of the host nations that the Peace Corps served, this was to prove to be disadvantageous to U.S. interests, as the leaders of some of these countries proved to be 'untrustworthy partners' – who used the local Peace Corps volunteers as 'pawns' in order to negotiate higher U.S. foreign aid payments or concessions – despite the Peace Corps was an independent agency, and had absolutely no influence on U.S. foreign aid payments.

This was to make the Peace Corps to feel that they were 'stuck in the middle' between the leadership in governments of their local host nation projects, and the diplomats in the State Department who in fact had full responsibility for such foreign aid negotiations.

After being 'blind-sided' on several occasions in which the planning and contractual agreements that had been previously signed between the Peace Corps and the local host government were effectively 'trumped' by secret negotiations with the U.S. State Department, the top leadership of the Peace Corps was soon to regret many of the implications of being an independent agency, and were to actually request President Johnson to create more formal direct organizational reporting to the Department of State.

Channels By Which Projects Were Selected and Managed

Peace Corp projects, after approval by the Director and government officials in the host country, operated through several channels.

First, according to the 1963 presentation of the Peace Corps to Congress, they operated through contracts or grants to private agencies engaged in similar activities:

"From its beginning, the Peace Corps has recognized the desirability of working closely with interested voluntary agencies operating in the host nation'.

The Peace Corps made volunteers available to reputable and experienced private agencies for projects.

In order to insure success of the projects, the Peace Corps partnered with private organizations having most recent experience in the country in which the project was established. Thus:

"Projects may be contracted with religious organization which meet our standards, and which do no proselytizing, and seek to further no sectarian causes."

For example, the Cooperative for American Remittances to Everywhere (CARE) administered a community action project in Colombia.

Thus, CARE was selected to directly administer a community action project for the Peace Corps in St. Lucia.

In addition to direct project administration, the Peace Corps drew upon the resources and experience of voluntary agencies for advice and problem-solution.

A second major channel of Peace Corps volunteers to underdeveloped countries was through the institutions of higher learning which had wide experience there. Approximately a thousand specialists from fifty-seven educational institutions had served under foreign-aid contracts in thirty-six countries.

Local host nation universities were selected to partner with U.S. colleges with technical specialty programs were especially valuable. Such U.S. colleges were also in a good position to screen potential Peace Corps volunteers.

Several leading U.S. educational institutions entered into joint cooperation agreement contracts with local host nation colleges for administration of projects.

Examples included the Chile project administered by Notre Dame University on behalf of the Indiana Conference of Higher Education, and the West Pakistan project administered by Colorado State University. The Peace Corps gained a wealth of knowledge and experience from such joint relationship between U.S. and foreign institutions of higher learning.

A third avenue of channeling volunteers was through the United Nations and its specialized agencies. Section Ten of the Peace Corps Act permitted the assignment of volunteers in special cases to temporary duty with international organizations and agencies such as U.N.

The number of these volunteers was limited to one hundred and twenty-five (most of whom were to be assigned to work directly with WHO on health projects).

Most Peace Corps volunteers to be surveyed agreed that the most valuable efforts in field of technical assistance to underdeveloped countries were undertaken by international organizations such as United Nations.

Many specialized agencies of the United Nations had all indicated great interest in broadening the influence of their programs through the U.S. Peace Corps volunteers.

Yet it was pointed out in the 1963 Peace Corps presentation to Congress that there were many in even the most receptive host countries who would criticize any activity sponsored by United States, and all projects could be subject to suspicion and even false accusation.

Participating in specialized agencies of the United Nations had prompted other governments to cooperate in the exchange of skills and ideas resulting in International Good Will and understanding, and this partnering channel with United Nations was to make many host nations to feel more comfortable with the Peace Corps projects; so this channel was encouraged to be included into every project to the fullest extent possible.

The fourth channel for Peace Corps volunteers was direct administration by the Agency. Because some projects were unique, they would require more direct supervision. The agency also used direct supervision to attain better standards of operation.

This channel was to become the most critical as so many underdeveloped host nations were to each have such a diverse range of incredibly different problems. By 1963 when President Johnson took over the White House, such special oversight of Peace Corps projects from Washington was increasing in volume and importance.

The Critical Importance of Local Host Counterparts

Whenever possible, the early Peace Corps aggressively sought out counterparts from the host country to work side-by-side with the volunteers.

It was also important for all volunteers to leave behind trained counterparts to replace them when they returned to the United States.

This was commonly known as the 'Teach a man to fish' rule, which applied to all Peace Corps projects.

The training of host-country personnel in the underdeveloped countries was often a missing element in most of all previous U.S. technical foreign-aid programs.

Yet, it was felt the efforts of a single Peace Corps

volunteer could be greatly amplified when they were applied in the right country at the appropriate time.

Such specific requests for specific projects that already had support from the local host country people were usually evaluated and approved higher than the usual applications for volunteer Peace Corps services.

The Peace Corps firmly believed that the risk of all projects could be reduced by proven value-added benefits for long-term success by tapping the latent energy of the host-country peoples.

Volunteers in the field were encouraged to look for additional projects that met the needs of their host community. Corpsmen were instructed to look primarily into four major areas of needs:

o Education
o Community action
o Agricultural extension
o Public health

The most important program was teaching. There was no greater need in the underdeveloped world than teaching people to read.

More than two thirds of the people of Asia, Africa, and Latin America were illiterate. Thus, slightly over fifty per cent of all early Peace Corps volunteers are assigned to host nation teaching positions.

On March 31, 1965, a total of 4,983 volunteers were assigned to regular classroom teaching.

Of these, 2,433 teachers were in Africa, 770 in the Far East, 722 in Latin America, and 672 in the Near East and South Asia. Seventy per cent of the teachers were assigned to secondary education.

In Nigeria, for example, 664 volunteers comprised more than one fourth of all degree teachers in that country's secondary school system. In many countries they were responsible for accelerating the rate at which teachers are being trained for expanding educational systems.

The contribution of teachers extended far beyond their classroom assignments. In some countries, where school vacations were as much as four months, agencies often planned vacation projects, such as census taking, inoculation campaigns, or community action projects.

The objective of community action often involved self-organization of individuals to take constructive action to satisfy their needs. It might begin with a vaccination campaign, formation of a cooperative, the introduction of a cash crop, the development of a cooking class, or the construction of a new school, a road, or a bridge.

Community action projects were energy-releasing and team-building activities, so the Corps had 2,142 volunteers assigned to such programs by March, 1965.

One such early community-action project was the Colombian middle school program. Middle schools were lacking and not often to exist in most rural Columbian schools. In order to get support of initiatives such as to build and staff a local middle school required a lot of local community organization in order to get local support.

As a result of the success of such programs, similar projects were requested and established in many other Latin-American countries.

Seventy per cent of all community-action volunteers were by 1966 serving in Latin America.

Many aspects of the Latin-American culture were conducive to community action, and several such countries were at the stage in their development when community action could be easily and effectively introduced.

According to the 1965 Congressional Peace Corps presentation, the Latin-American program was most largely involved in community action and development project work in rural areas. Volunteers were helping to propose and build schools, roads, and rural health clinics.

The volunteers spent much effort encouraging villagers and slum dwellers to organize themselves for their own betterment.

Outside Latin America, such as in Africa and Asia, there were usually more restrictions upon Peace Corp volunteer activities for community organization, due to greater tendency for third world government leaders in these regions to be more suspicious of such activities, due to common fears that local people would be indoctrinated, and converted to western religions or political views – as these nations had in the past had more often bad experiences with missionaries and communist agitators than was the case in many Latin American nations served.

The first urban community-development project in Peru was an experiment to see whether the same effect of volunteers in rural communities could be transplanted to a city slum. Over four hundred volunteers were involved in Peruvian projects, serving as construction tradesmen, social workers, and sanitarians for helping the town people to construct decent housing and improve standards of living.

Community, development was based on the simple idea that the best way to improve the conditions of life was to create a program that the people themselves can carry on after the Corps leaves. Activity of an underdeveloped country was largely agricultural.

Improvements in agriculture have the potential of directly advancing the living standards of eighty to ninety per cent of the people in most underdeveloped areas.

According to the 1965 Congressional presentation,

improvement in agriculture was the key to economic growth in these countries. Agriculture had to become more efficient to release labor and capital for industrialization.

Agricultural extension volunteers made up only eight per cent of the total Corps. Half of the agricultural extension volunteers were assigned to Latin America.

Agricultural volunteers had brought improvement to farming in the host countries. They had encouraged farmers to experiment with new crops, new methods, development of family gardens, and new marketing methods including cooperatives.

As the volunteers encountered illness, poor sanitation, and malnutrition of the people in the host countries, they naturally moved into public-health activity. This was to acknowledge the fact that the will to attempt self-improvement was often sapped by physical weakness.

Over 850 volunteers including doctors, nurses, nursing teachers, medical technicians, and sanitation specialists, were assigned to public health programs.

Most Peace Corps volunteers were involved in health work some time during their service. Volunteers deployed as teachers often promoted local programs for medical examinations, inoculations, and health training for all of their local students.

Community-action projects were often instituted to meet specific public-health needs: pure water supplies, latrine-building campaigns, and medical dispensaries.

Public Health Service doctors who served the volunteers spent all available time in health activities across their host country. They served in advisory roles for public health, and teaching of nurses and health care workers.

The public-health programs comprised ten per cent of the total volunteers in all host nations combined.

Yet in Latin America public-health volunteers were assigned to over sixty per cent of all projects, including those primarily for local schools health education, as well as for administration of vaccines to children.

Early Policies of Peace Corps Volunteer Living Conditions

All early Peace Corps volunteers were expected to live at the same level as their host country counterparts.

Despite some nations were to begin negotiations for a Peace Corps project with volunteer accommodations according to their culture to expect specific living conditions, the Peace Corps was often to push back on a project specific basis.

The critical rule for the Peace Corps was to define and profile the local project counterpart – who would be expected to take over the role of the volunteer after they were to return to the U.S.

Thus, if the project would be continued by a local counterpart who would be in an advisory or administrative role working with the local host government or at teaching hospitals, it would be appropriate that the Peace Corps volunteer should live in the same cultural setting.

However, if the project would be continued by a local counterpart who would be taking over a rural community project in a poverty stricken remote location, the Peace Corps would usually argue for arranging for the volunteer to live in same conditions as the local people.

The past experience of the assigned Peace Corps volunteer was not usually regarded as a top consideration.

A volunteer from the rural south raised on a farm with a graduate degree in agriculture might be assigned as an advisor to the host nation top government Ministry of

Agriculture, and thus be expected to 'hobnob' and live in the same conditions as relatively affluent elite officials.

A volunteer from an urban center in the northeast raised in affluent metropolitan lifestyle might be assigned as a local remote rural community advisor to live among poverty stricken and uneducated people, and to both accept and welcome differences in foods, attitudes and lifestyles.

Thus, one volunteer in Ghana was quoted in an interview as "awed" by his living conditions. He described his accommodations proudly: "I got a huge bungalow with three bedrooms, living room, dining room, family-size kitchen, huge bath facilities, the works. I had a cook and maid who fix the meals, washes, irons, and markets."

When asked to comment, Director Shriver assured the Committee on Foreign Affairs this was an isolated case. Mr. Shriver felt "Most Congressmen who have visited Ghana are aware that most of the volunteers are living below most Ghana teachers, not above."

The Peace Corps did not ever intend for any of the volunteers to live luxuriously in plush surroundings. In the case of the Ghana teacher, these were accommodations the Ghana government had provided, not the Peace Corps.

Nevertheless, Director Shriver also commented that the Peace Corps had never expected any volunteers to have to live in "mud huts":

"Corp volunteers receive a suitable allowance for subsistence, food, clothing, housing, local travel, and incidentals while serving abroad, that are intended to be healthy and safe within the range of teachers and doctors within each local project community, and we never intended to put volunteers at a level of local poverty".

The intention was that each Peace Corps volunteer was to have living conditions equal to a "modest mid-range compared to the local host community to be served". Thus, it was a fundamental objective of the Peace Corps that each volunteer would "live at a respectable level compared to counterparts among the people served, and yet not appear to be either more or less affluent than the average of the people they are there to serve".

This was to be one of the first of many formal policies established by the Peace Corp leadership.

It was commonly to be noted in presentations and documents that:

"Catholic priest missionaries in many nations in the past have been determined by history to not have been as effective as they could have been due to their 'vow of poverty'. In many of the cultures where they were sent, this lowered local respect. Yet in all nations, to appear to 'live in privilege' above local people creates resentment".

In addition to providing modest but adequate housing and food, the Peace Corps initiated a 'pocket money' fund for each volunteer. As part of their overall compensation, seventy-five dollars a month would accrue to a locally accessible host nation bank account.

If in any month it was necessary for the volunteer to access up to this amount each month for 'emergency unanticipated expenses' – all they had to do was contact their regional Peace Corps supervisor within one month to explain – and indicate if it was a one-time exception, or might require evaluation as an ongoing expense paid directly from Peace Corps local nation contingency funds, rather than another such emergency draw on the individual volunteer's contingency account going forward.

At the time when Peace Corps volunteers returned to the U.S., the full balance of this $75 per month contingency fund was paid upon separation as a readjustment allowance.

This money was intended to help the volunteer during the transition from Corps service to his next Job, or school. At the same time, it provided an effective cushion for field-deployed Peace Corps volunteers for fast access to a moderate level of cash to pay for unexpected but reasonable project expenses.

The volunteers had additional fringe benefits. They were given a $10,000 life insurance policy unless they waived coverage. Payments of National Defense Education Act student loans were suspended while in service. Interest did not accrue to volunteer student loans during service.

Also, many specialized programs of the U.S. government to 'forgive' student loan debt were expanded to include Peace Corps service. For example, complete medical school debt that was in the 1960's fully forgiven by 2 years of military or remote public health community service was also fully eliminated by 2 years in Peace Corps.

The volunteers were automatically credited with forty-five days of paid leave at the beginning of overseas service. This was for most of the teaching, engineering and medical professionals a minimum total accrued leave for one year prescribed term of service, and was subject to additional 'successful completion' payments, which was demonstrated as extremely successful to recruit an elite of Peace Corps volunteers.

For each day of this leave, $75 in addition to the regular living allowance was paid to cover extra expenses. This was clearly a way to accumulate a fairly substantial 'nest egg' for returning Peace Corps volunteers who successfully completed each one year mission. In most cases, this 'incentive pay' for successful returning Peace Corps volunteers was 'equal or above' most private sector compensation.

This program also involved legal requirements and obligations for the successful returning Peace Corps volunteer to "provide for the ongoing success of future Peace Corps activities related to their own experience and expertise". In effect, returning Peace Corps volunteers were expected not only to be 'available to consult future volunteers in their same area of professional expertise as well as all personal knowledge of local communities and projects for future success'.

This was also intended as policies to build an 'alumni' mentality to help create a public perception and understanding of both the sacrifices and value of past Peace Corps volunteers as they were to return and be integrated into professions in teaching, public health or engineering – and to both recommend Peace Corps service to others, as well as serve to recommend others to the Peace Corps – and this especially was to involve students.

In order that each early Peace Corps volunteer could obtain a broad knowledge of the areas they serves, the first year's leave was expected to be spent entirely in the country of first assignment. The volunteer was required to have advance written approval to travel outside the host country, and to report any contacts outside the U.S.

The normal tenure of service for a volunteer was two years. The volunteers agreed to serve up to two years, by mutual option. It was not an enforceable contract, and when presented with a letter to sign, the volunteer was told it was not a legally binding contract, and instead, 'a matter of personal honor'. The 'hook' was the contingency pay.

This was presented at the same time as details of the benefit package that would be available to each volunteer if they successfully completed their initial Peace Corps assignment. This was also another innovation of the early Peace Corps, and had been adopted by many large private corporations to recruit and retain prime talent since.

Such methods were confirmed by many studies to give all employers opportunity to not only recruit but also retain 'best and brightest' staff, using more 'positive reinforcements' rather than negative threats.

This was yet another very successful innovation by the Peace Corps, which was only able to bypass most of the usual permanent Federal Employee regulations because it involved temporary positions that were not regarded as 'grants and internships', with an 'at will' option to continue first year with Peace Corps at 'mutual agreement'.

The early Peace Corps administration at first discouraged the volunteers from extending enlistment beyond one, and at most two years.

The policy was based upon belief that if the objective of improving understanding of foreign peoples was to be fully realized if volunteers return 'to teach others' after at most two years service. This was later extended.

The early Peace Corps leaders felt that this was the intent of the original legal mandate from Congress in 1961. However, by 1964, after assassination of President Kennedy and start of administration of President Johnson, many in Congress began to express the belief that this was a waste of the critical experience of trained manpower.

There was a growing sense and sentiment of Congress and the American people of the need to not only stop the encouragement of returning Peace Corps volunteers to return to academic and private sector jobs, but to instead 'encourage' returning Peace Corps volunteers to take permanent positions in U.S. government executive branches, including U.S. State Department and Dept. of Defense, including any agencies that could benefit by underdeveloped nation cultural and political experience and insights (as well as advanced language training).

In 1964, the Peace Corps adopted a neutral position in the extension of the two-year service period.

Of the volunteers who had successfully completed a tour of duty, ten per cent desired to continue their assignment for an average of six months. Any extension of service beyond that had to meet Peace Corps approval.

Most of the surveyed volunteers were to report that they felt they could 'finish out' and fully accomplish their original project objectives by an additional 6 to 12 months in the nation. Notably, almost 100% of such requests for extensions after 1964 were approved.

As they had been regarded as 'temporary mutual at-will' employees, each volunteer member of the Peace Corps was entitled to resign or request a transfer at any point in his service, in order to formerly separate.

However, to do so was to always result in the volunteer to quickly receive a follow-up letter to summarize the 'contingency funds and bonuses' that would be lost if they confirmed to resign. Very few confirmed to resign.

The Peace Corps could also involuntarily return the volunteer to the United States and terminate his service, for any reason, and with no explanation other than 'for the convenience of the government'. This was not an exclusive innovation by the Peace Corps, but started to be more common during early years of the Johnson administration.

Despite this was approaching a time when 'Whistleblower' laws were to be implemented by Congress, in reality any situation or case where it was deemed in best interest of not 'embarrassing' or putting government in bad light, all temporary workers such as Peace Corps volunteers who did not agree to fully drop and agree to never talk about their concerns about any issues they had previously reported were subject not only to termination but loss of all compensation. So this was not actually to happen as often for the Peace Corps as in other agencies at the time.

This was not originated by Peace Corps, but was instead part of a growing division of culture over Vietnam War concerns both within and outside U.S. government, which were forced upon President Johnson, who were shown by historians to appall him, as he was to personally seek and believed his destiny was to create legacy to push for Peace Corps, NASA, War on Poverty and Civil Rights; yet he was to be increasingly drawn into War in Vietnam which he did not feel personally to put above Peace Corps, NASA and Civil Rights, yet he had no choice.

When a volunteer was terminated, the Peace Corps had the right to deduct return transportation from the volunteer's contingency pay. A volunteer terminated could have a personal review by a Director if he requested within one day of notification of the decision to terminate.

Out of the first four hundred sent overseas, only four were dropped for cause. Yet four per cent of the first 7,857 volunteers sent overseas came home because of 'inability to adjust'. Yet in nearly 100% of such cases, they had all reported concerns about their local assignment.

All persons employed by the Peace Corps were investigated by the Civil Service Commission to try to insure that their employment was consistent with U.S. national interest. If the investigation revealed any data reflecting questionable loyalty or security risk, the Civil Service Commission referred the investigation to the Federal Bureau of Investigation for a full field 'work up' conducted during the United States training period. Notably, it always did.

Although volunteers did not have access to classified materials and did not participate in policy-making decisions, they were serving in conspicuous positions. Every volunteer was looked upon as a private ambassador of the United States.

As a result, every volunteer was required to take the same oath of office required of elected and appointed officials of the United States. Yet they neither received same compensation or immunities.

As was in the fine print of their Peace Corps service as a volunteer "this shall not in any way exempt such volunteer from the performance of any obligations or duties under the provisions of the Universal Military Training and Service Act." The volunteer, who was subject to Selective Service, could ask his local draft board for deferment and permission to leave the United States.

Peace Corps service did not exempt the volunteer from military obligations, but the draft boards usually deferred volunteers while they are in the Corps.

The volunteer "was told he must deal directly with his local draft board on such matters as deferment".

Volunteers were not officers or employees of the United States Government, and did not possess diplomatic immunities, such as were held by any officials of the U.S. government that they were to offend.

Thus only a very small number of the early Peace Corps volunteers who were to make complaints or express concerns were not to drop them.

The legal status of an individual who accepted to join the U.S. Peace Corps were to change as a result of becoming a volunteer.

They had none of the full or limited immunity of was generally subject to the federal laws of the United States and to laws of the host country in which he served.

An agreement between the Peace Corps and the host country usually stipulated that Corpsmen receive the same treatment as that extended to private United States citizens residing in the host country, and was a unique aspect of the early Peace Corps volunteers in the 1960's that was not afforded to other contractors.

Fully 4% of all U.S. Peace Corps volunteers up till 1964 who were to file their concerns about situations and circumstances that they reported first up to their immediate supervisors were later to report that they felt they were threatened personally 'off the record' and 'without due process' to 'never speak or reveal details of issues' that had been elevated in good faith to their supervisors.

As a result, almost all complaint or disagreements with local hosts were either dropped or 'settled for mutual convenience' – most often at the express request of local host nation officials.

As a further result, such cases were closed by early Peace Corps, and volunteers received full benefits – but were usually advised to 'forget and move on'.

Notably, the United States Government did not accept liability for the actions of Corpsmen as it did for other government employees.

This was widely perceived as a flaw by host nations, who were to begin to regard U.S. Peace Corps as of mid 1960's as 'untrustworthy'. This was a major setback for the U.S. under President Johnson forward.

U.S. Peace Corpsmen often served in areas in which there were great hazards to health. A thorough and comprehensive medical program was established to insure that these health hazards were avoided as completely as possible, and to insure health risks were overcome rapidly and effectively, and to make sure to monitor closely.

The Peace Corps accepted a clear responsibility for the health of the volunteers from the start of training to their separation from service as described in the agency presentation to Congress for fiscal year 1963.

Yet, in many countries the potential health risks and hazard could not be completely eliminated.

To reduce its risks, attention was given to health considerations at every stage of planning and operations.

This included "health evaluation of proposed projects, physical and psychiatric examinations, health care and instruction during the training period and oversea assignments".

When a project was planned in a new nation or local area, usually a medical survey was made to determine the medical feasibility of the project and to plan overseas health supervision.

Medical hazards vary within a country, and evaluations required acknowledge of medical resources available locally.

If practical, surveys were carried out by the Corps physician chosen for assignment to the country.

These surveys enabled the physician to become acquainted with the country's medical resources and to develop plans for the health care of the volunteers.

Applicants who were selected for training took physical examinations at nearby facilities of "Veterans Administration, Public Health Service, Department of Defense, or by private physicians". This examination prevented applicants with any serious defects from being accepted for training.

The medical staff of the Peace Corps scrutinized the findings of the initial health examinations using methods similar to the Army to evaluate health status for potential soldiers, but excluded restrictions relating primarily to military service requirements.

The Peace Corps applicant's ability to meet these standards was studied in terms of the job and area to be assigned, potential physical effectiveness in the project, and chances of aggravating personal health condition.

In case of injury or disability, compensation was provided under Federal Employees Compensation Acts.

This was to prove to be one more of many confounds and even outright disconnects that limited the Peace Corps as it was created as a new entity that U.S. government struggled to fit between the existing U.S. Military and U.S. Dept. of State.

Since the Peace Corps was from the beginning envisioned as a humanitarian organization – and as such was not envisioned to be part of any government, no matter how benevolent or good; as well as to function alongside other independent organization such as the United Nations or religious missionaries.

Summary of the Early Operations of the Peace Corps

The early operations of the U.S. Peace Corps were greatly impacted by the unexpected and tragic assassination of President John F. Kennedy, and the many complications after he was replaced by President Lyndon B. Johnson.

Despite Johnson had been an early advocate and instrumental to the creation of the Peace Corps, NASA, and was early in his administration to champion Civil Rights and a 'War on Poverty', he was diverted to focus on many other major issues; primarily the War in Vietnam, which diminished his presidential goals.

The next chapter focuses on many of these issues, with more details about the methods that were used in the early U.S., Peace Corps to recruit and retain good qualified Americans to serve in the early Peace Corps missions.

CHAPTER III

EARLY PEACE CORPS RECRUITMENT, SELECTION, AND TRAINING

Men and women serving in an overseas community hold the key to the success of the agency. This had always been and will always continue to be the case, from the past origins of the Peace Corps, into the future.

For this reason, it was essential to recruit, select, train, and send the best possible volunteers in every professional field. The early Peace Corps was looking for people with specific talents, which were directly based upon the talents and skills that were requested by potential host nations. The most commonly requested skills of host nations were for agricultural and health technology expertise.

This was likely to be the same into the future of the Peace Corps, and all humanitarian aid from the leading technology and financially advanced nations, to assist less advantaged and emerging 'third world' nations, for many decades to come.

Reasons for Americans to Apply to Join Early Peace Corps

Almost all (fully 98%) of the early applicants to the U.S. Peace Corps reported in surveys that they had two common reasons to apply to join:

"1) They were inspired by the vision in speeches by new President John Kennedy to 'serve America by serving humankind'; and

2) They had a hope that 'U.S. Peace Corps can help prevent wars in the future".

This was common to results of early surveys prior to 1963, when the American people were to be historically more united than at any time since Lincoln.

This was prior to the assassination of President John Kennedy; yet after that event, the U.S. seemed to divide like never before; and the Peace Corps seemed to be at the heart of that dissension.

In fiscal year 1963, there were 38,000 completed applications for Peace Corps service. The number of completed applications reached their peak in fiscal year 1964 with 46,000.

This number dropped to 43,000 in fiscal year 1965, and ever since.

According to preliminary figures of recruiting officials, the number of applicants for each year seemed to have continued that downward trend.

These figures indicated beginning in 1965 that the Peace Corps had reached its peak in the number of applicants unless changes were made to motivate prospective volunteers.

In order that the Corps might increase the number of applicants, it was seen helpful to analyze what motivates an individual to become a volunteer. The answer to this question had intrigued many researchers.

The applicants and volunteers had been hard put to give a simple answer. Nevertheless, as of 1965, more than 175,000 Americans applied to become volunteers, with 17,000 making through rigorous selection process.

To be eligible to apply within these first years, an individual had to be over eighteen years of age, a U.S. citizen, single (or if married could apply as a couple, if with no dependents under age of 18).

As of the fifth anniversary of the Peace Corps under President Johnson in 1966, with the War in Vietnam and military conscription on the horizon, the Peace Corps had accepted and trained 12,330 volunteers, over 75% of whom had technical Associate and Bachelor of Science or engineering degrees.

Fully 82% of the volunteers were between 21 and 25 twenty-five years of age. Another 11% were between age 26 to 30, bringing to 93% in the 20-30 age range.

The original Peace Corps was almost exclusively a movement by progressive, and dominated by young recent college graduates.

It is also notable that more than over half of all Peace Corps applicants up until 1966 were also actively against the War in Vietnam, military service, and regarded the Peace Corps as envisioned by Kennedy and Shriver as an honorable alternative to military service.

Much more research indicated that the majority of early Peace Corps volunteers who actually completed training and assignments were in fact either officially Conscientious Objectors, or had considered to file as such, and regardless had strong sympathy and respect for those brave enough to file officially to resist the draft as a 'C.O.'.

Another significant demographic was gender. Nearly 50% of early Peace Corps volunteers were female, and fully 40% finished training.

This was in spite of the fact that in early proposals for the Peace Corps, only men were originally to be eligible.

An even more significant demographic of the first Peace Corps volunteers relates to the fact that most applications as well as the number of volunteers to complete the training came from only five states: California, New York, Illinois, Pennsylvania, and Ohio.

In addition, over 95% of the volunteers who finished training and received assignments were from the top 10 largest U.S. cities.

Despite the Peace Corps missions were in the most underdeveloped rural areas in the world, barely 10% of the early Peace Corps volunteers were from rural America, and thus the early Peace Corps volunteers from metropolitan cities faced personal culture shock issues.

Several early studies of the motivations of Peace Corps volunteers indicated their primary desire was to simply' help people.'

Despite the many origins of the concept of a Peace Corps based in Christian missionary movements in the early 1900's, over 80% of the early U.S. Peace Corps volunteers were self-reported as 'non-religious' or 'spiritual but not religious'.

What was even more interesting about these surveys was that not only were over 80% of the early applicants to the Peace Corps were not to identify with any organized religion.

Yet they also almost all universally expressed belief that 'America was best hope of world peace' and that 'America had a destiny to share freedom and prosperity to the world'.

These overwhelming responses to pre-1966 applicant surveys have been given again since 1966 many decades since – and results are almost always same.

Many such early applicants expressed a belief the Peace Corps itself was an alternative to both war and religions, and simply wanted to help further its goals.

To them, serving as a Volunteer was a way to work for world peace, serve the best humanitarian goals of United States, and help to improve international relations, or participate in the progress of developing nations – as a personal commitment to help make a better world.

Almost all such early Peace Corps volunteers also reported other motivations that were more personal. More than half of the applicants mentioned potential advantages to themselves, which they openly and proudly reported as 'selfish' – as personal opportunity to gain new experience, knowledge, and contacts to develop as individuals and further their careers or vocations.

Notably – almost all of the early U.S Peace Corps volunteers that finished training self-reported that their eventual goal was to take a job for a career as a U.S. Federal government employee.

Many noted the personal satisfaction which would result from helping others, or feeling they were identified with a worthwhile cause.

The advantage mentioned most often, however, was the opportunity the U.S. Peace Corps provides for learning about other cultures, getting to know and work with people of other nations, and to become familiar with their different customs, philosophies, and ways of life.

Several government research studies were to focus on these motivations, as there were several emerging psychological standardized tests that were showing very strong high correlations between the scores of the most highly motivated Vietnam War military volunteers, and the most highly motivated Peace Corps volunteers.

In both cases, a very significant factor related to measures of 'need achievement' and 'need for adventure'.

According to one of many government-funded studies of the early Peace Corps volunteers:

"The expository answers given by the applicants were classified by content-analysis techniques. Detailed statistical results appear in the study.

The most important point of the findings was that 93% of Peace Corps applicants reported a 'desire to give to others' as basis to applying, while only 65% reported a desire for personal gain.

Only 7% reported any concern with travel dangers, and barely 6% reported to be motivated with fighting against communism".

In fact, overwhelmingly over 80% of early Peace Corps volunteers that completed training to receive assignments were in such studies to fully agree that 'communism was a real world threat'; yet were also to express personal concerns regarding 'capitalism as greatest threat to the achievement of real world peace'.

When these early studies were reported to the Johnson administration by 1966, they created substantial concerns. The fact that fully 80% of early Peace Corps volunteers felt 'capitalism is an equal threat to the world as communism', was not well received by Congress or a vast majority of the American People.

Study of Peace Corps Applicants Who Decline Invitations

By 1966, after Kennedy and Shriver were no longer driving the future direction of the Peace Corps, there was fallout of 'declines' as an incredible 'reverse spike' and drop-off in the number of volunteers to accept to consider offers starting two years after death of Kennedy and even the election of Johnson as president.

There was a massive number of the approved Peace Corps volunteer applicants who declined for unstated 'personal reasons'; as reported to Congress in one study: "out of 300, 149 declined versus 151 to accept".

Notably, this study was reported to Congress in hearing of Peace Corps to emphatically declare:

"Over 50% best applicants who were accepted and offered a contract to serve in Peace Corps accept".

This was challenged by further Congress hearing questioning, and this among other problems resulted in severe Peace Corps budget cuts after 1966.

This particular Peace Corps consultant study reported to Congress that most Peace Corps volunteers who declined to accept invitations to move forward were: 'recent college graduates who did not have a job yet, and had between the time of their application already found a high paying job in private sector'.

Notably, this observation was not received very well by members of Congress oversight, one of whom made an observation that they were very concerned, as this finding indicated that many of the early Peace Corps volunteers offered invitations to move forward had in fact been offered a job in private sector, and simply had no other prospects or opportunities when they applied.

In response to this counter, the same consultants for the Peace Corps were awarded a study to 'discover whether the decliners were even qualified to receive invitation to join' the Peace Corps to begin with.'

Multiple follow-up studies were funded by Congress as the Johnson administration put a hold on Peace Corps deployments and increasingly again considered to put the Peace Corps under direct supervision of the State Department and AID.

The results of these studies were mixed, yet interesting, within the historical context of conflicted dynamics of the early presidency of Johnson as he was pulled by political influences of Civil Rights movement and his War on Poverty, while at the same time faced with increasingly dangerous confrontation by Communism as a real threat to the Free World.

In all due fairness, the complex domestic and international conflicts during the administration of President Lyndon Johnson was more complicated than any previous U.S. president, including Kennedy or even FDR.

As a result, Johnson took a 'back-seat' and 'hedged' position regarding the early Peace Corps.

On one hand he encouraged the Peace Corps and pledged budget support for it. But at same time he had to support the military as it 'geared up for War'.

Johnson later commented several times (off the record) that he felt he was 'between a rock and a hard place'. This was one of several, yet likely most significant reason, he did not run for second term presidency.

As for the specific results of the Peace Corps volunteers who had declined (which were reported to Congress and President Johnson), results were unexpected.

Fully 75% of the decliners indicated that although they had jobs in private sector, they wanted to be 'kept on file' to possibly apply again in the future, if 'conditions change'.

Notably, the 3 top ranked reasons for volunteer applicants to decline to accept to move forward were:

"1) danger of serving in remote locations without certain security protections;

2) reconsideration of the honest realities of living in the stark poverty same as the underdeveloped nations they honestly wished to serve yet were having second doubts about practical ability to do so;

3) realizing language and culture limits; and

4) realities of health conditions in other nations."

Nearly all expressed a continued wish to serve if these limits could be 'overcome'.

Another important finding of these studies involved a near 100% factor that their decision to decline the Peace Corps invitation (which was statistically confirmed to be insignificant with regard to whether or not they had another job already) was due to influence of advice from their discussions and consultations with others, including family and friends, as well as seeking out more informational resources after their combined concerns.

Early Peace Corps applicants liked to believe that they have made their own decision whether to accept or decline. However, most applicants consulted with other people, and research sources, about their decision.

More Surveys of Early Applicants to Join the Peace Corps

Most applicants felt that the views of others carried weight in their decision. A major finding revealed that influences exerted by friends and parents were among the most imposing factors that predisposed an applicant toward or away from the invitation.

Friends ranked first as advisors both in frequency of reference and in the weight given to their views. Eighty per cent of the applicants discussed the invitation with their parents, and over half felt that their parents feelings had considerable weight in their decision.

Acceptors made their decision in a social climate of support and approval, while decliners reacted to negative influences from those around them.

It was thus after many studies by the Peace Corps that consultants strongly suggested that informational material be sent to the family explaining Corps financial, health, and legal policies.

Thus, families of all future volunteers invited to move forward were sent many materials and contacted directly by phone or in person to make sure that they gave some thought to the immediate practical problems that would be created upon his acceptance.

The problems most frequently discussed were disposal of major property, payment of debts, and termination of job responsibilities (and opportunities)

Notably, the same and similar 'last will and testament' were actually derived based on same paperwork and counseling that was standard for military soldiers who faced mortal combat in Vietnam War.

This was unexpected by over half of the early Peace Corps volunteers that were accepted, as most also were surveyed to report that they had not really understood that they would be essentially 'on their own', without any promise of military protection in uncertain security areas; and after to discuss with their family and friends, many more were convinced to decline.

When asked what their concerns with an assignment that was to most influence the result in their decision to decline Peace Corps acceptance was that family questions of adjustments were most important concerns.

Despite the same subjects were surveyed again after the previous studies, most Peace Corps volunteers who decided to decline invitations did not cite either concerns for safety or career, and instead mostly to express increasingly fears that they 'could not make a difference'.

This new attitude from previously surveyed volunteers that were accepted yet declined to move forward when they were surveyed again was significant.

Most after one year not only expressed attitudes of futility of Peace Corps, and happy at new jobs, and no longer 'at all interested' in the Peace Corps.

These follow up Peace Corps volunteers who were accepted but declined twice were asked what the Corps might have done differently that would have made them feel more like accepting.

Fully 20% of the decliners felt that nothing the Corps could do would have made any difference.

According to survey of over 80% of declining respondents to follow up Peace Corps invitations, the greatest concern of the potential volunteer related to their 'second thought' considerations about the real difficulty of adjusting to strange customs (fully 80% felt this was the most important concern).

The second most important concern of the invited applicant was the chance of accomplishment – this was a very significant concern of over 70%, which was not as previously related to the challenge of adapting to strange customs, but a more complex awareness of their own personal sacrifice related to the potential success of their efforts to apply limited skills unrelated to their academic education in remote underdeveloped communities versus opportunities for careers domestically.

Another factor that was detected in the follow up studies was that most (again nearly 80%) of those early Peace Corps volunteers who had first declined, yet originally expressed desire to be considered for future acceptance – did in fact after one or two years formally withdraw their Peace Corps applications.

Notably, over 80% were within the one to two years after such invitation to join the Peace Corps were no longer even eligible, as they were no longer single and got married, so formally withdrew.

This again was a subtle criticism by Congressional oversight, who were to make stark observations that best Peace Corp candidates had no desire to marry.

Learning a language was the third most important concern of the early Peace Corp volunteers that chose to drop out. Over 90% of the early Peace Corps volunteers had some courses in secondary or higher education courses for languages such as Latin, French or Spanish – and as one survey respondent noted:

"I had two years of high school French and really struggled with it. I would be terrified of a really complex language like Swahili. I was thinking that all the Peace Corps services would be in English".

Most of the early Peace Corps assignments were in underdeveloped nations that were to involve very complex languages and dialects in Africa and Asia that were difficult for very advanced linguistic professionals.

To be able to combine the linguistic challenges with the scientific engineering and technical requests of underdeveloped nations were overwhelming to recruit.

Concern of medical facilities was the fourth important concern.

Most early idealistic Peace Corps volunteers had never considered the very harsh realities (which were honestly presented by Peace Corps recruitment and follow up materials by U.N. and WHO to graphically warn of the dangers of relocating to underdeveloped remote areas).

To understand to have very limited medicine or emergency health care services in most underdeveloped nation Peace Corps missions was a true reality test.

In addition, the extended follow up studies of the early Peace Corps volunteers to decline invitations to proceed, also included concerns that were ranked in importance by concerns of: isolation, separation from family, hazards, and weather.

The respondents (over 80% of whom eventually decided to permanently withdraw their applications) believed the Peace Corps could reduce the concern of future potential volunteer by better information from the agency at the time of application, not invitation to train.

Among the changes believed desirable by the invited applicant, in order of frequency, were:

1. More detailed information about the job to be done;

2. More rapid notification or better timing of offer;

3. More rapid processing and notification of status;.

4. Options for different types of work to help people;

5. More detailed information about the prospective country site.

As one survey respondent pointed out:

"Even the Army is better at recruiting volunteers. At least they give you a lot of information and options for different types of service, as well as approvals on the spot. A lot of that is scary, but at least it is up front, rather than at the last minute like with the Peace Corps".

Motivation of the College Seniors to Apply to Peace Corps

One of earliest Peace Corps consultant studies of motivation was conducted in 1964 among college seniors, the most important source of applicants.

The study concerned itself with the perceptions, value systems, and interests of college seniors. The sample interviewed included 388 students at twenty colleges dispersed geographically throughout the United States.

The students were shown eighteen statements which indicated various possible advantages and were instructed to rank each advantage regarding personal importance.

The statements which the students were shown centered around the concepts of national interest, self orientation, and social orientation.

Each of the statements was rated on a three point scale. Advantages that expressed the concepts of social orientation were considered most important.

The opinions of college seniors of the advantages of Peace Corps service stressed social concept of increasing knowledge of others as most important.

Most frequently considered as the most important was 'improving the status of the less fortunate', which was selected by 20% of students.

Other Important social concepts of advantages of Corps service included the 'promoting of international cooperation' and 'working for world peace'.

National concepts were believed to be an advantage to Corps service by college seniors.

The most important national concept was judged to be the 'presenting of a better picture of America'.

They also believed that 'improving American image abroad' was an advantage of the Peace Corps.

These college seniors believed that there are personal advantages to Corps service. Yet, the self advantage benefits were rated of less importance than social or national advantages

This survey also attempted to discover barriers to volunteering for Peace Corps service. Sixteen statements describing possible barriers to volunteering were rated by students according to personal feelings.

The statements rated centered about four different concepts in order of importance:

o   prior commitments
o   personal inadequacies
o   doubt that Corps needs me
o   general Peace Corps bad publicity

In terms of the specific statements that were rated, the two rated as most important in preventing application were 'desire to pursue a career' and 'desire to get married'.

The survey revealed that the desire for immediate employment was of greatest mean importance for not joining the Corps.

In addition, there was a significant high reason for not joining that was related to the honest desire to 'use their college degree to not only get a good job in the U.S., but also their greatest desire to marry and raise a family'.

The desire to attend graduate school was the second mean important reason for not joining the Corps.

This was also confusing, as this same desire response was given most frequently, by forty per cent, as the first choice reason not to become a volunteer.

Reasons for this have been subject of many studies since then, but they all seem to be explainable by the common need for recent college graduates to seek multiple resolutions for their best opportunity in Peace Corps, graduate school and family with career.

Students rated reasons for not joining the Peace Corps in order of importance:

o salary too low
o unfamiliar with Corps objectives
o afraid of hardships,
o contemplating marriage
o concerns about Corps objectives
o family disapproval.

Fear of being rejected was actually rated lowest, with only a very small percent to be self reported.

Major Drop Off in Peace Corps Applications

As the number of Peace Corps applications began declining since 1964, it became increasingly a focus that was funded by government studies to attempt to understand the reasons for this drop.

Despite both the Kennedy and Johnson administrations had put so much effort and resources into the Peace Corps, and had been the focus of major Federal legislation for both budget and unprecedented new organization of independent bureau of the Executive Branch for an American Peace Corps, almost immediately after the Peace Corps was permanently established by Congress, the level of applications dropped off sharply.

Several studies have analyzed the rise and fall of the early Peace volunteers. There were many complex variables. Yet, the most critical seems to have been the popularity of President Kennedy.

Within the year before his death, the number of Peace Corps volunteer applicants rose to an all-time high (both for the Peace Corps as well as any other similar American government program).

Yet, after President Johnson assumed office and was elected, the same level of support and applications declined almost immediately, as rapidly as it had risen.

These were many studies about the Peace Corps and other government programs during the mid-1960's.

This included studies that included the areas of economics, psychology, and sociology.

For example, level of economic activity may well have been a factor for decisions by individuals to volunteer or to accept invitations.

In the early 1960's there was massive unemployment. Yet by the mid-Sixties, there was a major economic boom due to Vietnam War Preparations.

As the level of unemployment declined, the availability of jobs increased. As jobs increased, potential volunteers had a choice between Peace Corps and private sector (including military-industrial) employment.

Beginning in the early 1960's, the U.S. economy was in yet another down-turn, and up until 1963 to 1964 many recent college graduates had only two options, to choose either to volunteer for the Peace Corps service or unemployment.

Many of the early Peace Corps volunteers were later surveyed to self-report that they 'had only applied to the Peace Corps' as a 'back-up' plan if the economy did not improve. By the mid-1960's, most did. Yet, by that same time, graduating American college students were more worried about the Draft, rather than about Jobs.

As the likelihood of a War in Vietnam increased, recent college graduates began to have another option, as the number of war preparation jobs in the military-industrial sector increased dramatically by 1965 to 1966.

Also, new college graduates in the mid-1960's had yet another option. They could volunteer for Officer Candidate School, which gave them a chance to make much higher salaries than drafted or enlisted personnel with no college education – and ROTC was also to be increasingly taught on college campuses for immediate military officer commissions upon graduation.

Notably, very few military officers with the same technical education that was being recruited by the Peace Corps would ever even be close to combat in Viet Nam. Thus, a growing number of the college students that were being recruited by the Peace Corps chose careers as military officers in a wide range of technical positions.

Thus, almost ironically, only a few years later, nearly one-third of the original applicants for the U.S. Peace Corps, actually took instead much higher paying jobs in either direct or indirect support of war effort in Vietnam, as either military officers or for military prime contractors.

A vast majority of these recent college graduates were to report in multiple surveys that their decision to turn down invitations to accept assignments in the Peace Corps was mostly based upon the much higher pay, security, and ability to start and raise families instead.

Wage differential between Peace Corps service or employment in the private sector had in fact been a major early matter of concern by Director Sargent Shriver, as well as Hubert Humphrey and others in Congress.

Yet, the objective to assign Peace Corps volunteers to live and work in local villages with the same standard of living as natives resulted in Congress to limit the salary of Peace Corps volunteers in the field to what was regarded by many as a 'bare level of subsistence.

Thus, salary for Peace Corps versus public sector was always significant, but began to be more important.

Under President Johnson, Peace Corps volunteer wages remained constant, meanwhile starting wages for college graduates vastly increased.

In addition, the number of job openings in private sector, either directly or indirectly related to war preparations, began to increase exponentially.

The economic advantages for the massive turn downs by the number of accepted Peace Corps applicants were likely a dominant factor, but there were also the security issues. As one declining Peace Corps applicant was reported to comment:

"I finally realized that at least if I join the military, even if I have to go into harm's way, I will know that there will be a lot of others to protect my back. But if I join the Peace Corps, I am more likely to be alone in the dark".

What many surveyed volunteers would also commonly comment to criticize was what many were coming to regard as a 'near-priesthood culture to remain single subject to being terminated if they married or even dated to express consideration to marry'.

This was also to be highly correlated to the growing ambivalence about Peace Corps security risks of going into remote area where there was minimal military protection from the dangers of communist violence – as America as a whole became increasingly aware of risks due to graphic presentation of communist atrocities on TV.

One researcher, David Sills, a specialist in recruiting volunteers for nonprofit organizations such as the Polio Foundation, stated that:

"Corps volunteers receive intrinsic rewards for participating in a voluntary association, and from being a part of a social movement. But violence is more concrete."

In the early life of the Corps movement, there was a sense of pride in the unique identity of being a volunteer.

But barely five years after the Peace Corps was started, with twelve thousand active volunteers, much of this uniqueness had been lost.

The volunteers did not receive as much attention in their local community, their friends, or even their own family as at inception of the program.

As the ambivalence and confusion of most Americans about the growing reality of the Cold War and increasing threats of communism to America, returning Peace Corps volunteers were faced with much of the same mixed reactions, and even hostility, as was beginning to be directed at the first American soldiers to volunteer for military service in Vietnam.

Although the idealism and charisma of President Kennedy had united and inspired the nation, after his assassination there was a growing cynicism and even anger that the Peace Corps was 'unable to really change anything'; and many anonymous phone survey opinions indicated that 'the Peace Corps makes U.S. look weak'.

Some in government simply believed that the Peace Corps was losing its freshness.

Congressman Ed Derwinski, a member of the House Committee on Foreign Affairs, stated simply:

"I would simply presume that the drop in applicants had been caused by the novelty and newness of the program wearing off."

Congressman Roy McVicker, also a member of the same Committee stated that he felt number of applicants dropped simply because "the thrill is gone".

Followers of social movements are often characterized by psychological frustration of some kind.

Fully one-third of all volunteers applied for the Peace Corps 'without knowing what was really involved'.

Some initial Peace Corps volunteers later confided they felt they had been "running away from responsibility" or "delaying a decision of what to do in life".

A large number of volunteers readily admitted that they welcomed at the time they had first applied the option for the delay of two years, before making many more important decisions about careers, marriage, and the entire course of the rest of their lives.

Yet, Dr. John Sullivan, a psychologist at New York University who evaluated many volunteers, did not feel that deferring a decision was the same as running away to escape. He observed that the volunteers expected to get many experiences to benefit them in future careers, and also made the comment that "it has not been all that different for many military volunteers'.

Arnold Green, a sociologist, observed that "participants in social movements are generally at odds with themselves and the world about them".

He also observed, and proposed, that "since there are only a limited number of alienated individuals, this source of recruitment does not increase proportional to increase in quotas" – just as in 'supply-demand' economics.

Another member of the Committee on Foreign Affairs, Congressman Clement Zablocki, felt the number of applicants had dropped for the same reason:

"When the program was begun there was a reservoir of people in this country interested in going abroad as Peace Corps Volunteers. Over the past five years that reservoir had largely been tapped".

This was a much less direct comment than Green, yet was a reflection of the growing sentiment in Congress for multiple reasons, to limit Peace Corps budgets.

The American attitude may well have contributed to the reduction in enthusiasm for an opportunity to serve in this program.

The attitude of the average American traditionally favors quick solutions to all problems.

Five years, in many American minds was sufficient to solve the problems attempted by the Peace Corps, even though the problems have long existed.

One reason for the early popularity of the Peace Corps was that within its first five years was that it served as an outlet for idealism of American youth.

Yet, in the following five years, that idealism was redirected, and more idealism of youth was manifested toward pushing back communism by the Viet Nam War.

In the early 1960's, potential service in the Peace Corps was widely looked upon as youth's contribution to mankind. Yet, the next five years came to be more widely regarded by young people to look to the Viet Nam War as their generation's contribution to society.

Thus, by the mid-Sixties in America there were origins of a vast cultural divide that lasted for decades, which impacted the Peace Corp with the rest of the world.

Furthermore, the great number of young people required for the military operations in Viet Nam also increasingly reduced the number of potential applicants.

The implementation of the draft and the realities of military conscription further complicated this division on many personal and emotional levels.

But a simpler impact was the fact that as a result of the draft, a major portion of the best candidates for college education were sent to War, with several complex impacts on Peace Corp recruiting remaining graduates.

The spirit of Peace Corps idealism was symbolized by President Kennedy, but it quickly forgotten.

The Peace Corps had been living off the past capital of President Kennedy's memory for several years.

Yet as President Johnson and budget resources of America were more and more drawn into War in Vietnam, that all changed.

The conclusion was that most potential volunteers fail to join for a combination of reasons.

The Colorado State University feasibility study, which proved to have been so accurate in most predictions, had estimated there were sufficient qualified individuals for about ten thousand volunteers.

In 1965, there were 9,787 volunteers abroad. It seemed that the predictions of 1960 Colorado State University study had been very accurate.

Although some minor adjustments were indicated in order to increase number of Peace Corps volunteers, it was unlikely for all the reasons that were encountered within first decade that major increases would be useful.

Significant Drop Offs in Public Interest in the Peace Corps

The number of articles written in newspapers and magazines about the Peace Corps was greatly reduced after the death of President Kennedy.

The number of articles listed in _Readers Guide to Periodical Literature_ averaged twelve per month in 1961. The average number of articles listed in 1964 was one per month. The average per month for the years 1965 and 1966 was less than two. Almost as many articles were written in 1961 as in the following five years.

This sharp reduction in number of articles about the Peace Corps in newspapers and magazines was reflected in the interest of Congress to budget and appropriate more funding to the Peace Corps.

Consequently, American youth, and Americans as a whole, were by the mid-Sixties, reading less and discussing less about the Peace Corps as much as in the early-Sixties.

Furthermore, the number of articles written that were written about the Peace Corps began to have an increasingly critical and unfavorable tone that questioned its usefulness in the time of a growing Cold War world.

Stepped Up Peace Corps Recruiting in Late Sixties

Former Director Shriver held that recruiting was a matter of informing the American citizen about eligibility and opportunities for service.

It was also an attempt to fill an ever-increasing demand for volunteers with specific skills. Increasing coverage by radio, press, and television helped dispel some of the misconceptions about skills needed for service in this organization into the late Sixties. Recruiting efforts were reported by the Peace Corps to cover two main areas.

"First, colleges and universities receive seventy-five per cent of the effort; and second, agricultural and technical professions receive twenty-five per cent."

The Corps maintained a harmonious working relationship with colleges and universities through paid liaison officials on campuses. They competed with ROTC for prospective officers, as well as Army recruiters who were quickly to contact students who 'dropped out'.

From these campus liaison officials, news items and general information were passed to the student body.

Although college students were the prime recruiting targets, many surveys and studies indicated they were not well informed concerning possibilities for service.

Many analysts reported this as growing lack of interest in the humanitarian goals of the Peace Corps, versus a growing consensus of discomfort of American security in a growing Cold War.

The Peace Corps did not have recruiting stations scattered across the nation or personnel exclusively assigned to speechmaking, which was a disadvantage versus the wide locally distributed and growing networks of military recruiters in most small towns in rural America.

The Peace Corps was instead mostly focused on major urban area college campuses. All coordination of recruiting was from Washington DC administrators, who had limited understanding of the heartland of America.

This was especially a limitation to the Peace Corps to achieve their goals of either agricultural specialists, or scientific and engineering recruitment.

As a result, the vast majority of Peace Corps applicants who were accepted to be actually trained and deployed were instead mostly liberal arts majors with limited practical skills, social science majors – and other volunteers who were not what host countries needed most and had asked for.

These recruitment challenges posed yet another major problem to the Peace Corps by the late Sixties.

Many host nations, who had been accustomed to getting exactly the agricultural and scientific technology expertise that they asked for, from both American and European nonprofit missionary organizations, actually withdrew their requests to participate as host nations for any future projects proposed by the U.S. Peace Corps.

Even more to become a matter of concern to highest levels of U.S. government, was the fact both Russian and Chinese communist regimes were offering, and delivering, effective agricultural and scientific local 'technical advisors', as a very real and dangerous threat to humanitarianism – as such communist advisors were able to build support for communist rebel infrastructure in remote local areas that were of direct substantial current and future threats to the U.S.

These growing concerns were increasingly reflected in articles in newspapers, magazines, and major TV networks, which focused on stories about dangers facing Peace Corps workers in remote areas, and atrocities of communist rebels. The American public was increasingly to feel concerned and confused.

The official response from the Peace Corps during the last half of the Sixties was that it had purposely concentrated its recruitment on large universities in the North for two reasons:

"First, the response to Peace Corps recruitment campaigns in the South had never been very successful.

Second, the civil rights problem had discouraged recruiters in the South, who are targeted for violence."

This was while all of the Peace Corps' own research and official publications continued to highlight almost exclusively volunteers from the Southern rural areas had distinguished themselves in Africa as well as other parts of the world, especially with regard to dissatisfaction of the host countries versus volunteers from urban North.

By the end of the Sixties, the Peace Corps was no longer the same grass roots humanitarian organization as had been the model from the first Christian missionary as well as multi-faith and secular humanitarian organizations.

So by the end of the Sixties the Peace Corps had become a very bureaucratic quasi-government organization that was dominated by an 'elite' of liberal arts and social science academia from the urban Northern universities, who had very little in common with, and actually had greater difficulty to serve in same conditions as Third World local native populations.

Notably, most of the rural Southern university graduates were not interested in Peace Corps service, and most were instead to take positions as officers in the military, or to work for military prime contractors.

Additional surveys of the local people as well as leaders of the emerging 'Third World' nations that continued to accept Peace Corps volunteers to assist in their projects were often to comment that they 'wanted more of the same kind of volunteers who were from the South or West of U.S., and were experts about agriculture and construction projects, and accustomed to 'camping out' and 'hunting', and were equally comfortable in high society balls as on expeditions into the jungle.

Several independent surveys of local people as well as leaders in Africa after successful Peace Corps projects expressed greater comfort with Peace Corps volunteers from the South who could live in same modest conditions as their people (despite most were White) – versus their experience to work with Peace Corps workers from privileged urban Northern universities who were not able to live among the local people, and were 'not as easily able to understand their needs' (despite many of them were not White). This was to become yet another factor in growing complications in the Peace Corps.

Although there were many other countries that were to feel comfortable with Peace Corps volunteers from the urban metropolitan cities, this mostly to include only those assignments and projects that were more focused on government ministry advisory and consulting positions, rather than projects with direct contact to local peoples.

This was learned by Peace Corps studies to assign urban volunteers to work out most effectively with Asia projects, versus rural volunteers to work most effectively with Africa, with a mix of both in Latin America.

The problem of obtaining sufficient volunteers to meet Corps requirements was an overriding one. If this problem was to be solved, new techniques must be developed and existing methods improved. It was recommended by one consultant that:

"The Peace Corps should establish a permanent well-trained staff of recruiters numbering approximately fifty. These recruiters should be assigned to areas of the country so that all colleges and technical schools will be visited at least twice a year.

These recruiters would maintain a close relationship with the college liaison officials. More effort should be spent to recruit Negroes from the rural south colleges in order to increase their representation."

It was believed that the Corps had failed to encourage retired people to serve their country. This idea was reinforced by the fact that barely seven tenths of one per cent of volunteers (0.7%) were over sixty years old.

Retired persons had much to offer in experience and would likely respond if properly recruited.

The Peace Corps was urged to expand its recruitment efforts for retired people. A special training program should be implemented for the older volunteer, with less emphasis on rigorous physical training.

As previously mentioned, more attention was given by the Peace Corps to motivation studies, and parents of potential volunteers were supplied information about the Corps policies.

The Corps decided to expand its efforts to increase the acceptance rate of those who initially decline the offer to train.

The Corps administration also decided to intensify its efforts to reduce the time period from original application to invitation to train, in order to increase the acceptance percentage.

Considerations of Training for the Early Peace Corps

In order to be selected for training, the prospective volunteer had to fill out a lengthy and comprehensive questionnaire, furnish double the usual letters of reference for a public sector job, undergo written and psychological examinations, and pass a physical examination.

In many comments from past Peace Corps volunteers, it had widely been observed that: "It just seems like it is easier to be an Astronaut at NASA than to be approved to pass training as a Peace Corps volunteer'.

Yet the formal qualifications for Peace Corps service during the Sixties were not all that numerous.

The minimum age for volunteers was eighteen, with the stipulation that anyone under twenty-one would have to show parent's or guardian's permission before being accepted.

There was no maximum age stated in the original charter of the Peace Corps program. Married couples could serve if both were qualified to contribute to the Peace Corps (as a team as assignable to the same locations), and if they did not have any children under eighteen.

Peace Corps volunteers in the Sixties needed to demonstrate their technical ability, physical stamina, and emotional stability.

They needed to be able to adapt themselves to an unfamiliar way of life and to work overseas with peoples of all colors, religions, races, and cultures.

The qualified potential Peace Corps volunteer in the Sixties was given a thorough physical examination at Federal facilities near their homes.

These medical evaluations, like all background materials, are sent to Washington headquarters to be analyzed by Peace Corps administrative analysts.

It was clearly not as difficult as passing a 'NASA astronaut' exam; yet it was understandable that many of the Peace Corps volunteers were to feel overwhelmed by the exam process.

By the time that Peace Corps applicants had completed the screening process, the Peace Corps selection officials had a sizeable file on the applicant.

The dossier included results of many placement tests, information secured from the volunteer questionnaire, information derived from references, and preliminary medical reports.

Information from these sources was evaluated and correlated with current and projected needs.

If an applicant was judged to meet desired standards, a letter invited him to assign them to a specific training group at a particular university or college. Only one candidate in four was found suitable for such training.

Individuals entering the training program from this elaborate process of selection for training were expected to be superior. Yet, only 60% of applicants invited actually were to accept the invitation to train.

Those who accepted underwent an elaborate training program. It was in fact in many ways similar to the training programs for astronauts, as well as for special forces in the military – as many of same scientists and consultant for military programs also helped to design much of the Peace Corps training.

Trainees recruited for any given project (or to be deployed to the same host country) were trained together. Yet, no two groups for a given project or location had exactly the same schedule.

These training programs depended on facilities and faculty available at the training institution, and on the type of work to be performed in the field.

However, all Peace Corps groups during the Sixties were trained according to a three-phase pattern:

"1) ten to twelve weeks basic training, obtained in the United States;

2) field training, usually given at one of the Peace Corps field camps; and

3)overseas training in the host country."

Phase I – Peace Corps Training at U.S. Universities

Most of the first basic training programs of the Peace Corps during the Sixties were conducted in cooperation with, and located at, top rated colleges and universities.

Many institutions of higher learning were not fully equipped with the staff, physical facilities, and curriculums to meet current Peace Corps requirements.

The problem was to supplement regular services of the collegiate institution in such a way as to create environments simulating to the Peace Corps trainees to be better able to adapt to situations in which the volunteers were to labor, and to give them the knowledge, skills, and attitudes necessary to function successfully in new jobs.

In the early years of the Peace Corps there was from the beginning an emphasis upon applying many of the same methods used by the military for 'boot camp' (although it was regarded as an intellectual and cultural 'boot camp' rather than simply physical training for military combat). Consistent with the objectives of the Peace Corps versus the needs of military, such as in Army conscript and Marine volunteer 'boot camps', a primary goal was to 'shake up' recruits by putting them into strange new surroundings and then begin to build them into teams to learn new skills.

For example, the Southern rural recruits to Peace Corps were sent to train at Northern urban universities (and vice versa). This was a good strategy, founded on many scientific studies – yet it presented many complications that were not easily applied from past research military recruits, involving greater 'culture shock'.

Therefore, it should not be surprising that by the last half of the Sixties, there were many problems with use of institutions of higher education in training volunteers. This was partly due to serious problems of security and political Anti-War activism that was not easily mobilized on college campuses, and complicated Peace Corps training.

Even beyond these security problems were more essential and practical issues, such as described by Joseph Kauffman as follows:

"The traditional method of instruction in American colleges and universities was simply lecture and examination. If we are to introduce effective and achievable goals into the Peace Corps training process, it becomes necessary to make alterations in traditional didactic approaches".

Simply put, some things colleges do well and were useful to Peace Corp; but some were not.

Training Peace Corps volunteers for effective service abroad involved necessity of teaching foreign languages and dialects.

Colleges could do this very well, so this became a major focus of Peace Corps training. Yet colleges were less able to prepare them for culture shock.

Such Peace Corps training at universities for what was often to be referred to as '90 Day Wonder Camp' was most effectively linguistic. After completely one training rotation, the Peace Corps trainee could apply to ask for another training in another linguistic area.

In one case from the beginning of the Peace Corps at the start of the Sixties until the end, that there were several Peace Corps trainees that actually were to complete training to speak, as well as speak and write multiple languages without actually deploying to the field (also notably, by the end of the Sixties, many trainees reportedly joined other international agencies instead).

Peace Corps trainees tend to be a heterogeneous lot, in some programs combining high school graduates and graduate students – all going to the same country as 'buddy teams', yet usually to perform different tasks.

They were all trained and evaluated in team simulations – which were equally effective as training methods of field agents for many military intelligence and as quasi-military organizations from late Sixties.

The university based phase of Peace Corps training programs were designed as the final opportunity to determine the suitability of the trainee to undertake a specific assignment abroad.

It was considered as an extended comprehensive exam. However, according to the training model that was first developed by the first Director Sargent Shriver and his senior staff:

"This does not mean the candidate fails to gain knowledge and skills during this period, but rather the program concerns itself primarily with testing his ability to focus his skills on a specific job".

The objectives of the training program for the candidate were described by former Director Shriver as: "1) a guide to his strengths and limitations; 2) a demonstration of techniques and attitudes required for the actual assignment, and 3) an experience in performing his expected role critical as those he may encounter abroad".

In order to meet these objectives, the Peace Corps in the early Sixties first established a tough training program including eight main areas of study conducted sixty hours per week.

The schedule utilized lectures, seminars, simulated field work, language laboratory, and films.

Again, the models for this Peace Corps 'academic boot camp' were based generally upon the same 'boot camp' 90-day training as for military recruits.

However, this training was more like the training for military officer recruits, and for reserve officer training at universities that encouraged ROTC training, which was mostly group team exercises that were routinely tested and reinforced by films and field exercise simulations.

The first main division of the curriculum was area studies were to mostly include historical, economic, political, and cultural aspects of the host country.

Second, American studies included an analysis of our American democratic institutions, history, and current social and economic problems.

Notably, any political or religious views were discouraged, and a major condition of approval to proceed in training was related less to academic or linguistic skills than to expression of not only a strong desire to help people in other nations, but that they were equally to be committed to help people in other nations using democratic processes.

The third area of study included world affairs dealing with Sixties contemporary international problems, including communist strategy and tactics, and America's role in the improving world scene using democracy and capitalism as the prime alternative to communism.

Religious beliefs were not discouraged, yet the training was to encourage all Peace Corps trainees to be not only tolerant of all religious faiths, but to be eager to accept and encourage all faiths with humanitarian goals.

The fourth area of study was health and medical training. This was to include first aid, personal hygiene, and preventive measures required in the country of assignment.

A major emphasis of this training was to be able to identify and respond to the most basic critical first aid without immediate benefit of antibiotics and other medicines, in favor of available herbal or other practical treatments, as well as how to use field military triage methods to decide when to elevate to emergency medical treatment requests, including priority requests for transport.

The fifth area of study was composed of personal physical training and recreation, including personal conditioning as well as practice of both American and host nation sports. This was usually baseball and soccer.

Learning of such sports as soccer, a very common worldwide sport not widely known in U.S. during the Sixties, was a major focus of Peace Corps training – as well as local host nation sports that were not widely known outside of the host nation country.

Thus, knowledge of many variations of team sports such as soccer that had very local meanings to the many host nation peoples were critical to host acceptance.

The sixth division of study was orientation which described the aims and organization of the agency, and the volunteers' role within it. This was an attempt by Peace Corps to collect information about individual trainees, as well as prospective Peace Corps proposals to Congress.

Seventh, the curriculum for technical studies includes training for knowledge and skills required to perform the assigned job in the host country.

Primarily, the primary focus here was to compare the most current state of the art for their own academic specialty to the most current status of the best experts in their own field that they would likely meet in the host country (and role playing in how to overcome barriers).

Finally, the eighth division of study was the language-training curriculum, which included basic knowledge of the structure of the indigenous language, basic vocabulary, conversational practice, idioms and technical terms appropriate for successful completion of the assignment.

Phase II – Direct Training by Peace Corps in the Field

Secondary phase training was provided at the sites such as the Peace Corp camp 'Field Camp' in Puerto Rico.

As a result of a successful pilot project conducted in the spring of 1965, the training center was converted to provide full-scale training where trainees receive all their training, including language, cross-cultural and American studies, and physical training, as a 'Fast Track' for combined training to include all of the 8 components in the usual Phase I training – with field 'Boot Camp' simulation to include rapid 'virtual immersion' into situations where increasingly only language of the assigned host nation were allowed, with additional benefit of native speakers contracted from the host nation.

This was to prove to be a highly successful accelerated training program, and was to be a future model, only for the Peace Corps, but other agencies as well.

The Peace Corps by 1967 indicated that "this training was superior to university training for certain kinds of activities and it had the added advantage of permitting the utilization of former volunteers as instructors and staff in all aspects of training."

The results were not only less costly, but greater performance to combine in some assignments.

The Corps expected to give full training to 800 trainees at the Puerto Rican camp in 1966.

The total cost per trainee was $2,060 compared to $2,700 at the university – which was a very big (over 20%) reduction in total costs per year to train over 10,000 volunteers, and from that alone was very popular to Congress; thus this innovation was to be very long lasting.

But even more importantly, within the next two years, the better performance in all Peace Corps objectives of the 'Fast Track' training, including the satisfaction of the host nation, versus the traditional university trained Phase I volunteers – was very impressive – as the university trained had about 50% success rates, compared to over 80%.

Thus, by 1967, with Congress encouragement, in view of the favorable results at Puerto Rico, the Peace Corps began to explore the possibility of integrating similar 'Fast Track' and 'field boot camp' training.

The Congress GAO auditors confirmed that at least $36 Million per year could be saved to train same level of 10,000 Peace Corps volunteers using this method. This led to changes to accelerate training past 1968.

Phase III – Host Country Training for U.S. Peace Corps

Those selected at the conclusion of field training were sent to the host country for Phase III. This phase of training ran from two weeks to three months with an average of one month.

Phase III was conducted by the host country, and its content, format, and personnel involved were selected by the host country in consultation with Peace Corps officials. This final phase included an orientation to the host country.

The host-country training afforded the Peace Corps volunteers an opportunity to become accustomed to new environmental conditions prior to the actual start of their assignment. In addition, it provided elements of training not available in other phases.

It enabled the host country to contribute to the preparation of the volunteers for their future assignment. Increasing emphasis was being given to health instruction at the training site in the host country.

This approach promised to increase the effectiveness of health instruction by making it possible to use instructors with a greater knowledge of local health conditions and by providing health information at a time when it was of greater immediate interest to the volunteer.

A volunteer overseas needed to be aware that his activities were judged according to standards of the host country and the village in "which he was living. These standards were often different from those to which Americans are accustomed.

The volunteer had to attempt to understand the foreign culture and standards. This could not be accomplished without studying the history which had conditioned the culture and institutions of a host country.

The volunteer did not have to adopt the host country viewpoint, but his effectiveness depended on his being aware and sensitive to it. Upon successful completion of this third-phase training, a trainee became a full-fledged Peace Corps volunteer and was sent on for his assignment.

Aspects of Assignment Selection for the Early Peace Corps

Selection as a volunteer was a two-phase process: first, selection for training, based on a review and evaluation of paper qualifications; and second, selection for overseas service, involving additional reviews and assessments of performance during training. The selection process was lengthy and detailed, designed to ensure that the best possible people are selected.

Selection for overseas service was based on a continuing comprehensive exam test throughout training. The training program had been designed as the final opportunity to determine the suitability of the trainee to undertake a specific assignment abroad.

The program concerns itself primarily with testing the ability of the volunteer to focus his skills on the specific job to which he could be assigned under social, economic, political, and cultural conditions often markedly different from those in the United States.

The trainee was periodically evaluated by the selection board during training. The board was made up of a doctor, a psychologist, training instructors, group training officer, and a representative of the host country. Upon completion of the field training program, a final selection meeting was held.

One of three recommendations was made concerning each candidate; "First, the trainee may be assigned overseas with the group; Second, the trainee may be separated from the group and recommended for another project; or Third, the trainee may be separated from the Corps."

The selection of volunteers was a difficult and exacting endeavor as the job of a volunteer was a complex one: "The volunteer must demonstrate his technical competence in a foreign environment; he must become a special kind of community leader; he may need to communicate in a foreign language; and he must maintain his own physical as well as psychological well-being in essential isolation from his own culture."

These requirements indicated that selection procedures must go beyond aptitudes and achievement.

At the same time, the performance of the Corpsmen was of such great potential importance that strong demands were made in the selection process:

"Failures in the field may be so costly in their total effect that the selection apparatus was designed to determine fitness, in order that failures may be held to a minimum."

An Overview of the Selection Process

Prior to the last week of training, a dossier was prepared on each trainee. It included information from the questionnaire, the letters of reference, entrance tests, a full field investigation by the Civil Service Commission, ratings by supervisors and psychologists in the training program, and personal medical history records.

On the basis of this complete record the selection board composed of representatives of the Corps, the training institution, and the embassy of the host country, recommended those candidates that it believed should be assigned to the specific project overseas.

Ratings were based on careful observations of the trainees as they proceed through the various stress situations. The selection officials, particularly psychiatrists, placed great emphasis upon potential volunteer reactions to hypothetical as well as simulated stress situations.

Psychological screening was made by a psychiatrist or psychologist engaged by the Corps.

The psychiatrist counseled, tested, and closely scrutinized each applicant during training to make selection recommendations.

There was one psychiatric consultant for each fifty trainees at the training sites, who served ten to twelve days in each training cycle.

Success of Early Methods of Peace Corps Selection

The general impression was that the overall selection process was working fairly well, but the validity of personnel selection procedures can never be assumed.

A survey of forty returned volunteers conducted in April, 1966, by the author revealed that ninety-four per cent did not believe that the present twenty-five per cent attrition rate was excessive.

Only one volunteer felt that ninety-nine per cent was not too high if they are not qualified.

The assumption seemed to be that all of those rejected were unqualified and those selected were qualified.

A survey at that time of twenty members of the Committees on Foreign Affairs and Foreign Relations showed acceptance of the Peace Corps 25% attrition rate.

Congressman Peter Frelinghuysen, New Jersey, member of the Committee of Foreign Affairs, did not feel that the number rejected during training was too high.

Congressman Clement J. Zablocki, Wisconsin, member of the Committee on Foreign Affairs considered a "twenty-five per cent rejection rate during training an indication of the rigorous standard which the Peace Corps had successfully maintained. If this rejection rate fell off too drastically I should then become concerned about the quality of our volunteers."

Congressman Edward Derwinski, Illinois, member of the Committee on Foreign Affairs, concluded that the percentage of rejection during training was too low and that consequently undesirable individuals are being selected for service abroad.

Controversies Over Performance Rating Methods

As previously noted, it was important to send only qualified volunteers overseas. On the other hand, it was expensive to reject qualified volunteers. The cost of a trainee investment at time of selection was over $2,600.

Some of those rejected face a psychological problem resulting from their failure.

Furthermore, recruitment officials at Peace Corps headquarters expressed a belief to the author that the rejected trainees adversely influenced recruitment.

The fear of being rejected after public reporting of several rejected volunteers experience seemed to prevent some prospective applicants from joining.

For example, the idea of giving the psychological tests and interviews for four days before training actually begins, and then selecting at that time on this basis would lessen the distraction of selection with little loss effectiveness of this ineffective system.

Lloyd Morgan, volunteer in Tanzania, in a letter to the editor of the <u>Peace Corps Volunteer</u> journal suggested changes in the selection process. He recommended the elimination of peer ratings, and all of the intensive psychological investigations.

Al Carp, Director of the Division of Selection, replied to Morgan's letter:

"In the summer of 1965, about 5,000 trainees were asked to respond to a questionnaire about the selection process.

A sample analysis revealed that about sixty-five per cent felt that the present methods of selection had contributed significantly to securing the best trainees for overseas service."

Dr. Carp looked upon this as conclusive evidence of a successful selection system.

Yet this was alarming, as for thirty-five per cent to believe selection was flawed appeared very significant.

Dr. Carp revealed that forty per cent of attrition in summer of 1965 was brought about by 'self-deselection' (in far simpler terms, this means that they 'dropped out).

As Director of Selection, Carp felt that the effectiveness of the selection process was demonstrated by the performance of volunteers overseas. He seemed very defensive to the complaint of volunteer Morgan.

However, the complaint seemed to be validated by surveys of a large segment of volunteers as verified by the forty-one volunteers in Peru. It was questioned by many letters from Volunteers 'how Director of Selection Carp can be so emphatic about validity of selection procedures in light of independent research findings sponsored by Peace Corps'.

Excerpts from one letter stated: "We know that the Brewster Smith report was read by a large number of psychologists who serve as Field Assessment Officers or Field Selection Officers for Peace Corps.

We also know that there were at least two major messages in the Smith report. The first of these was that a variety of personality styles were associated with adequate performance as Peace Corps teachers in Ghana.

The second was that concepts derived from psychiatry and clinical psychology, what Smith called 'mental health concepts' were not particularly useful in distinguishing among levels of adequate performance.

In a sense then, Smith was suggesting that beyond identifying cases of clearly abnormal behavior, the psychologist might well permit himself to be somewhat less 'clinical' in his performance in Peace Corps selection. Smith wrote: 'I am certain both of these messages were understood by the reader. I have no hard data concerning the effect of either message on the behavior of the reader'."

The author sent the letter to the Director of Selection and Training, as well as editor of the Peace Corps Volunteer requesting comments on any changes brought about by the independent study of Dr. Brewster Smith, Professor of Psychology at the University of California.

The letters were referred via Dr. Robert Krug, Peace Corps Director of Research, to reply to the author. Dr. Carp, Director of Selection, was also sent a copy of Dr. Krug's letter in case he did not concur with it.

Dr. Krug also commented that "a large number of psychologists used as Field Assessment Officers and Field Selection Officers have read the findings of Dr. Smith's study with the Corps without knowing what influence it had on selection procedures". The response was confusing.

It was inferred from this correspondence that the Division of Selection made no policy change as a result of this study. It was implied in Dr. Carp's article in Peace Corps Volunteer in response to letter by Mr. Morgan that the Corps was fully satisfied with its selection procedures.

Analysis of Early Selection Criteria and Performance

Dr. Robert Krug in an analysis of eighteen Corps projects evaluated various criteria used by selection boards. The basic method of analysis was the correlation between the rated criterion at selection and rated performance of the volunteer in the field.

Entrance tests showed low positive correlation, with the language aptitude test as the most consistent.

Letters of reference were the most important criteria that were reported across all 18 projects to have been used for selection of Peace Corps candidates. Standardized reference forms asked for evaluation (on a 5-point defined scale) of job competence, emotional maturity, relations with other people, and an overall evaluation.

The numerical ratings obtained from referees showed consistent predictive validity. Yet letters of recommendation were considered as the most useful qualification for most acceptances by the Peace Corps.

Dr. Krug suggested two kinds of investigation to maintain or improve their usefulness:

"First, referees should be categorized by class and relationships to check on potential differential validity.

Second, the validity of references should be watched over a period of time."

The personal interview record asked for rating (on a 5-point scale) of competence, maturity and emotional stability, motivation, morale, interpersonal relations, and prediction of success as a volunteer.

It was designed to be completed by the Project Selection Officer during training. Results were available for only five projects, yet revealed positive correlations.

Psychiatric evaluations included ratings (on a 5-point scale) of psychopathology, character structure, object relations, reality testing, ego functioning, motivation, and prediction of overall success as a volunteer.

Results of fourteen projects revealed disappointing correlations: "Judgments of motivation do not agree to any greater extent than was evident in any randomly chosen cell of the matrix."

The final rating by the selection board was compared to overseas ratings. This comparison showed "low positive relationships which support the use of Selection Board Rating, as an interim criterion onto which to validate selection procedures.

These findings led Dr. Krug to conclude that it was "essential to conduct more intensive research on the selection process for a few projects. The general intent should be to collect more data:.

Krug recommended that a "full-time research person should be assigned to a project during its training phase, to collect data which are crucial to an understanding of the total assessment process. The independent judgments of all members of the selection board should be collected prior to their meeting as a board. Studies of this type are essential if the dynamics of the Corps selection process are to be understood and improved".

Detailed Evaluation of Peace Corps Teachers in Ghana

Dr. Brewster Smith and assistants of the University of California compared the rated actual performance of forty-four volunteers in Ghana with their predicted performance at selection.

In general the records of the various measures of success prediction were poor.

The most promising results came from a novel procedure, the mock autobiographies.

In regard to selection, his evidence suggested that the key positive qualities to be sought are competence and commitment. On the other hand, the negative qualities to be avoided are dependent, anxious immaturity:

"The clinical perspective of psychology and psychiatry, with its emphasis on psychopathology, seems not to have been very helpful in predicting different levels of performance, once the extremely disturbed individuals have been eliminated."

His findings revealed that if a volunteer was not "certifiably ill," other qualities than mental health could predict how well he will perform.

A main practical purpose underlying this study was to determine extent to which effective performance overseas can be predicted from measures during training.

Most significant relationships come from either the Stein Self-Descriptive Test, Mock Autobiographies, or Peer Nominations.

Peer ratings were an attempt to use trainees to select those of their group to be sent overseas.

The Corps looked upon peer nominations as a part of the responsibility of the trainees to assist in the selection program and to do their part in making sure that only qualified persons are sent abroad.

As previously noted, Lloyd Morgan recommended the elimination of this technique of selection.

However, Dr. Smith found encouraging strong correlations between training peer assessments and local host rated performance overseas.

Psychological Tests and Psychiatric Appraisal

Psychological tests and psychiatric appraisals employed in Ghana were not very useful as a basis for predicting the effectiveness of the trainees subsequent performance. Dr. Smith explained his findings thus:

"Apart from the still crude state of development of psychological and psychiatric technology, we think that there was another reason why psychological and psychiatric assessments proved to be of relatively little value here. Quite properly, a major focus for clinical psychologist and psychiatrist must be to screen out those who are actually mentally ill or likely to become so. This focus on psychopathology seems to lead to limited predictability about relative degrees of effectiveness among those who pass the initial screening. Our evidence strongly suggests that provided a volunteer was not certifiably ill, other qualities than 'mental health' decide how well he will perform. Our analysis of patterns of personality and performance indicates that there are many personal avenues to entirely acceptable performance as Peace Corps teacher, and some of which do not correlate well with prevailing purely psychiatric view on mental health values."

Dr. Smith pointed out that many teachers that were originally rejected by Peace Corps consulting psychologists nonetheless performed in an outstanding manner in Ghana: "For Peace Corps volunteers in Ghana, the actual performance as evaluated by host nations points to the need not to lose such outstanding potential volunteers to the Peace Corps."

Thus, in general, neither selection boards or psychiatrists, did as well in the prediction of volunteer performance as recommendations by academic references, and most significantly by active Peace Corps volunteers.

Early Peace Corps Recruitment and Selection for Training

There had been a sharp drop in applications for Peace Corps service by the mid-1960's. An attempt was made to understand the reasons for this drop.

In order to understand recruitment, an analysis was made of the typical volunteer and his motivation for joining the Corps. An analysis of a declination study revealed techniques to increase the acceptance rate.

Some suggestions were made to improve recruitment policies.

A brief analysis of the three phases of training and some of the training problems was presented.

Changes were suggested for making the training program more effective. An overview of the selection process was presented.

The selection process was believed by most people to be satisfactory; however, others feel that the selection procedures need a systematic analysis and revision. Independent research studies raised serious questions about the selection and assignment procedures.

The various techniques used at selection were evaluated. Peer nominations and letters of reference provided the best predictors of volunteer performance.

Psychologists and psychiatrists were poor predictors of performance. After these findings were validated by future research, the use of psychologists at selection was limited to screening to filter out only "certifiably ill" trainees.

In the next chapter, additional challenges are presented in a historical perspective related to early international territorial disputes, national instabilities, and problems of personal adjustment and culture conflicts that were to impact the early years of the U.S. Peace Corps.

CHAPTER IV

PEACE CORPS LOCAL HOST NATION
PROBLEMS AND RISKS

In addition to the previously discussed problems of recruitment, training, and selection, the early Peace Corps had a number of other problems.

These problems primarily involved security and risk concerns of sending Americans innocently into troubled areas, without reasonable protections of U.S. military normally available to all embassy and consulates in other nations at the time.

This was in effect one of the most significant of the many new dilemmas and paradoxes that were posed by the new concept of the U.S. Peace Corps, as proposed by President Kennedy and others in its early years.

The primary purpose the Peace Corps was to overcome the fears that created distrust among leaders and people of underdeveloped host nations, who were concerned about the influence of American military power and financial interests of large U.S. corporations.

Yet the original model of the U.S. Peace Corps as it was originally to be funded and organized in 1961 made the assumption that the local host nations 'would and could' be able to protect volunteers of the U.S. Peace Corps in their local host nations and project communities.

In reality, then and since – such underdeveloped nations 'could not and would not' – from then and every year since – for political and security reasons that evolved from the early years of the Peace Corps until now.

As a result, even the most dedicated and well received Peace Corps volunteers faced the same local personal risks that missionaries faced, before the Peace Corps was enacted as an Agency in 1961. There were no reasonable protections or assurances for missionaries, or for Peace Corps volunteers when they go out of U.S., or even at U.S. embassies or consulate offices.

Early Peace Corps Volunteer Removal from Trouble Areas

The greatest challenge for the U.S. Peace Corps within its early years involved the harsh reality that the Peace Corps volunteers would ultimately have to face the same personal dangers as all of the previous humanitarian organizations before the Peace Corps, including Christian missionaries, and even Philippine Teachers of U.S. Army.

By assigning Peace Corps volunteers to projects and missions in host nations with severe poverty and political conflicts, especially in remote locations without nearby protection of U.S. military, they became a target of enemies of the U.S. seeking to build communist or rebel support in the same remote areas.

Yet, even worse, even for Peace Corps volunteers assigned as teachers in cities of host nations, risks of violence due to civil conflicts became an increasing cause for evacuations and termination of many projects.

Barely one year after the start of the Peace Corps, it was forced to withdraw to cancel a host nation program because a shooting war eliminated Peace Corps volunteer jobs in Cyprus.

In September, 1962, twenty-three volunteers arrived in politically tense Cyprus, which was focus of dual claims made by two governments, Greece and Turkey.

The Corpsmen had to walk cautiously between hostile Greek and Turkish communities to avoid criticism and charges of press in both countries of spying for the U.S., which was to become an increasingly common claim by pro-communist press in many nations.

Some of the Cyprus Peace Corps volunteers worked with Greek communities, some with Turks, and some worked for government agencies serving both communities – as well as directly for independent Cyprus.

In the first eight months, the volunteers came under heavy attack of the left-wing press, both in the host nations, as well as in the U.S.

Yet, these volunteers had been making steady progress in all of their assignments when extensive fighting broke out on the island in December, 1963, less than a month after President Kennedy was assassinated.

Both Greece and Turkey had demanded that Peace Corps volunteers leave the war zone, as they both regarded the presence of the 23 Americans as an open invitation for the U.S. to send troops and get directly involved in the conflict – which was something that neither Greece nor Turkey wanted.

With all of the chaos in Washington DC within the first days after the death of President Kennedy and the transfer of power to the new President Johnson, Director Shriver quickly began to evacuate volunteers from Cyprus.

If the War in Cyprus had not started at this time, it was possible the volunteers might have reduced tensions in this country, as they were working with both the Greeks and Turks in Cyprus as well as in Greece and Turkey.

But because of the fighting, schools were closed and volunteer teachers could no longer teach. Because of fighting in the countryside, the geologists and agricultural workers could not continue their field work. Therefore, Director Shriver had no other choice.

The last volunteer left Cyprus on March 19, 1964. This was the first time volunteers had left a country because of war – yet the action was preventive, as at no time had hostilities been directed toward the volunteers.

For this reason, many in the U.S. press felt that Shriver should have supported the view that there was no direct danger to the 23 Peace Corps volunteers, and that they should have been ordered to remain, to take on local roles as diplomatic intermediaries under orders from the State Department.

But Director Shriver and top Peace Corps officials feared they would become hostages, and President Johnson reluctantly agreed.

Peace Corps Returns During Dominican Civil War

During approximately the same time period, there was a temporary withdrawal of Peace Corps volunteers due to the break out of a civil war, and coup in that country which was compared in many ways to the takeover of Cuba by Castro a few years prior.

The decision was reversed by the new military government in the Dominican Republic, so the tasks of the volunteers were only temporarily interrupted.

Within three months, the United States recognized the new government in the Dominican Republic. At the same time all U.S. foreign aid that had been paid to the previous regime was reinstated to be paid to the new military backed government.

In retrospect both the Cyprus and Dominican Republic withdrawals appeared relatively early in the history of the Peace Corps.

There was a lot of harsh criticism from both extremes in the U.S. press – one which felt that the Peace Corps had abdicated its responsibility and should have left the volunteers in both countries, despite the danger to each of them personally as well as the danger of escalated military involvement of the U.S. – and the other side felt that these volunteers should not have been deployed to such highly volatile locations to begin with.

In retrospect, more Peace Corps due diligence was implemented during project risk analysis and other project planning.

More administrative experience might have prevented entry into Cyprus or the Dominican Republic, as the internal situation in both countries was already known by the CIA and State Department to be 'very volatile' at that time when the volunteers to both countries were originally deployed.

Yet, on the other hand, more analysis of local intelligence and experience might just as likely have called even more for deployment to these locations – however, in such a case, there would likely have been more resources deployed that included military advisors and personnel.

Yet, surveys and polls after these actions by the Peace Corps tended to agree with the evacuation decisions. There are no indications that the United States lost prestige from either the Peace Corps deployments or withdrawals.

Peace Corps Withdraws from Ceylon For Lack of Interest

The Peace Corps terminated its program in Ceylon in the spring of 1964 after thirty-four volunteers assigned there all completed their two-year term of service.

All projects were completed successfully as they were originally agreed, and there were no complaints by the hosts. None of the volunteers were asked to leave, and there were no requests for them to be replaced.

Talks between the Peace Corps and the Government of Ceylon simply did not reveal any further Ceylon interest in continuing the programs and projects.

Surveys of the Ceylon local people and government administrators indicated they were 'not dissatisfied'. Yet many had 'somewhat expected more' and felt Ceylon local residents 'are just as qualified' as the Peace Corps volunteers assigned.

It was noted by Peace Corps analysts that Ceylon was like many host nations which had asked for more agriculture and scientific help than was provided.

It was also noted by the surveys that the Ceylon government and people felt that the Peace Corps volunteers were 'good administrators and managers' – which may reflect the early shortage of scientists and agriculture engineers, versus the over-supply of liberal arts and social science graduate applicants in the first years of the Peace Corps – or may have also have provided insight into the failures of intensive basic training in science or agriculture for liberal arts and social science applicants.

Notably, this mission was not ended due to any potential danger or security issues. This was first of many future examples of instances where the volunteers simply did not gain host-country acceptance for complex reasons.

Peace Corps Expulsions of All Volunteers From Indonesia

President Sukarno issued a terse statement in early 1965 stating all Peace Corps volunteers would be expelled from Indonesia unilaterally because of 'irreconcilable' tensions following American support of the Federation of Malaysia, which recognized Malaysian claims of territory that had also been claimed by Indonesia.

The growing communist rebel attacks on both Christian and Moslem populations that were difficult for Indonesian military to prevent, let alone for U.S. military to assist in preventing, across literally hundreds of remote islands, made the Peace Corps and administration of President Johnson very easy to accept – and most likely actually relieved, to be given a way to 'save face' – while the U.S. government quickly withdrew all Peace Corps volunteers from the increasingly unstable and troubling situation across the Indonesian islands.

It is worth noting that no Peace Corp volunteers will harmed due to the fast evacuation – yet within the upcoming months, many Christian missionaries and their converts were the target of pro-communist attacks, which were to include burning of churches and killing of their Christian converts – and missionaries were also soon after to be evacuated back to U.S. by missionary organizations.

It was also worth noting that within the previous year, all U.S. Foreign Aid to Indonesia had been reduced from over $100 Million to only $3 Million (97% reduction).

This Foreign Aid had been paid directly to Sukarno regime prior to this decision by the U.S. State Department at the direction of President Johnson administration – which was increasingly worried that Sukarno was 'playing both sides' – and even concerned that Sukarno was warming up to communist China and even Russia – which could have had disastrous implications as the U.S. prepared for a War in Viet Nam.

Ironically, shortly after the Sukarno expulsion of the U.S. Peace Corps volunteers, and the pro-communist rebels upon Christian churches that prompted a large evacuation of missionaries back to U.S. as well – there was a massive and unprecedented uprising from both Moslem and Christian Indonesians against the communist and atheist rebels – and which was also shortly after to result in yet another military coup, this time to oust Sukarno.

In each of these cases, the Peace Corps left not because of any failure, but because of the general deterioration and instability of very complex and fluid international relations, often in which the U.S. was in effect only an 'impartial third-party'.

Yet, these early cases all demonstrated the difficulty of the Peace Corps to remain in any potentially unfriendly or unstable host country.

The failure to remain in each of these countries ran counter to the early claims of the Peace Corps agency, after Director Shriver resigned, that all host countries were demanding more volunteers – which was the basis for most of their budget requests to increase, and even double, the number of Peace Corps positions.

Yet, in all fairness, there were in fact many host nations who did in fact ask for expansion of projects and more volunteers, and in many other troubled areas, the Peace Corps had actually been very successful.

Peace Corps Lessons After Coup in Dominican Republic

On September 25, 1963, the leadership of the Dominican army overthrew the government of President Juan Bosch and established a new government.

Notably, this was in the days between the failed attempt of the Bay of Pigs invasion of Cuba, and the assassination of President Kennedy.

There was initially immediate fear that there was another coup that might involve communist rebels with support of Castro's Cuba, and as a result Director Shriver was to recommend immediate withdrawal of all volunteers in Dominican Republic, which began the next week.

The U.S. Government had also immediately suspended diplomatic relations, and its military and economic assistance programs to the Dominican Republic.

Yet fully one hundred and fifty Peace Corps volunteers remained in rural areas after the coup and suspension of official relations by the State Department.

Yet, even as the 150 Peace Corps volunteers were being recalled and there were arrangements for military support to protect them as they left, the U.S. State Department also made many attempts to reach out to the new military regime, originally in order to attempt to negotiate safe passage for the 150 Peace Corps volunteers.

Instead, the new military regime leadership expressed no intention to harm the Peace Corps volunteers, and even 'asked to allow them to stay'.

The new military regime in the Dominican Republic was instead mostly interested to negotiate with the U.S. State Department to renew diplomatic relations (and also the Foreign Aid), as they contended that they were in fact pro-U.S. and not at sympathetic to communist rebels, from Cuba or any other communist country.

As a result, in early December, 1963 (again just days after the death of President Kennedy and assumption of power by new President Johnson), with the approval of Johnson and direction of the U.S. State Department, the

150 Peace Corps volunteers in rural areas were ordered by Director Shriver to stay, and resume work on their projects.

Peace Corps Confusion of Over Missions in Ghana

During the violent civil war disturbances in Ghana in the spring of 1964, four American University teachers were identified as 'U.S. Peace Corps spies' by new Ghana leaders reportedly supported by communist rebel forces, and after one of several military coups, were ordered to leave the country.

However, these 4 teachers were not in fact even Peace Corps volunteers, and were instead independent humanitarian mission volunteers.

The official U.S. Peace Corps programs in Ghana, had concentrated in the areas of geological survey and secondary education, and had been attacked sporadically by Ghana left-wing pro-communist newspapers.

The most critical attacks had curiously been made by papers dominated by a radical group of opponents to the pro-American president of Ghana – who also received substantial Foreign Aid directly to his regime, which was recognized by the U.S. State Department..

The Ghana President Nkrumah prior to 1965 had assured the Peace Corps as well as U.S. State Department and Congressional oversight visitors that such 'left wing' and 'pro-communist' press criticism did not represent his own feelings nor the feelings of his Government.

However, early in 1965 President Nkrumah harshly criticized the Peace Corps in interviews to the press – yet at the same time was requesting even more U.S. Peace Corps volunteers directly to the State Department.

In several anonymous reports that surfaced in the U.S. press, there were allegations the Ghana President was also reportedly 'shopping around' to communist nations for technical agriculture and scientific advisors and other manpower – and was open to 'either side' to provide them.

The Peace Corps in 1965 promised to deliver superior technical advisors, despite they knew that there were not enough Peace Corps specialists in these two high demand areas with the needed African language skills.

At the time, there was still a wide belief in the Peace Corps that liberal arts and social science graduates could be quickly 'retrained' for agriculture and engineering project management with their '90 day' intensive 'university boot camps' – despite research data was starting to come in to indicate otherwise.

As early as 1961, Ghana President Nkrumah had asked only to receive science or mathematics teachers – and 'highly skilled plumbers'.

There had never been a plumber to apply for the early Peace Corps even as late as 1965. But the Peace Corps was sure that they could deliver enough qualified teachers of 'math and science' – and also, as one U.S. official was to comment 'off the record': 'Surely somebody in the Peace Corps waiting to be assigned can be trained as a plumber'.

In fact, there was a wide belief in U.S Peace Corps administration at that time, that the many liberal arts and social scientists that were in surplus in the ranks of early accepted Peace Corps volunteers could be 'easily trained as educators to teach math, science and even plumbing'.

Yet, only thirteen of original fifty-one Peace Corps volunteer teachers sent to Ghana had any background in science or math.

This was based upon the official criteria to require such volunteers to have at least 6 college courses in math and/or science (thus, 38 out of 51 math and science teachers sent had 5 or less courses in science or math).

This inability of the Peace Corps to deliver teachers of math and science to Ghana was easily detected by college students in Ghana, who most often already had more academic courses in math and science than the Peace Corps teachers sent to teach them.

Ghana President Nkrumah was furious when he discovered after the complaints of Ghana students that more than half of the Peace Corps volunteers sent to Ghana were actually trained in American History and English, which was exactly what Nkrumah had particularly specified that he did not want (this was made even worse when a Peace Corps volunteer trained in liberal arts showed up to make 'skilled plumbing repairs' at his private palace).

The result was that Nkrumah made it clear that he did not want any more U.S. Peace Corps teachers, and as he began to expel them from Ghana, he also began to more seriously negotiate with communist nations to provide the technical talent that he had originally asked for in 1961 (this was also reportedly to have included as a top priority the need for 'expert plumbers' – and it seems USSR had many).

As the American Peace Corps volunteers were being removed from Ghana, two volunteers who were among those who actually held degrees in science and engineering made a series of interviews critical to the Peace Corps for sending them into an 'impossible situation' and 'putting us at risk' in a dangerous 'banana republic country'.

Yet, the Peace Corps by 1966 was to include Ghana among their 'success stories' – since there was yet another military coup to remove Nkrumah from power, the next regime was quickly to be officially recognized by U.S. State Department, who approved restoring both U.S. Foreign Aid, as well as Peace Corp humanitarian aid in the form of math and science teaching projects. Notably, the new regime was reportedly 'not interested in plumbers'.

Peace Corps Diplomacy During the Civil War in Panama

When anti-American riots broke out in the Panama Canal Zone in January, 1964, fifty-five volunteers were in process of being deployed to projects in Panama.

Some volunteer activities were halted temporarily during this time, but the Peace Corps decided to continue deployments on a selective case-by-case basis.

Although Panama temporarily severed all diplomatic relations with the United States at that time, the Peace Corps program went on, with the promise of 'extra protection' by Panamanian government.

The Peace Corps was curiously the only agency of the United States Government that continued throughout the crisis, and it was specifically requested by the Panama host government. The reasons for this were unclear.

In retrospect, many independent analysts have raised the possibility that this unexpected exception by the government of Panama to continue to invite and accept Peace Corps volunteers was most suspicious in light of the fact that despite tension between Panama and U.S. State Department, the Foreign Aid to Panama increased dramatically following the anti-America riots and severing of all other relations by Panama to the U.S. government.

The strange turn around in the relations between Panama and U.S. that followed the increase in Foreign Aid was noted by many in U.S. press at the time – but was overshadowed by many other confusing and chaotic events.

In all of these troubled areas, the Peace Corps volunteers were asked to quickly leave, or stay, based on rapidly changing orders. As reported in one letter to the editor of the <u>Peace Corps Volunteer</u> internal magazine:

"In many cases, we have faced serious possible harm. The local people in Panama are friendly to us, but there has been much protest that is violent as well as often nearby to us. We are concerned about no formal diplomatic relations, with a U.S. embassy and security support".

During these early years, leadership at the Peace Corps contended they were making difficult but wise decisions about evacuations when host nations had more risk; yet official policy was to try to remain if at all possible.

There were two purposes for the Peace Corps 'Prime Directive' of remaining in a host country:

First, the agency felt that its prestige would be elevated by remaining.

Second, the Johnson administration believed that the Peace Corps had the best chance of all U.S. Government agencies of remaining in the host country in a political or military crisis.

In fact this was by the late Sixties a reflection of the reality U.S. Peace Corps was increasingly a 'quasi-agency' reporting to the U.S. State Department.

Problem of Part-time Peace Corps Director Under Johnson

Leadership of an organization determines its spirit, its morale, and the motivation of its employees and thus often makes the difference between successful and unsuccessful performance.

At a Congressional Hearing on the Future of the Peace Corp in 1965, a witness commented: "Leadership creates a spirit of cooperation and teamwork throughout the organization. The Peace Corps had suffered from violation of this principle. A part-time administrator for the Peace Corps cannot effectively furnish this leadership."

This was a reflection of concerns within the Peace Corps that by mid-1964, the new President Johnson effectively put them 'on the shelf'.

Within less than one year after the death of President Kennedy, Johnson had quietly fired or transferred most of the Kennedy administration to other positions. In the case of Shriver, because of his close family ties to Kennedy family as the husband of Kennedy's sister, Johnson seemed careful to avoid criticism or scrutiny, and assigned Shriver to two other difficult positions also reporting directly to the White House at the same time.

Johnson asked Shriver to not only continue as the Director of the Peace Corps, but to also take on the dual roles as Director of the newly created Office of Economic Opportunity, which was to focus on the most critical new initiative of the new President Johnson, his 'War on Poverty' – and to pilot programs that were envisioned to create a 'domestic version' of the U.S. Peace Corps, which was commonly described as a "U.S. Job Corps".

In effect, Shriver was asked to do 'double duty' to be responsible for the two most difficult agencies in Sixties.

Even more important to note – this was the first time that any top government official other than a President of the United States, had even been given the responsibility for both 'Foreign and Domestic' duties, and command authorities, at the same time.

Within the first year after Johnson asked Shriver to take on the dual Director roles, the toll on the morale and effectiveness of the U.S. Peace Corps was severe.

In surveys of returning Peace Corps volunteers, over half felt that 'having only a part-time Director hurt the mission and effectiveness of the Peace Corps'.

This was reflected in both the U.S. public opinion polls, and also in votes of Congress on its budget.

In addition to serving as Director of the Peace Corps, Sargent Shriver had served from September 9, 1964, to January 17, 1966, as administrator of the newly created Office of Economic Opportunity. As he said openly in many interviews, Shriver was 'exhausted and disillusioned' over his ultimate 'inability to burn the candle at both ends'.

After over a year of criticism directed at Shriver – by what was to coincide with well-orchestrated strong pressure from Congress, Johnson accepted the resignation of Mr. Shriver as Peace Corps Director. Shriver was among last of Kennedy era appointees to be replaced by Johnson.

Some in Congress that had been close to Kennedy believed that Johnson had made a mistake by permitting the Peace Corps to run almost eighteen months with a part-time Director.

Many felt that most problems that surfaced during the first two years after Johnson took office could have been prevented if Johnson had transferred 100% as new Director for his 'War on Poverty', rather than to have asked Shriver to fill two such critical positions at the same time (and even worse to simultaneously head one agency that was international, and another that was domestic).

In his own personal interviews, Shriver admitted that he devoted only two days per week to the Peace Corps.

The two Jobs of directing the Corps and administering the Economic Opportunity program were believed by several Senators, including Senator Javits, to be too demanding for one individual:

"The Peace Corps suffers as Mr. Shriver devotes most of his energy to the new and larger agency. It is felt that the Economic Opportunity program is also more involved in domestic U.S. politics, and may have hurt the image of the Peace Corps by foreign nation leaders.

Mr. Shriver by necessity has reduced his overseas trips to meet directly with them and their host country administrators after 1964, and thereby lost some of his personal touch he previously had with them, as well as personal contacts with the Peace Corps volunteers".

In several personal interviews, memos and letters to friends and professional colleagues, Director Shriver was to 'sadly agree'; and asked to meet with President Johnson.

President Johnson, in April, 1965, named Warren Wiggins as Deputy Director of the Peace Corps. The new Deputy Director had been the 'confidential assistant' of Director Shriver, and performed multiple complex functions for the Director, including all coordination with the U.S. State Department and host nations.

The position of Deputy Director of the Peace Corps had been vacant for seventeen months before it was filled by Johnson, despite Shriver was effectively filling two primary Director roles at the same time.

The appointment was regarded by many in the press as a 'likely transitional bridge to appoint Wiggins as an Acting Director of the Peace Corps if and when Shriver would step down or resign'. This was a common way that most President administrations transitioned leadership of a critical agency during their terms, to assure for continuity.

This was all during a time that Johnson was increasingly to add cabinet and director staff that had long history of employment within the military-industrial complex that Eisenhower had warned against in his last speech as President.

So despite the official statements by Johnson after Kennedy was assassinated and he assumed power, by the time that Johnson was starting his first elected term as President, he had replaced almost all of the Kennedy administration, and his early commitment to 'War on

Poverty' and 'Civil Rights' that were initially intended by President Johnson to assure his legacy – most of this was superseded by growing needs to focus on 'War in Vietnam'.

Early Peace Corps Image of Peace Corps by U.S. Public

The public-relations staff of the early Peace Corps had first promoted a myth of a volunteer stereotype in the minds of the American public.

The stereotype was a sweaty but wholesome American youth, motivated by visions of self-sacrifice and adventure, living in a mud hut in a jungle across the sea.

This was in fact actually the opposite, as a vast majority of the first Peace Corps applicants, as well as those that were to fully complete the process to be selected as volunteers, were mostly highly educated ivy league youth with affluent urban backgrounds.

The reason for the original public-relations experts of the Peace Corps to promote such stereotypes was reportedly as an attempt to try to attract more rural and state 'A&M' university graduates, which were more in line with what was most often requested by the third world underdeveloped nations the Corps was created to serve.

The response to this initial image was two-fold. Not only did it fail to attract more such 'sweaty but wholesome' youth with rural backgrounds and experience; but it also was to 'turn off' the early flood of applicants from urban affluent backgrounds as well.

There were a great many research studies that were to study the reactions of both groups to posters and other imagery to motivate young college graduates to join the Peace Corps, using both focus groups and surveys.

As one student commented: "These posters seem to be very close to Army military recruiting. They do not seem to reflect what we thought about the Peace Corps."

In fact, many other students surveyed were to confirm this sentiment by comments such as: 'most of the volunteers I know of wear glasses and are more brainy than brawny'; and 'I might respond to posters like this if I was more interested to join the Marines and volunteer for War'.

These survey responses were quickly noted by the Peace Corps and Congressional oversight that paid close attention to such research, and the posters and recruiting materials were from then on to focus on images that were to show Peace Corps volunteers more often in schools and meetings around tables discussing white board and black board drawings with charts all showing 'upward trends', more similar to what might be typical marketing or sales meeting at a successful American business.

This was to resonate much more effectively to the traditional base of Peace Corps volunteer applicants, and was demonstrated to result in a partial recovery from the drop in all Peace Corps volunteers. However, it had become clear that the 'sweaty and adventurous' college graduates mostly only interested in military recruitment.

Actual Experiences of Early Returning Volunteers

Much of what had been written about the volunteer presented, at best an incomplete picture, and at worst a distorted one. Though the volunteers were told they would suffer extreme physical hardships, only a minority have experienced them. Some volunteers lived better overseas than they did in the United States.

The Corpsmen had suffered four times as many lost live from jeep accidents and bad roads as from disease.

A survey of forty returned volunteers conducted in April, 1966, revealed that over thirty-five per cent did not encounter hardships overseas.

Volunteers generally did not live on a level as high as State Department officials but often have facilities above nationals performing comparable work in the host country.

Yet, the volunteers often had a problem of living up to this Peace Corps public relations stereotyped image.

By March 1966, a total of 6,937 volunteers had completed their service. By 1970, the number was over 30,000 so there was a much more substantial data base.

The early Peace Corps volunteer was relatively well prepared for the culture shock before he was assigned to his host country; however, practically no preparation was made for the volunteer to return to ordinary life after completion of his tour of service. As one returning Peace Corps volunteer was to state:

"The change from conditions in the overseas assignment to American life was sudden, requiring only a few hours on a Jet plane – but often a lifetime to adapt".

A few volunteers landed smoothly beck in the U.S.. Many more were jolted, but slowly returned to normal life. But some would carry permanent, often bitter scars.

In one way or another, the re-entry crisis was inevitable. Most people returning from overseas service have a similar adjustment.

The problem of the volunteers returning was described by Richard Stolley, a returning volunteer:

"The volunteers feel unwanted, uncomfortable, apologetic or defensive, sometimes all of these."

The question of what to do about the re-entry was at the top of the Corps problems.

Typically, these difficulties begin as the homecoming welcome congeals rapidly into disillusion.

For the United States had changed mysteriously and uncomfortably while he had been away.

Once the joyous spasms of reunion are over, his family sees that their son had changed in disturbing ways.

He seems moody, preoccupied, irritated by their well meant questions.

In considering the matter of re-entry, Corps psychiatrists had come to two conclusions. The first was that major readjustment shocks are inevitable:

"On an average the initial and most severe phase falls approximately four months after returning with the duration varying with the individual.

The returned Corpsman goes through another phase of the crisis after about a year in which he begins to question the value of whatever he happens to be doing.

For instance, a returned volunteer to become a student returning to graduate school may begin to question the whole philosophy of education".

The second conclusion by Corps psychiatrists was that the discontent which produces this crisis was healthy and reassuring:.

"The Corpsmen performed key and responsible jobs abroad and returned to the United States loaded with self-confidence.

Many expected favorable consideration for employment upon return as a reward for their service".

Peace Corps literature had made such promises as that the returned volunteer was "particularly employable;" school systems are "eager" to use volunteer teachers; "most governmental agencies have made special request for returned volunteers;" and "two years in the Peace Corps today was more significant than a Rhodes scholarship."

This kind of recruiting literature was to anger many returned volunteers, who wanted to warn recruits.

Except for a few receiving favored treatment from the Government and college scholarship selection boards, the early Peace Corps volunteer had had to take his place in the competitive society like everyone else.

The distress of the volunteer was quite open, as sometimes a returnee obtained a good job, and then quit without explanation after forty-eight hours. Again, as another returned volunteer commented:

"When the returning Corpsman discovers that no business is anxious to hire him, he feels like he has been double-crossed. A lot of us feel that the agency itself is largely responsible for this reaction".

From college to college, Peace Corps recruiters asked students to sacrifice two years of their lives to make a better world – and broadly hinted the pay-off would come when they returned. Recruiting pamphlets promised 'new opportunities for men and women with experience abroad'.

Congress had early recognized the potential significance of the returned volunteer. The third purpose of the Peace Corps Act in its original charter was 'to help citizens of the United States to become better acquainted with the foreign peoples of the host countries'.

It was suggested by one research study that the agency should devote more effort to prepare volunteers for the readjustment to American society and acquaint them with what to really expect in the competitive labor market:

"The Career Information Service should start working with the volunteer several months before the end of his tour of duty. This would tend to reduce the impact of the inevitable re-entry crisis.

The returned volunteer truly can contribute substantially to fulfilling this third purpose. The contribution of returned volunteers to society constitutes a major potential impact of the future Peace Corps.

The agency should do its part in aiding the returned volunteer's adjustment. Volunteers are changed by their service and return searching not merely for a job, but for work which will carry some of the responsibility and satisfaction experienced in the Peace Corps."

Ongoing Early Peace Corps Security and Mission Problems

In an effort to attain its objectives, the Peace Corps had encountered a number of problems. In this chapter, these problems were treated in a descriptive and interpretive manner, and, where appropriate, suggestions were made on how to alleviate.

While in the host country, the volunteer was plagued by a number of problems. However, most volunteers remained less than two years in a host country. Volunteers were withdrawn from several countries for various reasons. The Corps administration had volunteers, with very considerable success, in other troubled areas.

The Peace Corps administration was handicapped by a part-time Director and no Deputy Director for seventeen months. This brought criticism from the Congress. The Congress had established a five-year limitation on staff employment and the wisdom of such rigid management principles was questioned. The organizational staff structure was adequate with the Peace Corp representative being its weakest link.

The Corps attempted to improve its policies and procedures by an organized system of program evaluation. The evaluators recognize existing problems and anticipate others, but Corps administrators have been slow to adopt certain of their recommendations. They attempted to improve effectiveness. Meeting these problems received continuous attention of the early Peace Corps.

CHAPTER V

EARLY EVALUATIONS OF
THE PEACE CORPS

As of 1966, it was still too early to place an accurate evaluation on the U.S. Peace Corps.

Nevertheless, dozens of preliminary evaluations of the first five years of Corps operation were undertaken with significant funding by Congress.

There were by that time a great many concerns about how the early Peace Corps was going to fit into the many new emerging threats to the U.S. abroad, as it faced increasingly the threats of communism and its allies that threatened the very basic goals of the U.S. Peace Corps – and all humanitarian efforts for freedom and democracy in all nations, as most early Peace Corps applicants espoused.

These early evaluations provided many insights from the early experience of the U.S. Peace Corps that can be applied even to this day. One member of Congress was to comment: "Early Peace Corps results are very mixed',

All together, both the experience and learnings of the early Peace Corps projects and the surveys of its initial volunteers and applicants, as well as their impressions and opinions are valuable for future efforts to apply from the historical evidence to create a better future world.

Following are results of several such early academic research studies and surveys that helped to guide early Congressional oversight and amendments to the original Peace Corp Authorization Act of 1961. There are many insights to be gained to reconsider such studies today.

Early 1966 Peace Corps Evaluation of Crossroads Africa

Dr. James H. Robinson, Director of Operation Crossroads Africa and member of the Peace Corps National Advisory Council, felt that the first five years laid an important foundation upon which the Peace Corps can build. He contended that the volunteers have lifted horizons of both the people and the governments with which they have been at work. Dr. Robinson contended that "these horizons are beyond what Peace Corps, as it was presently constituted, can help them to reach."

Dr. Robinson believed the future would demand more skilled and seasoned personnel to meet the requests of the nations they seek to serve.

Arnold and Marian Zeitlin, a returned volunteer married couple, both over age 60, contended that the most important measure of the success of the Corps was how much it increased living standards in countries where it operates. They felt professional competence was the first test of a volunteer's usefulness.

Chester Bowles, 1966 United States Ambassador to India, felt that in the future years the Corps would be judged less and less by ability to recruit and train dedicated volunteers to live and work in faraway places, and more and more by accomplishment in behalf of the underprivileged people it served.

He contended new organizational concepts would be in order to raise the standards of performance.

196

Ambassador Bowles concluded that the standards of performance should be raised:

"The most obvious way to move toward this objective was to select experienced professionals in those fields in which the Peace Corps was concentrating and to place each of them alongside, say, 20-year-old to 30-year-old volunteers, in positions where their technical skills can have a multiplier effect".

A number of host governments contended the skills and the quality of the volunteer's performance were inadequate for their needs.

Increasingly, Peace Corps host-country officials were requesting a larger proportion of professional and specialist personnel rather than any more generalists.

The most critical problem with this trend was that such professional technical specialists were not possible under current or past budgets, which had been approved by Congress based on the assurance that such generalists were both affordable and readily available – whereas to begin to hire significantly more advanced professionals would have required a major budget increases by the Congress, which everyone at Peace Corps knew was not likely to happen.

Harris Wofford, Associate Director of the Peace Corps, was convinced that "ways must be found either to recruit more highly skilled volunteers or to train liberal-arts volunteers in the special skills or to provide more skilled personnel either supporting professional staff or from other sources outside the Peace Corps."

This was a serious problem for the Corps. There was agitation both from within and outside the agency for more technical emphasis.

It appeared that the Peace Corps must have more technical skills at its disposal, either from within the Corps or from some other government agency, to survive.

Rather than to even attempt to prepare to build a case to ask Congress for more funding as an independent agency, most of the Peace Corps leadership felt that the time had come to instead begin to court both the State Department and AID, as well as military and intelligence agencies, for direct partnering in return for 'inter agency agreements' of mutual interest. This decision was obviously a very drastic turn around in Peace Corps agency policy.

One of the keys to the past success of the Peace Corps was that the volunteers had not gone as an adviser to foreign institutions, but as an local host country contract employee of those foreign institutions.

The unique contribution of the Peace Corps had been to bridge the "gap between technical and human development. Skills and economic aid have not achieved the desired ends in the past.

Congressman Richard Ottinger, former Peace Corps administrator who left to run for Congress, felt the Corps had proven use of 'generalists' in primitive societies:

"There have been complaints that we have not satisfied the technical needs of these countries, but a highly trained technician has an excess of knowledge for a primitive community. Thus it appears close coordination with other agencies to better advise for the most appropriate level of technical skills for each Peace Corp host nation and project is most likely the best answer."

Study of Performance In Colombia

The Peace Corps furnished the author a copy of this unpublished independent study by Dr. Morris I. Stein, Professor of Psychology New York University.

The purpose of this study was to determine opinions and attitudes toward the first group of volunteers who were involved in a rural community development programs in Colombia.

Data was gathered by four graduate students using standardized questionnaires in interviewing 33 Colombian community groups.

There had been twenty-five volunteers stationed in the fifteen sites where the respondents were interviewed. Sixty-four per cent of the local host community respondents had worked with the Peace Corps volunteers.

The questionnaire was established to gather information on the effectiveness of the Corpsmen and their program. The volunteers worked in cooperation with local host community councils to administer the research.

Seventy-one per cent of the people interviewed believed that the community council could not have accomplished its work without the aid of their volunteers: "The volunteers stimulated interest, instructed, worked, organized the people, and provided critical direction".

Of those twenty-nine per cent who felt the community council could have accomplished its work without the aid of the volunteers, twenty-two per cent complained about the volunteers. Some felt:

"The volunteers did not work properly, did not contact the people, or did not cooperate".

The remaining individuals felt that the council was capable, the people were capable, volunteers were capable, or that the work had been successful because of all groups.

Evaluation of Activities

Evaluation of the activities of the volunteers was established by four sets of questions.

Fully ninety-two per cent of the respondents reported they were positive when they heard that Peace

Corps volunteers were coming. The most frequent belief was that the U.S volunteers were coming to help.

Only four per cent of the respondents had negative expectations, believing that the Corpsmen 'would be spies, would exploit the people, or would make war'.

Ninety-nine per cent of the respondents felt the volunteers performed well in some activity for the benefit of the community. Only one per cent felt that 'the volunteers did not do much'.

When the respondents were requested to rate the value of different programs in Colombia, the Corps program was regarded as 'very high in value'.

In this regard, it should be kept in mind that there were other organizations involved in direct aid to the community other than the Peace Corps.

A little more than one fourth of the people "stated specifically that they were satisfied with what the volunteers had done." Seven per cent felt that Corpsmen's activities were hampered by others.

The respondents also overwhelmingly desired more help in the form of concrete constructions such as schools. The same 99% who were positive about the performance of the volunteers were to also admit that they were 'hopeful the U.S. will help us build more schools'.

Evaluation of the Volunteers

The use of the Questionnaire to determine the host people's evaluation of the volunteers was limited to those respondents who were directly acquainted with them. An average of sixteen host persons evaluated each of the 25 returning volunteers.

The results of this questionnaire revealed that the respondents thought the volunteers' ability to speak

Spanish was "only average" on their arrival, but when they left their ability to speak Spanish was "very good."

Eighty-five per cent indicated that when the volunteer's Spanish-speaking ability improved, their effectiveness at their projects also improved.

Two thirds of the local survey respondents had visited their Peace Corps volunteer home, and had shared meals together to include both American and local dishes.

Ninety-two per cent of the respondents believed that the volunteers were 'very dedicated to work for the benefit of the community' and were 'very likable'.

The respondents felt that the relationships of the volunteers were good with the people, the community council, government officials, and the host-country counterparts. Ninety-four per cent of the respondents felt quite congenial toward the volunteers.

Less than ten per cent of the people rated the volunteers as reserved, lazy, unpleasant, or argumentative.

The Corpsmen were quite positively rated by the host people who mostly wanted 'to continue friendships'.

Evaluation of the Peace Corps

Ninety-four per cent of the people returning the questionnaire felt the Peace Corps was worthwhile and six per cent felt it was not.

The 6% felt the Peace Corps was not worthwhile felt that it 'did nothing' or that 'the volunteers brought nothing new to us'. When asked what they liked best about the Peace Corps, nine per cent replied, "Nothing."

The remainder felt very positively, and pointed to the volunteers' general behavior or their useful work. This is to reflect over 90% of Returning Peace Corps Volunteers (RPCV's) were proud of PC service, yet fully 6% were not.

Evaluation of Attitudes Toward the United States.

Less than twenty-four per cent of the respondents knew that the United States paid the volunteers – and had been under assumption that they 'paid their own way here'.

Ninety-five per cent of those interviewed said that the United States aids Colombia 'out of purely Good Will'.

Eighty-two per cent felt that United States aid was of great benefit to their own local communities.

Ninety-two per cent of the respondents had positive opinions about the United States and the most frequent reason for the positive opinion was that the United States 'helps us to be smarter and more secure'.

Only eight per cent of the respondents had negative opinions about the United States because they felt that they were being exploited politically.

The results of this study appeared very favorable toward the United States.

One fourth of the respondents reported that they had previously known an American before they met their Peace Corps volunteers, and they were 'mostly what they expected after good experience knowing Americans'.

Two thirds of those interviewed considered the volunteers different from Americans they had known, and were 'more friendly and helpful so had improved in their views of Americans after knowing Peace Corps volunteers'.

They mostly regarded Corpsmen more positively than the other Americans that they had known.

The respondents all had positive attitudes toward the United States, agreed that 'the United States aids Colombia as a nation and their local community.

The Peace Corps was seen as a form of humanitarian 'Good Will' aid, and it reinforced positive feelings toward the United States.

The early Peace Corps volunteers in Colombia had enhanced the American prestige in that country. This was to be as critical for future U.S. activities during the 'War on Drug Cartels' as the Philippine Thomasites to build local support during WWII.

However, despite the 'Good Will' and positive feelings toward the U.S. that were created by the early Peace Corps in Columbia, this was to be very troubling into the next two decades, when Columbian Drug Cartels were to commit violence and atrocities on both the many local people that had been helped by the Peace Corps, as well as violence against Americans, which led to far different action by U.S., and restricted Peace Corps projects there.

A Study of Performance In Ghana and Volunteer Reaction

Dr. Brewster Smith evaluated the Peace Corps project in Ghana. Dr. Smith permitted the author to receive one of his "very scarce remaining copies of the final report" of his study. The appraisal by Dr. Smith was based upon observation during three field visits to Ghana. According to the Smith study:

"The Corps has contributed some badly needed teachers to the operation of the Ghana secondary school system. The long-run consequences of this short-run contribution cannot be established at the present time.

Underdeveloped countries are interested in raising level of education, but contribution of education to political and economic development is not simple or automatic. One short-run effect may have long-run consequences: the infusion of a substantial group of American teachers into a British model educational system seems sure to contribute to a desirable greater flexibility of traditional Ghana educational practices.

203

In a time of delicate political relations between Ghana and the United States, the presence of fully committed volunteer teachers who pursue tact and informality can only serve to counterbalance and in the long run, possibly to mitigate politically generated tensions.

The Ghana hosts who deal directly with U.S. Peace Corps volunteers soon learn there is a difference between Americans and Europeans. However, the long-run effect of volunteer presence in Ghana will depend on political developments beyond the scope of the Corps.

A remarkably firm consensus developed among the volunteers that their main reason for being in Ghana was to teach. Their high commitment to teaching was a major reason for their fine performance.

The volunteers insisted that neither political propaganda nor establishing personal relations with Ghana was a much a part of their job as simply to teach".

Dr. Smith agreed that their committed devotion to the Job was admirable, and agreed with the volunteers that their relationships with their students were more important than those with others.

He further agreed with volunteers that 'relations with students were likely to be superficial on both sides'.

Despite his substantial agreement with the volunteers on these matters, he felt there was an element of bias in their perspective, possibly due to a tendency to be defensive about missed opportunities.

The Smith study revealed that the volunteers tended to regret missed opportunities for rewardingly close relations with their highly educated adult Ghana hosts:

"Two reasons are suggested for their relative backwardness in establishing such relationships: the language handicap from which virtually all of them suffered, and the fact that to cultivate such relationships requires a good deal of initiative and effort."

The Smith study stressed the importance of adequate language instruction which will pay rich dividends In their increased ability to communicate with their students and Ghana higher education colleagues.

Only a minority of volunteers reportedly made real lasting friendships that opened windows to the intellectual and cultural life of the country. Many reported they were 'more often to make lasting friendships with their students rather than any teaching colleagues in Ghana'.

There was a tendency for the Ghana volunteers to flock together. Smith noted:

"Training should stress the fact that they should endeavor to establish meaningful relationships and that the benefit of such relationships was worth the effort.

The training program for Ghana was put together too hastily to cover many important aspects.

A high proportion of volunteers felt that it had taken them entirely too long to achieve adequate communication in the classroom.

The volunteers criticized that the health training as too theoretical and too time-consuming.

They felt that too much concern was given to culture shock, which was not as likely to arise in Ghana as in many other African nations".

The Smith study also revealed in another series of Ghana local host interviews of volunteers that:

"Too much time is spent arming the volunteer against sharp ideological challenges which did not arise.

The Ghana volunteers performed their jobs efficiently, but felt little need to establish meaningful relationships with Ghana.

The Corps should stress in training that two of the three legislative purposes of the Peace Corps are to create better understanding between the American and foreign peoples".

This was to be generally regarded as 'very useful' feedback by most of the top leadership of the Peace Corps; yet it was also to create controversy as this analysis was not always received well by mid-level bureaucrats of the agency.

Effects of Corps Service on Volunteers

The value of the Corps may rest as much in the effects that it had on the Corpsmen themselves and on American life as In the effects of its accomplishments abroad. Corps service provides an ideal occasion for the stimulation of maturing change in volunteers.

Many volunteers welcome two additional years to find themselves and decide what to make of their lives.

This effect of Corps service was described in detail by Dr. Smith:

"Volunteers tend to take advantage of the 'moratorium in life' decisions options provided by their two-year jobs in the Peace Corps, and to leave the Peace Corps with a clearer sense of personal direction than they had when they entered.

For a number, however, the two year interlude with its involvements and self-testing does not fully solve the personal dilemmas that many of them face.

We have been led originally to the impression that the substantial flow back to campus represents not only the search for advanced training to prepare oneself for more ambitious career goals, but also, to an appreciable extent, their reported need for still further 'moratoriums and sabbaticals before final decisions have to be made".

Notably, Smith was to also show in follow up studies that most of the volunteers returning from Corps service in Ghana eventually chose U.S. careers in teaching, but substantial proportion of the volunteers also sought careers in government service and international relations.

Cornell Study of Performance in Peru

Three anthropologists directed the massive research that resulted in the Cornell Peru Report, which was the story of the performance (or lack of it) by fifty volunteers in the Andes. It was the story of fifteen villages and what happened to them because of the volunteers.

The researchers were familiar with community life in the Andes long before the volunteers arrived.

They measured every aspect of volunteer activity over the period 1962-1964 in a study published by Cornell.

A comparison was made of fifteen specific Peruvian communities to which volunteers had been assigned with five comparable communities to which volunteers were not assigned. The aim of this study was to measure the differences that may occur in such variables as economic self-sufficiency or local initiative.

A major conclusion of the report was that Peace Corps communities developed at a rate of nearly 3 times as fast as comparable communities without volunteers. The Peace Corps paid $82,168 to Cornell University to study the impact of the volunteers. Yet the cost benefits of the conclusion of their study were estimated at over $3Mil/yr.

Allan Holmberg, one of the researchers, made the observation that: "The Federal Government hasn't paid much attention to careful evaluation of the promising results of its community action programs."

Peace Corps Director Sargent Shriver commented in personal interview to the author that he felt "this report was clearly a significant scientific study showing measurable cost benefit improvements in a society of people due to proactive action on part of individual volunteers in Peru".

When asked for elaboration, Shriver was to comment instead that: "Cornell University has been and will continue to be a source of both academic studies of subjective performance, but even more for objective and operational manpower optimization to help cut our costs".

Effectiveness of Peace Corps Volunteer Work with AID

Direct American aid to Andean communities proved to be even more effective when it was distributed by Peace Corps volunteers. A Cornell research team reached this conclusion after it carefully observed the distribution of material aid to these communities.

In a number of instances, purely on an experimental basis, the Agency for International Development afforded Peace Corps volunteers material resources for work on larger-scale development projects, which they could not have managed on their own or purely Peace Corps resources. The volunteers aided Agency for International Development by providing its staff with information on local and regional area community needs.

Such mutual reinforcement was advantageous to both agencies. The report revealed that: "U.S. material aid dispensed under volunteer supervision achieved greater impact than either volunteers without materials, or goods without volunteers. Yet, U.S. aid without a lot of fanfare and local press coverage as such does not necessarily make communities better off. Peace Corps helps to fill that gap".

The report pointed to an example of an irrigation project that did not improve a Peruvian community, yet provided critical intelligence and local good will to AID.

The research team observed the distribution of material aid in communities where there were no volunteers, and concluded the Agency for International Development program was roughly twice as effective working with volunteers as it was working directly with rural community leaders.

Specifically, AID credited the Peace Corps volunteers for passing on significant information about future needs of nearby areas as additional needs for more effective AID funding, and for consideration of future Peace Corps projects in those areas of mutual benefit to U.S. and Andes.

Thus, the Peace Corps volunteers simply provided the Agency for International Development with Information about possible programs and future material needs, and when approved, helped to coordinate it. Even more successful was for them to identify to AID possible synergies to combine or coordinate multiple projects.

For example, in one case the Peace Corps volunteers had a project to teach sewing lessons on machines that had been provided by the Agency for International Development, which gave opportunity to meet a business need, yet had insufficient financial benefits to apply their new skills to stimulate the local economy.

Yet, due to the recommendations of the same Peace Corps volunteers as they interacted with other nearby local area communities, AID was convinced to invest to fund agricultural irrigation equipment and pumping stations that also stimulated a surge in local area farming and agriculture economy, which created shared opportunities for the development of agriculture and textile product transportation delivery routes, which together became a major success for both Peace Corps and AID.

The increased effectiveness of material U.S. AID dispensed by volunteers was measured by community scale indices and by observation, to be regarded as very positive.

Furthermore, the findings of the study reveal that residents of rural Andean communities where volunteers worked during this period achieved only eight per cent of their total increase due to community action by their own unaided efforts.

Ninety per cent of the rural community scale increases achieved during this time were determined to be due to the combined efforts of local residents, Peruvian governmental agencies, the Agency for International Development, and Peace Corps volunteers.

Resulting Favorable Attitude of Peruvian Press

As a direct result of the success by the Peace Corps working with AID in the Andes, the resulting positive coverage by the press in Peru was overwhelming and positive.

More significantly, this press coverage was credited with creating a shift of positive host nation attitude toward the U.S. in Peru, which also led to greater academic cooperation between U.S. and Peru universities, as well as an increase in financial funding by private U.S. banks and investors in business partnerships.

This early Peace Corps success was studied widely by researchers in order to attempt to replicate and leverage to other nations.

Cornell researchers credited considerable attention to Peace Corps coverage in Peru newspapers and concluded that the reporting was "overwhelmingly favorable in tone. More than half of the articles appearing from 1961 to 1964 were rated positive by the researchers."

According to the report, 375 articles about the Corps success in Peru appeared during the period covered in the research. Overwhelming positive articles made up fifty-six per cent of the total coverage, and even the most critical were in fact mixed to admit positive influence of the Peace Corps and U.S. upon Peruvian communities.

Within this, forty-two per cent of all articles were rated as neutral with straight news treatment. One story in twenty reported criticisms and anti-Peace Corps reporting was conspicuous by its absence. Yet the Peace Corps had no public information operation in Peru at the time.

Importance of Job Assignment

A job assignment was very important to the success or failure of the volunteer, according to the study. The research team stated that volunteers assigned to relatively ill-defined jobs felt most dissatisfied with their accomplishments.

Of the volunteers sampled, the report revealed that "lone volunteers had one chance in ten of achieving significant impacts, while volunteers working with other agencies or in large project teams had nine chances in ten of succeeding" in rural community development assignments. Correlations showed that the size of the project had greater impact on success than any other factor.

This demonstrated the need for better project planning and needs assessment, and to increase the push to actively seek partnerships with other agencies..

Volunteers in smaller unsuccessful on their first assignment succeed in two thirds of their assignments when given a second chance, to work on larger projects.

Need for Language Fluency

The volunteer needed command of the local host country language in order to win the respect of its citizens.

The Cornell Peru Report suggested that fluency in Spanish according to early Peace Corps standards was only a minimal requirement, and did not guarantee success.

Yet, fluency of Spanish as measured by the Foreign Service Institute correlated well with volunteer achievement in fifty-eight per cent of the sample cases.

Ironically, shortly after the success of Peace Corps and AID in the Andes to result in a large number of new projects in Peru, which were notably staffed primarily based on Spanish language fluency as the most important criterion for selection, the early Peace Corps received one of its most painful set-backs up until that time.

This failure was also analyzed by the Cornell University studies, as a parallel to previous Andes success.

Reason for Expulsion of Thirteen Volunteers in Peru

Barely two years after the success in Andes by Peace Corps working with AID, in a newer Peace Corps project in the village of Vicos, Peru, a local host council voted to notify the Peace Corps thirteen volunteers were not meeting expectations and decided to expel them. Vicos had a self-governing Peruvian Indian local host community.

As the Peace Corps volunteers were expelled from the Indian village by a vote of the local council, the Peace Corps agreement required that they be immediately withdrawn from Peru; their projects were terminated, and the volunteers were all placed on suspension and recalled.

This vote came after the volunteers had been in Vicos for seventeen months. The Cornell Peru Report cited "numerous accidents, blunders, and misunderstandings" that brought about their expulsion.

The American Peace Corps volunteers had shown great proficiency in written and oral Spanish language understanding, yet had very little cultural understanding of the Peruvian host community they were assigned to.

They had been expected by the Vicos hosts to be living among them with same standard of living, and to communicate with them with respect to local customs and sensitivities. Unfortunately this did not happen.

The first priority of the U.S. Peace Corps volunteers to arrive at the Vicos community was to set up an inexpensive cooperative "diner" where they all agreed to spend an average from $1.10 to $1.45 per day for food.

To American cultural standards by young college graduates who were accustomed to spending 10 times that amount daily, this amount was very much in line with their 'worst' expectations of poverty, and they were unable to hide their dissatisfactions to have to eat and live on such meager provisions.

This was to have even worst impact since these volunteers invited local people to share meals with them 'for free' – which they thought was a good way to build local relationships. However, many of the volunteers were to denigrate, and even 'express disgust', at the food they were able to buy on this budget – which was noticed by the local community, and was regarded by them as an insult.

As part of the contract agreements between U.S. Peace Corps and Peru, the host nation provided Peace Corps a stipend for total boarding as well as house meals at average of thirty-five to forty cents per day.

The difference was by mutual agreement of the 13 Peace Corps volunteers paid out of their daily Peace Corps per diem, and it was pointed out by the analysts in the

Cornell study interviews that they had all felt this was a generous and humanitarian sacrifice on their part, as they invited to share their food at their "diner" to local Vicos Peruvian Indians in the community.

Yet, The average local population subsided on diets and economy of between 3 to 5 cents per day – which was barely 10% of the amount that the Peruvian government gave out of credits against U.S. Foreign Aid – but even worse was barely 1% of the amount the American Peace Corps volunteers gave out of their meager Peace Corps salary (which they also felt such a sacrifice as less than 10% of the food costs equal to experience as college students in U.S. they were not able to hide it).

So for local Vicos people accustomed to living on diets costing under 5 cents per day per person, the food that was to be available locally to Peace Corps volunteers at over 20 to 30 times greater cost was considered by them to be an incredible feast. This might have been actually to be regarded positively by the local people – except that they were to observe (and report to Peruvian press) that many volunteers 'acted disgusted and refused to eat the food'.

The result was a major PR disaster for the early Peace Corps. Many Peruvians felt that the American Peace Corps volunteers were simply arrogant, and showing off their superiority and wealth.

As a result, they were unhappy and unsupportive of the Peace Corps project in their own community from the beginning. All of the early positive press and reactions by the people of Peru were to quickly plummet.

Despite all of the good intentions of the Peace Corps volunteers assigned to Vicos in Peru, they were never to be accepted from before their project began, until they were all voted to be all expelled in one petition to the Peace Corps by the local community council.

The 13 Peace Corps volunteers, who all spoke fluent Spanish, were stunned and unable to understand why. Some analysts were to comment that 'if they had all been less proficient at Spanish language and idioms the situation might have been different – but what they may have thought was joking offended Vicos locals instead'.

The experience of one volunteer leader showed some of their frustration in community development.

The volunteer leader, a Harvard graduate who had worked on a farm, was attempting to promote improved livestock horticulture and veterinary handling practices, to encourage stock vaccination and de-worming of livestock.

He had been educated as a veterinarian and practiced the very best proven methods of modern horticulture to manage livestock populations, according to most advanced veterinary standards.

At the advice of cutting edge veterinarians that he knew in the U.S., this Peace Corps volunteer used a new method to castrate a local resident's donkey, in an attempt to prevent a serious infectious condition that the entire Peace Corps team had agreed to be a threat to the entire local livestock population of the local Vicos community .

The procedure may or may not have helped to stop the infection, which the local uneducated community had very great difficulty to understand anyway; but worse, the donkey died as a result of complications from the procedure – and the dire warnings of possible infections to other livestock never happened (largely due also the fast quarantine of the first reportedly infected animal – but because the local people did not understand any of the modern reasons for either quarantine let alone an advanced veterinary surgical procedure – the entire Vicos community was outraged). There were immediate repercussions.

Understandably, the result of the death of the donkey was to greatly anger the owner, who mobilized the local residents. Even worse, the Peace Corps volunteer leader further irritated his rural Peruvian counterparts by attempting to round up other local residents donkeys and livestock to put them in a corrals for quarantine – which was a standard practice in the U.S. when livestock may be infected – but when he was to explain that these livestock might need to be 'put down' if they were infected, this was far too much for the local Peruvian Indians to understand.

The matter got even more out of hand when another local Peruvian Indian resident was to be reported to attempt to 'run down' same Peace Corps volunteer with a motor vehicle, as retaliation for quarantining his donkey.

After this, two other peer Peace Corps volunteers notified their superiors of the incidents and requested that the veterinarian be reassigned to another location; yet was included at the top of the list of several expulsion requests by the local Peruvian Indian community council.

Thus, this was from beginning of the Peace Corps project at Vicos in Peru a troublesome assignment overall. Yet, this was only the beginning, and even more unsettling consequences were to result from the rapid deployment of 'fluent Spanish speaking' Peace Corps volunteers, who were all very well-intentioned, yet mostly lacked cultural understandings that challenged their communications.

Another Peace Corps volunteer had proposed and received approval from both Peace Corps and local community for an expensive but promising re-forestation project, after a large nearby area to Vicos Peru had been decimated by wildfires. Hundreds of local Peruvian Indians planted tree seedlings, provided by the Peace Corps and AID, with great expectations for success all around.

Then the Peace Corps volunteers and the local Peruvian Indians all left for two weeks according to a local Peruvian holiday. But when they returned two weeks later, over 10,000 tree seedlings were dead from lack of irrigation. No one including Peace Corps volunteers, or the local community Peruvian volunteers, or their government would accept responsibility, as each was to claim that others had been responsible to provide for water irrigation.

The U.S. Peace Corps volunteers appealed to both AID and the Peace Corps offices in Washington, DC for a solution. They were able to locate a nearby project that was building a public hot-shower facility, got funds from the community council, and laid the foundation for piping off-flow from showers to attempt to irrigate new tree seedlings, which were replaced by AID for Peace Corps.

However, due to 'various unexpected technical problems', the intended irrigation system design did not work, and again to much dismay by local Peruvian Indian volunteers these tree seedlings also died; and the project was abandoned and never completed. Yet this was also not the last of failures at Vicos, Peru.

In yet another Peace Corps project accepted during this same period by Vicos, Peru, a Peace Corps volunteer was a talented classical musician with extensive musical education, who had proposed to teach the local native Peruvian Indians in modern western music. He got funding from AID to buy modern instruments for an orchestra of young Indian boys.

Again, cultural differences, despite both the Peace Corps and the local Vicos Peruvian Indians were at first enthusiastic – plagued the best intentions of the project from both directions. The Peace Corps volunteer tried very hard to teach the Indian boys how to read modern sheet music and play the various instruments, but the Vicos

Indian boys never accepted or liked the music from the modern instruments, and preferred to play their native Peruvian flutes and drums instead. Even worse, the Peace Corps volunteer was not flexible to accept their music, and both parted ways feeling offended by the other.

Worse, without even to ask for yet receive approval from the Peace Corps main office, the volunteer packed all of his electronic audio equipment, lights and power generators on a pack horse and left in the middle of the night to travel to other villages to try to drum up support for his vision to teach modern classical music to Peruvian Indians, until Peace Corps officials were able to catch up with him and send him back to the U.S.; where he was transferred to a U.S. agency to research music therapy.

These and other mistakes led to the expulsion of the entire thirteen Peace Corps volunteers assigned to Vicos, Peru. The Peace Corps representatives at capitol of Lima, Peru attempted over more than a year to correct this situation on several occasions with little success despite the volunteers had all agreed ready to render their resignations.

After at two weeks some most favored volunteers were asked to return; however, most of them did not. They continued to believe until they were to be totally expelled by the local Vicos community counsel that they were right.

These incidents reinforce the previously expressed need for the Peace Corps representative to have a more effective means of disciplining the erring volunteer.

The Peace Corps representative attempted unsuccessfully to correct some of the shortcomings that led to the expulsion. The 13 volunteers finally responded altogether by offering joint but angry resignations.

The shortcomings of the volunteers in Vicos reveal defects of recruitment, training standards, and selection.

Frank Mankewictz, Latin American Regional Director, simply said that the "research findings prompted changes in volunteer selection, training, and field operation. These include better language training, more emphasis on selection of volunteers with adequate education or technical knowledge, and improving relations between volunteers and host country citizens and institutions".

The shortcomings, however, could not be completely blamed on recruitment, training, selection, standards, and administration. The researchers also blamed the affluent society in which the volunteers were reared.

As the researchers commented, the majority of incidents cited were "examples of behavior engendered by the tremendous accumulation of wealth in the United States that alienates their citizens from the majority of the globe who are uneducated and poor."

The researchers noted that the gulf could not be completely overcome, even by a highly motivated volunteer with proper training.

Volunteer Carelessness

The Cornell research team found that one of the most significant Impressions that Corpsmen as a group conveyed to Peruvians by their behavior. The shortcomings of the volunteers in Vicos reveal defects of recruitment, training standards, and selection.

Frank Mankiwitz, Latin American Regional Director, also said that the "research findings prompted changes in volunteer selection training, and field operation."

These included better language training, more emphasis on selection of volunteers with education or

219

technical knowledge, and improving relations between volunteers and host country citizens and institutions.

The shortcomings, however, could not be completely blamed on recruitment, training, selection, standards, and administration. The researchers also blamed the affluent society in which the volunteers were reared.

The majority of incidents cited were "examples of behavior engendered by the tremendous accumulation of wealth in the United States that alienates their citizens from the majority of the globe who are poor." The researchers all noted that the gulf could not be completely overcome, even by a highly motivated volunteer with proper training.

The report cited numerous examples of volunteer carelessness, which were recorded but not elevated:

"We received last week lumber warped; twenty bags of cement turned to stone; tools and Jeep parts scattered; ten thousand seedlings dead; a bumper from a Peace Corps vehicle lost and ignored; and vehicles neglected are all but one broken down."

All of these were very serious examples of carelessness to the poor local populations.

However, as many of the 13 expelled Peace Corps volunteers were to express: "What do we know about things such as these details? We all assumed that somebody local was responsible for such matters. We never heard about or even imagined they were not being handled".

Retreat from a Culture

The Cornell researchers found that most volunteers established "little Americas" by banding together, rather than by mingling with the Peruvians. Some volunteers retreated to their rooms to read six hours at a stretch to escape the strange culture.

These are all results of the work – or lack of work – of trained volunteers in Peru.

This might have been a matter similar to fairly typical adjustments and 'kinks' during the first years of a start-up of any American company or business.

The problem was that the host countries had often been led to believe that the Peace Corps was and official part of the U.S. government and there would be no 'kinks'; so they were understandably dissatisfied.

The Cornell study had revealed evidence of the overall effectiveness of the Peace Corps volunteers.

However, it had also revealed a number of problems, failures, and shortcomings of the volunteers in their efforts.

The three independent studies as just presented in this chapter would prove useful for evaluation and changes during the first years of the Peace Corps.

The volunteers in the Peace Corps had by 1966 been surveyed and interviewed to obtain thousands of highly personalized experiences, not one of which was fully typical, and no two of which are completely alike.

For one volunteer there were the comforts of home; for another the primitive conditions in a mud hut. For one volunteer there was quick, measurable success; for another, merely promises for future accomplishments.

The Peace Corps experiences determined the view of the volunteer.

The realities of early Peace Corps life mostly had little in common with the stereotyped image which persisted in the minds of the American public, in order to present the feelings of the volunteer, so those most representative of stereotypes were most often cited.

Yet, excerpts from the report on community development in Peru showed the frustrations of trying to achieve 'impossible goals' of one twenty-two year old volunteer, Tom Carter, from Portland, Oregon, who worked in a slum in Peru:

"My job was to get these people, to raise their standard of living. I taught in the local school during the day, and I taught carpentry to adults at night.

Both were important jobs, but I considered them only a beginning.

For example, our school had no roof. It should have been a simple ten-dollar project and about one day's labor for two or three Peace Corpsmen to build that roof.

Yet we couldn't do it. If we gave my school a roof it would always be simply that, a gift, 'the Gringo's roof'.

When it needed fixing, no one would fix it. If it takes me a year to talk my neighbors into putting on that roof it will be worth it. Because it will be their roof and their school."

Notably, this was not exactly in official line with the early Peace Corps policies.

So this was the crux of the dilemma. If the Peace Corps volunteers did not do all of the work of a day it often did not get done.

Instead the culture of the Peace Corps was to live among the local people they had to try for most of their year to convince somebody in the community to fix it for free, and take responsibility to check to maintain it for a few hours every year or so in the future.

Meanwhile, tens of millions of U.S. Foreign Aid dollars were spent, yet nothing gets fixed.

As one humble anonymous source was to say to Peace Corps Director Sargent Shriver: "Why not just pay $10 USD to a local to fix the roof for an honest day of work, and tell him next year there will be another $10 to maintain and fix it again?

That would save a lot of millions of U.S. Foreign Aid waiting for somebody locally to do something for free right?" Shriver reportedly said: "Exactly."

But Shriver also provided a file folder from a direct report that had been distributed in Peace Corps training guidelines:

"A volunteer has to be careful to not become too much of a leader – we must simply hint at things and let locals come up with ideas themselves – we must always let them lead the action.

A really good Peace Corps volunteer receives little credit. Keep that in mind wherever you read Peace Corps stories, expect a lot of failures, a few tangible successes, and a great deal of frustrations, we are making silent sacrifices to help others help themselves".

Volunteer Mark Ruwet, of Torrington, Connecticut, described his experiences in Brazil as follows:

"A year has passed since I arrived in Brazil to begin work. There have been encouraging moments.

Encouragements have come easily, particularly in the beginning part of my work.

But at first it was the language, then the customs, then food, and then you get past all of that, and realize the real work didn't seem to progress at all.

I have finally began to accept the fact that I should not expect to see the quick results that most Americans are accustomed to at home.

Volunteer Ken Van Sickle, North Dakota, described after his year in Nepal:

"Our Peace Corps volunteers failed to obtain community support in building a latrine in Nepal.

After a year the locals still did not have any understanding of why it was needed, and some even feared it could somehow 'cause the end of their world'.

Few people ever got very sick, so that they could understand why that when they did get very sick it was mostly caused by bad hygiene.

What we knew to be deaths and illness caused by lack of something as simple as a latrine was often explained by community leaders by superstition and myths."

Eventually this Peace Corps volunteer and his team built the same latrine themselves, without any help from the local community. Yet, few of the local community ever used the latrine, and avoided it as if it was a taboo. According to Van Sickle after this he later wrote:

"In calmer reflection, I realized two things. First, we made mistakes in conceiving and organizing the project.

We had failed to make the locals see that the latrine, and its relation to health and sanitation, was something of immense importance to them.

Enthusiasm for any project arises only if the project aligns to the experience of local people. So locals never accepted it, and so did not use it."

Volunteer Jim Grandel, after a year of service in Niger, related his reactions:

"Language proved a problem at first as we found many of the terms taught in training weren't useable here; but it didn't take too long for us to adapt new terms and vocabulary needed for our work.

I lived in what they call a compound, which includes three houses enclosed by a mud brick wall. I had no electricity or running water, and use kerosene lamps, and the water was carried in daily by porters.

This past year has given me a chance to see America and the American way of life as others see it.

This picture many times has been an ugly one from the view of the locals, and it was hard not for us to develop a sense of sympathy to appreciate their views."

By 1966, at the end of the first 5 years of the Peace Corps, as the volunteers returned individually and in groups, there were an increasing number of mixed reviews of the experiences of the early Peace Corps volunteers.

Increasingly, these returning volunteers felt so strongly that many were obligated to independently contact Congress to express concerns, which commonly stated their opinions on what was required to improve the Corps.

Three Volunteers in Ethiopia

A letter to Senator Russell, written by three volunteers who were teaching in the area of Addis Ababa, Ethiopia, gives their reactions to the Corps service. The three volunteers were Raymond Donaldson, Thelma Bingham, and Philip Bingham. They wrote:

"At present, information concerning the Peace Corps comes almost exclusively from Government sources. We believe that the information available through Government sources was inadequate.

The Government may not deliberately be trying to manage Peace Corps publicity; however, we believe that since the Peace Corps staff was already convinced of Peace Corps success, they tended to be biased in the information that they released to the general public.

The presentation of such one-sided view does not give the public an objective view of the Peace Corps merits. Biased Peace Corps publicity is not only detrimental to the general public, but is also detrimental to prospective Peace Corps volunteers.

Misrepresentations before and during our training sometimes requires extensive readjustment by the volunteer after arriving in the field. Though we were told we would suffer physical hardships, and though we expected them when we came, it was our opinion that very few volunteers in Ethiopia actually experienced physical hardships.

Yet, the publicity at home appears to emphasize minor hardships that were easily a minority when in fact a majority of volunteers had a wide variety of personal hardships. This includes even cases where volunteers lived in comparative comfort relative to local people, yet there were always lack of same healthcare or the little necessities of life that all Americans are accustomed to. When the volunteers showed stress or strain to adapt to their new surroundings, this is recognized by the local people and becomes a barrier to our sincere desires to help them.

Because volunteers do not live on as high level as State Department officials or Peace Corps administrators and PR agents in Washington DC, they all felt they were making a great personal sacrifice, which we were; yet compared to the local people, we were all privileged compared to them, and this was a real barrier."

The returning volunteers tended to become more opinionated after their separation from the Peace Corps, for many common as well as individual reasons.

This was demonstrated by an editorial in the Michigan State News, July, 1965, concerning Peace Corps trainees becoming highly incensed at the requirement of Case Dining Hall that they wear shoes in the dining hall at breakfast and lunch, and shoes and socks at dinner.

This was an issue that was widely published in a hand-out distributed at the campus by a group of returning Peace Corps volunteers, who had observed that the trainees should be prepared to learn to walk barefoot from the point of their first acceptance to training – since they pointed out that in all of the current field assignment locations of the Peace Corps at that time, very few of the local host community had ever even owned a pair of shoes.

226

This was to became an embarrassment that the Peace Corps tried very hard to suppress in the mainstream media. Many of the Peace Corps volunteers in training who asked about, let alone supported initiatives by not wearing shoes or socks to classes or dinner, were very quickly disciplined, or even expelled from training.

For many who had just accepted to join Peace Corps invitations, they already had prospective or full offers of employment for advanced and highly competitive technical and engineering education, and quickly backed out of training, or future candidate consideration as well.

Early Experience of Volunteer Couples in the Peace Corps

Arnold and Marian Zeltlin, early Peace Corps volunteers who became a famous first 'senior' retired couple, after their service, spent two years in Ghana.

They became very critical of the Peace Corps. They believed the Peace Corps had "sold the public a bill of goods", and was failing to fulfill its promises.

They contended that often volunteers join the Peace Corps just to prove they have the stuff to rough it, and were 'adventurers'. They commented after return to U.S. on their impressions of the Peace Corps as follows:

"The Peace Corps shapes its projects to provide work for the people it recruits. As a result, 75 per cent of its work involves school teaching and community development assignments that mere generalists can fill at least some extent after quick orientation."

The Zeltin's also commented to report what other returning senior married couple volunteers were saying:

"Local host countries and communities are very disappointed. The volunteers are asked to make contributions that are small by U.S. standards.

Yet for most local host communities such projects rank high in their local economies, yet often reduced from their U.S. Foreign Aid, and they frankly feel cheated.

They expected top experts in both Agriculture and Engineering, yet usually get only newly graduated U.S. college graduates with no practical experience other than teaching of very basic courses, which the local host countries have already to teach after similar coursework by locals, who already speak their language.

It was our experience, and it talking with other senior volunteers, that most underdeveloped had special respect for older people, probably because there were not many in their local population because of much shorter life expectancies.

In many cases, local 'elders' who were most often the local community leaders, were only in what would be regarded as middle-aged in the U.S. – yet were the oldest people in the community.

This often creates cultural conflicts with much younger volunteers in their twenties were telling older local community leaders what to do, as it was often resented.

We believe that most local host countries expected older volunteers with a great deal of experience rather than just a general higher education.

We feel that the Peace Corps has missed a great opportunity by not recruiting more older people with long career experience as volunteers. "

These comments were also to be widely circulated among the Peace Corps leadership, and the general consensus was the Zeltlin comments were highly useful.

However, in the final reality, there was very little interest among senior couples and retired career technical experts to volunteer to serve in the Peace Corps; and all of the pilot projects to recruit them were to largely fail.

Early Random Survey of 250 First Peace Corps Volunteers

In the summer of 1962, a reaction survey from the first wave of Peace Corps volunteers assigned to overseas projects was conducted by Velma Adams, on 250 volunteers in twelve countries in which they were operating at that time. This was mostly 'half-way' through projects.

Ninety-five per cent were glad they joined the Corps. Only five per cent felt they would not volunteer if they had a chance to reconsider.

Yet, seventy per cent stated that there had been problems that they did not expect.

These included having to plan their own projects, lack of privacy, and 'relentless curiosity' of the host people.

Only fifty-four per cent of the volunteers felt that training was adequate.

Twenty-three per cent felt they failed to receive ongoing support from the Peace Corps headquarters in their host nations, or from the U.S.

Reactions From Among First 850 Returned Volunteers

In March, 1965, about 850 former volunteers were paid to participate in a conference by the Peace Corps on the future career goals of returned volunteers.

In a preconference report, prepared by Neil Boyer, a former volunteer in Ethiopia, the agenda and issues of returning Peace Corps volunteers were summarized and presented to the Peace Corps leadership in Washington, D.C.

This included their reason for joining, experience as volunteers, and their uneasy adjustment after they returned from abroad to America.

Notably, this was at a time that the Peace Corps was also considering to change the policy to not allow former Peace Corps volunteers to accept full employment as Federal employees to work in Peace Corps leadership. Most of the 850 invited volunteers were aware that they were being informally considered for high level Peace Corps leadership position as this ban was lifted. Mr. Boyer spoke in a welcoming speech as follows:

"Despite all the diversity, you came to the Peace Corps with many common characteristics. In general, you were all to learn as volunteers that host nations are distraught at the supermarket image of American life".

Many who volunteered describe themselves as 'idealists.' Very few who came home two years later would use the word. If they had idealism, they ran headlong into a thing called reality.

For many this was a violent crash between ideals and the real world. The one thing most every volunteer can tell you was that he learned how to be patient.

He came to know and appreciate more his own country's strengths. But he also saw the deficiencies of American operations in his adopted country.

So if you ask a volunteer what he accomplished, he probably won't be able to tell you in very concrete terms. But his real accomplishments were more personal, as a basis of understanding, to urge others to help themselves, of broadening horizons.

Of course he went through periods of depression and loneliness and great frustration. But when the volunteer returns home, he has a greater commitment to what he wants for America.

The volunteer hopes that he can put his knowledge and experience to work to bring about change.

He views himself as one possessing great energies in a country that does not yet know how to use them.

The returned volunteer has often been disappointed by the United States. The returnee finds discomfort in having his situation suddenly reversed upon his return as, he is often no longer accorded great respect he had during the great responsibilities he had overseas."

Journalist Eric Sevareid believed that the re-entry problem was caused by an excess of acclaim on their departure. This was also built upon obvious comparisons of parades for military enlistee soldiers marching to war, versus the greater lack of parades or even acceptance of soldiers who return after military service, despite they come back damaged both mentally and even physically, to live the rest of their lives in very tragic circumstances. He said:

"Despite few of the returning Peace Corps volunteers returned with similarly damaged bodies as soldiers, many or most had just as severe mental and emotional problems after their return.

This was to be expressed by many returning Peace Corps volunteers as even more difficult to endure since they felt they were led to volunteer as a way to help to secure 'World Peace' and prevent wars, yet they mostly felt they had to be put in harm's way to support intelligence gathering and even preparation or helping to build infrastructure in the Third World that was to be known by and used in future U.S. military operations.",

As the reports and interviews by unhappy returning Peace Corps volunteers began by 1966 as the War in Vietnam seemed inevitable, Sevareid commented that:

"The shock felt by these returned volunteers was the inevitable backlash of the publicity that surrounded the birth and recruitment of the early Peace Corps."

Mr. Sevareid also suggested that:

"The returning Peace Corps volunteers might consider the contribution of soldiers in war, before feeling sorry for themselves. The spirits of the volunteer have been enlarged as he matures from his tour of duty; therefore, he should be grateful, not resentful."

Random Survey of 40 Returning Peace Corps Volunteers

A random survey of forty returned volunteers was conducted in April, 1966 by the author, with the assistance and support of the Peace Corps Director Sargent Shriver, as a random sample from Peace Corps volunteers that had successfully completed their assignments and returned to the U.S. with good recommendations from their host nations and local communities.

These returned volunteers had completed at least two years of service, and at least one year of which was in foreign field service.

```
RANDOM SAMPLE SURVEY OP FORTY RETURNING VOLUNTEERS

Glad they joined the Peace Corps                     100%
Believe Peace Corps service a positive contribution   90%
Changed career goals as a result of Corps service     79%
Encountered personal hardships serving overseas       65%
Received full support from Peace Corps headquarters   63%
Felt Peace Corps basic language training was adequate 63%
Felt Peace Corps Director holding two jobs detrimental 51%
Decided to continue education after Peace Corps       51%
Felt Peace Corps publicity was biased or inaccurate   43%
Believed mountain climbing training was necessary     39%
Considered rejection during training excessive         6%
Considered over-supervised by Peace Corp HDQ in field  3%
```

Overall, the questionnaire revealed that the returned volunteers were unanimous in being pleased that they had joined the Corps. The reasons for being pleased with their Peace Corps service were undefined.

A substantial number of volunteers cannot state specifically why they joined. Ninety per cent felt their service was a positive achievement for their host country.

Yet, a significant ten per cent did not consider their service a positive achievement for their host country.

Thirty-seven per cent did not receive all the support they needed or asked for from Corps headquarters, either in their host country or from Washington, DC.

The survey revealed a number of shortcomings in Peace Corps training.

Thirty-seven per cent of the returned volunteers felt their language training was inadequate. In follow up interviews, these volunteers felt they got 'basic language training but limited true basic understanding of idioms and cultural matters including body language.'

Over half of those surveyed did not consider their overall training adequate. Sixty-two per cent did not believe mountain climbing and "drown proofing" training as necessary (many pointed out that there were assigned to arid desert locations with 'very little chance to drown').

The Peace Corps from the beginning had stressed that physical hardships would not be experienced by many volunteers in their assignment abroad. This idea was rejected by over thirty-five per cent of those surveyed.

Most of the surveyed returned volunteers felt that selection during training was adequate, with only six per cent believing that in the early quota that 25% rejected during physical training was excessive.

An overwhelming majority of all complaint mail from volunteers who were accepted to Peace Corps training related to the level of these rejections for physical training, versus their feeling that the main focus of their Peace Corps training was very basic language proficiency,

which should probably have been at more advanced levels
As one Peace Corps volunteer stated:

"The PR of the Peace Corps seems to act like
Peace Corps training was similar to training for NASA
astronauts. This was ridiculous.

The only training we seem to get was mostly very
basic foreign language syntax and vocabulary, but very little
culturally useful."

The same questionnaire indicated a number of
reservations on Peace Corps administrative policies.

Fifty-six per cent felt that Corps publicity had
been biased favorable toward the agency.

Thirty-six per cent felt that the Corps had
overemphasized the benefits they would receive at the
completion of their service.

Almost one half of those surveyed concluded that
former Director Sargent Shriver had hurt the Corps by
'holding down two jobs'.

In the opinion of thirty-two per cent of the
returned volunteers, the five-year limitation on staff
employment by volunteers was unwise legislation.

The reactions to the survey demonstrated the
profound effect of Peace Corps service on the personal
lives of returned volunteers.

An impressive total of seventy-nine per cent
revealed that their career goals had changed as a result of
service. Peace Corps service tended to raise the volunteers
self-esteem, and improve their self-confidence.

A natural result was to seek additional education.
An impressive fifty-one percent reported that Peace Corps
service had caused them to further their education.

Thus it was seen that Corps service influenced the
lives of returned volunteers in various ways.

In an effort to obtain current reactions of the members of the Senate Committee on Foreign Relations and the House Committee on Foreign Affairs, a survey of ten members selected at random from each Committee was conducted by the author.

Some of their opinions revealed in this survey made in May, 1966, are presented to show the prevalent attitudes of the House Committee on Foreign Affairs. This was to reflect that 8 of 10 Congressman replied.

Congressman Peter Frelinghuysen (R-New Jersey) was of the. opinion of the Peace Corps today was more favorable in 1966 than at the beginning, of the agency. He was not concerned that the Peace Corps consistently missed its annual quota. The Congressman expected the number of volunteers to level off close to the present number. He did not consider the twenty-five per cent rejection at training as too high.

Congressman Edward Derwinski (R-Illinois) had considerable doubts at the time the agency was created and his opinion had not changed. He felt the fiscal operations and projection of quotas had been poorly handled. The Congressman believed that the Peace Corps had been less than honest with the public and the Congress in regard to its failures and problems. He felt the Peace Corps had been too concerned with building a positive image. The Congressman expected the number of volunteers to level off close to the present number. He concluded that the rate of rejection during training was too low, permitting too many unqualified Individuals to go overseas.

Congressman Clement Zablocki (D-Wisconsin) opinion of the Peace Corps was as favorable in 1966 as it was at the beginning of the agency. He felt that the Peace Corps quotas were realistic as the Peace Corps had projected. He believed the number of volunteers was likely to level off close to present rates at the time in 1966.

Congressman Roy McVicker (D-Colorado) opinion of the Corps was about the same as at its beginning. He was concerned, however, that the Peace Corps had consistently missed its annual quotas, and yet used up all of its administrative funds. He feels the Peace Corps had been somewhat unfair to Congress and the public by projection of unrealistic quotas. The Congressman expected the number of volunteers to level off close to the present number as of the end of 1966.

Congressman Spark Matsunaga (D-Hawaii) affirmed that he had paid tribute to the Peace Corps on its fourth anniversary. He stated: "Without a doubt, the Peace Corps had proven itself to be the most effective instrument for bringing about understanding between the United States and other nations of the world. Through Peace Corpsmen it had helped to create a new image of our country abroad, and a change from one of the acquisitive, materialistic society of fortune-seeking individualists, to a great nation of good will seeking to help all those in need."

Congressman John Brademas (D-Indiana) also wrote to comment: "We recognize the great importance of increased capital in underdeveloped areas of the world. The underdeveloped nations need trained and skilled people in technical and economic fields to move their countries economically and socially into the Twentieth Century."

Mr. Brademas also further recognized both the importance and limitation of the Peace Corps: "Obviously, the Peace Corps cannot fill this serious gap in all these areas. But what the young Americans taking part in the Peace Corps can do was to help some areas in some measure, and, perhaps more to the point, can serve as a positive and dramatic example of the awareness of the people of the United States of our desire to see the peoples in the underdeveloped areas improve their own economies, to develop free societies, and free political institutions".

Congressman William Bloomfield (R-Michigan) questioned the advisability of having 56 volunteers in the Philippines and only 168 in a large country like India. Mr. Bloomfield felt this was "totally out of proportion."

Mr. Bloomfield was also critical because the Peace Corps had sent volunteers to Indonesia to teach physical education. He questioned the assignment of physical education teachers to a country when we are supporting them with substantial foreign aid.

Director Shriver defended this policy by a letter he wrote to Joseph Clark, and copied to Mr. Bloomfield, that quoted Shriver in a letter from the author requesting further clarification on May 23, 1966, as follows:

"Stating that things move slowly in India, and that India has a large number of unemployed educated people, is already well known.

However, the Peace Corps has gradually increased its program in India to 695 as of March 31, 1966, and within another year may reach 3,000, according to the predictions of the new Director Jack Vaughn."

As Director Shriver commented to the primary in a personal interview as Shriver was preparing a response:

"This is exactly kind of correspondence that takes up most of my time and my entire staff as well, while we all serve double duty. This kind of criticism could not have been anticipated by any planning, as the decision to put 56 volunteers in Philippines versus 168 in India were based on a long series of comparative analysis of cost-benefits that are far beyond the understanding of Mr. Bloomfield of what was truly proportional."

Director Shriver believed that teaching physical education was a good way to develop close personal relationships with the people of foreign nations. Shriver was also to comment to effect that: "a Director of the Peace Corps needs more press staff than a U.S. president".

None of the ten members of the Senate Foreign Relations Committee 'had the time' to answer the survey questions submitted by the primary author. Yet, two of the Senators did acknowledge by personal letters to comment, after they also stated that their busy schedule did not permit time for answering the specific questions.

Yet, Senator Joseph S. Clark (D-Pennsylvania) stated by letter to regret not having either time or expertise to answer questions in detail: "I can state, however, that I continue to have a very strongly favorable impression of the Peace Corps, and the fine work which it is doing."

Senator Jennings Randolph (D-West Virginia) felt that "the program of Peace Corps Volunteers was needed now just as much or even more than when it became law." He was confident "that their past record of achievement will be sustained in future endeavors."

There was one other of the 10 Congressmen from the House Committee on Foreign Affairs that not only answered the survey questions, but also enthusiastically wrote a very long letter, and sent several large documents that reflected his own personal commitment to the U.S. Peace Corps, including his own published research (which he commented in his letter that he had been personally asked by Director Shriver to send to this author).

Congressman Richard Ottinger (D-New York), was actually the second original senior staff member of the Peace Corps that had been hired by Sargent Shriver, and he took part in the original early Peace Corps task force reports. He decided to run for Congress was to 'champion the Peace Corps' after the death of President Kennedy.

Ottinger had served as Director of Programs for the Peace Corps for the west coast of South America. The Congressman was personally motivated to run for office based upon his commitment to advance and support legislation and budget for the Peace Corps and related programs, based largely upon his honest analysis of real data on the Peace Corps to make a five-year evaluation of the Peace Corps and all of its related agencies.

Reportedly, Ottinger was a protégé of Sargent Shriver, and his top choice to replace him as Director.

According to the report of the first five years of the Peace Corps that was headed up by Mr. Ottinger with the review and comments by Director Shriver:

"The Peace Corps seems to be running out of steam. The exciting innovations of yesterday are becoming routine. The Peace Corps will be swallowed up whole by the Agency for International Development if it doesn't rejuvenate itself.

Degeneration of the Corps would be tragic because the agency has demonstrated success in working effectively with underdeveloped countries where other approaches have failed to a greater or lesser extent."

Congressman Ottinger thus suggested in 1966 that the great potential in the world, both economically and politically, lies with the underdeveloped countries, as they will largely decide "future balance of Freedom". Thus, as Mr. Ottinger observed:

"The Corps has demonstrated efficacy of recruiting and utilizing 'generalists' without a high level of technical expertise in dealing with primitive societies."

Mr. Ottinger contended that "a highly trained technician in a primitive society had a great wealth of knowledge, which can be effectively utilized in underdeveloped countries, and has critical opportunity to impress local populations if they can selectively present advanced ideas in a very simple way".

Ottinger also observed that "the high-level technician can frequently become frustrated at inability to utilize his sophisticated knowledge, yet a greater value was to the quiet hero who can find the ways to help people in remote assignments to understand simple science".

This was also proposed as a determinant of future success of both the Peace Corps volunteers as well as Peace Corps itself. If an applicant was "more interested in an academic career or to be a scientist or theorist on the cutting edge of advanced technology, they are probably not a good candidate for Peace Corps service. However, if they are more inclined to be a humble teacher or humanitarian in order to teach and help to build understanding for good of people, they are.

The Peace Corps has proven their ability for building from the bottom up rather than from the top down. This is in contrast to the Agency for International Development. Thus, the Peace Corps may be better a personal and career move for teachers and humanitarians who may come back to U.S. to teach in public education and serve in nonprofits, rather than those that seek to be career bureaucrats as appropriate for AID.

The Peace Corps has demonstrated the value of coming to the host country as an equal rather than as an adviser. The Peace Corps has proven the efficacy of living in a community where our young people work, receiving comparable compensation, and living at a comparable level. The Peace Corps has shown the critical importance of separating development aid from purely political goals".

Congressman Ottinger believed size was a chief limitation of the Corps: "All of the Peace Corps volunteers serving worldwide in 1966 could have been placed in India alone without fully satisfying the vast needs there".

Mr. Ottinger was convinced that to succeed, the Peace Corps must expand. These are his recommendations on how to expand:

"First, to utilize higher-level technicians;

Second, to make married couples with minor children eligible for service;

Third, to permit Corps service to substitute for military service;

Fourth, to encourage non-college skilled workers to join by extending training periods for them".

Each of these recommendations had been the subject of pilot studies and analysis under Director Shriver, yet had each been characterized by mixed results.

The Congress had generally supported the Peace Corps. However, the members individually and collectively appear to be taking a more critical look at the organization and its activities. The expected normal reaction would be for the Congress to evaluate a new agency more critically after five years, and to carefully consider such proposals.

The United Nations Educational, Scientific, Cultural Organization sent a young British sociologist, Glen Roberts throughout Africa studying the work of Peace Corps volunteers.

In his first report, he had praise for the volunteers but also gave suggestions for improvements. He praised the care with which volunteers were selected and trained.

However, Roberts believed far greater care was needed in planning the projects undertaken. His chief criticism of U.S. Peace Corps was over-supervision:

"The result of this micro-management supervision seems to be that the volunteers never get far away from the United States, either in spirit or in practice."

Awards to the Peace Corps

Awards show favorable reactions to the Peace Corps. The Corps received the Ramon Magsaysay Award for International Understanding on behalf of the volunteers in eleven Asian countries.

This award, which was established in 1958 to honor the late President of the Philippines, recognizes persons in Asia that exemplify the late President's "greatness in spirit, integrity, and devotion to liberty."

It had been termed Asia's equivalent to the Nobel prize. The volunteers are the first nonresident Westerners ever to win it. The board stated:

"This 1963 award is given to the Peace Corps for their contribution to work among people and service to the cause of peace and humanity in a direct and personal way."

The problem of achieving peace amidst the tensions and dangers of a nuclear age occupied the minds of much of the volunteers, yet few within it were to they had discovered a fully useful way to contribute.

Yet, he Peace Corps volunteers belonged to a small but growing fraternity who felt that at least a small part of their individual efforts did in fact make a difference.

Halfway across the world in South America a similar award was given to another group of volunteers. The Silver Medal of Areaulpa was presented by Peruvian President Fernando Terry to the forty-five volunteers working in Peru's second largest city.

The award each year was presented to the individual or group which had most helped the city of

Peruvian city of Arequlpa. In 1963 the volunteers were judged the most deserving group.

This was the first time that a group of North Americans had received the award. These awards demonstrated the feeling of the host people toward the volunteers and indicate success for the Peace Corps.

However, the backlash against the Peace Corps in Vicos, Peru the very next year were effectively to create conflict, and to encourage pro-communist supporters.

Reaction of Worldwide Communism to U.S. Peace Corps

The most concerned populations in host nations that were disturbed by the U.S. Corps within its first 5 years were undoubtedly the local press and organizations either directly or indirectly supported by Communism.

In the eyes of the Peace Corps and the U.S. government, the surest sign of its success in any local host country or community was the corresponding intensity of attacks on it by the Communist propagandists.

Within the first five years after the U.S. Peace Corps was created, both Soviet and Red Chinese broadcasts beamed to Africa and Southeast Asia increased by over 400%, and predicted that no country in the areas of their influence would ultimately accept the Peace Corps.

Also, it was to be immediately of concern to American intelligence communities, with very advanced regional African and Asian language and cultural expertise, that these increasing broadcasts conveyed very dire and serious threats to any host nation or local community to 'accept' to 'harbor' any Peace Corps projects or volunteers into their communities.

Although there was strategically absolutely not even one Peace Corps volunteer that was to suffer violence that could be directly linked to communist supporters who opposed U.S. humanitarian aid, there were a very large number of reports of violence to local supporters of the U.S. Peace Corps and its missions, including many deaths.

This was once again to be most often to occur in Africa and Asia, although it was also to be suspected in many Latin America and South America incidents during that same time period, as these regions were increasingly the focus of the Communist nations to build support for their anti-American agendas.

In the years immediately after the assassination of President Kennedy, as the new President Johnson struggled to balance many of the domestic civil rights problems with the growing threats from the Communist powers, the local political propaganda attacks became common place.

Peace Corps volunteers were increasingly described in local press of all host nations and communities as an arm of the U.S. Central Intelligence Agency.

Castro joined the attack by claiming the U.S Peace Corps was preparing the way for a new invasion of Cuba, and after that the world.

Despite it was ridiculous to Americans and most of the educated world, the uneducated in many underdeveloped nations leaning to communism believed it.

It was also interesting that Russian propaganda usually attacked the Peace Corps as a whole, but the Chinese communist press usually was to attack the integrity of the individual volunteers, versus projects, that they Chinese were proposing to replace them.

It was also interesting that during this time, Japan was to also be coming to regional host nations and local communities to consider to propose projects similar to the Chinese, but with more financing over longer terms. This was ultimately to lead to many Japanese investments.

So although they did not encourage or support U.S. Peace Corps, the Japanese were to indirectly to support the gradual transfer of new Japanese technology by Peace Corps similar to what had been provided by U.S. to Japan, and this was effectively to neutralize a lot of unchallenged support for many Communist influences.

Together, these issues all converged to create many complex underdeveloped host country situations.

Host Country Reactions

Most host countries had welcomed the Peace Corps, and asked for an increase in the number of volunteers. The Prime Minister of Nyasaland, Kanaza Banda, wrote Sargent Shriver expressing his country's appreciation of the work of the volunteers, and requested additional volunteers. The Prime Minister on June 23, 1964, wrote:

"They have made, and are making a great contribution to our country.

They have been true ambassadors of your country and have rendered my people invaluable service.

Their departure will leave a grievous gap in our educational system.

I would earnestly ask you to reexamine your plans for next year and see whether there was any way an additional number of Peace Corps volunteers might be sent to my country." Prime Minister Banda offered to pay half of the cost of an airplane ticket home for any of the volunteers that would sign on for an additional year.

Mr. Ahmad Wuric, Sierra Leone's Minister of Education, spoke to a group of Peace Corps teachers:

"The Peace Corps has in a very real sense opened new windows in our schools, admitting a breath of fresh air to many stuffy corners, and revealing new horizons of interest to many pupils.

This has been perhaps your greatest achievement. We did not lack academic challenges in our schools. What we did lack in all too many schools was an adequate range and variety of non-academic activities, both inside and outside the classroom.

The first Peace Corps volunteers arrived just over two years ago, and to them must go a good deal of the credit for the changes in attitude in many of these matters which we are just now beginning to see".

The Corps was sufficiently popular to be imitated by the governments of several countries. By June, 1965, nineteen countries had established international programs similar to the American Peace Corps.

Countries establishing volunteer service programs include the following Argentina, Australia, Austria, Belgium, Canada, Denmark, France, Israel, Italy, Japan, Netherlands, New Zealand, Norway, Philippines, Sweden, West Germany, Switzerland, and United Kingdom. Also, a total of twenty-eight countries had established domestic programs modeled on VISTA, which was regarded as domestic equivalent of American Peace Corps.

The United States Peace Corps also took the lead in establishing an International Peace Corps Secretariat of the United Nations in 1962. This Secretariat rendered advice and coordination to concepts of national voluntary middle manpower as a tool of economic and social change.

Increase in Numbers of Americans Overseas

In addition to performing a vast amount of service to the host country, the Peace Corps created a reservoir of personnel who, as a result of their experience continued to serve the United States, the United Nations, and other countries.

In June, 1965, one hundred and seven volunteers have returned to their host country for employment by the United States government. Seventy-three ex-volunteers had gone back to work in a Peace Corps country other than the one in which they had originally served.

A total of seventy-three had gone to non-Peace Corps countries for various reasons. Foreign governments often tried to employ volunteers at end of their projects.

The Government of Turkey actually made an across-the-board offer to hire every Peace Corps teacher in Turkey upon completion of his service – at double the rate previously paid for their service in the Peace Corps..

Voluntary Community Service

A Career Information Study, revealed that of 3,222 volunteers who completed service before December, 1964, fifty-two per cent are since engaged in some form of voluntary community activity. Voluntary service work enables many returned volunteers to continue the sense of "challenge and commitment offered by overseas work, regardless of the nature of their primary activity."

Service in the Corps had a significant effect upon their future career choices. Before joining the Corps, thirty-four per cent of over two thousand included in a survey made by the Corps had no career goal.

After completion of service, only twelve per cent were still uncertain, and many of these had general plans toward which they were working in graduate training.

While in the Corps, fifty-four per cent of the same group of volunteers made a change in their career goals.

This does not include lateral or vertical changes, such as a secondary teacher changing to university teaching.

A profound effect on international careers was evident. When they entered the Corps, only eight per cent of the volunteers desired permanent careers overseas; after their Peace Corps service, almost a third desired some form of international career.

The number desiring careers in teaching increased five per cent as a result of Corps service. Nine per cent more were seeking government jobs after Peace Corps duty. Seven per cent more were pursuing goals in social service than before joining the Corps.

Approximately forty per cent of returning volunteers decided to continue their educations after Corps service. Two thirds pursued graduate degrees and one third entered undergraduate or special education programs.

As half of the volunteers are serving in teaching programs, many develop a career interest in education.

Despite their two years of teaching experience, most volunteers found "state teacher-certification regulations a formidable barrier to full use of their talents."

Both President Kennedy and President Johnson had encouraged government agencies to hire returned volunteers. By June, 1965, six hundred former volunteers were working for federal agencies and for state and local governments. There were 317 former volunteers on the Corps staff who were hired in positions working for private corporations.

The fact that the number hired by American private industry employers remained relatively low may be partially explained by the number of liberal arts students that were accepted into the Peace Corps who had no technical credentials to be qualified for U.S. industry positions. Thus the number of returned Peace Corps volunteers who elected to pursue technical and graduate university education did better than non-RPCV students.

This was emphasized by a study taken in 1965 by Career Information Service and the Peace Corps Division of Research. For more than one hundred volunteers, seven out of eight are getting higher grade point averages, and continuing follow up studies showed similar results.

Summary of Early Peace Corps Evaluations

Three independent government sponsored studies revealed a number of measurable positive effects of the Peace Corps. Also, a reasonable number of problems, failures, and shortcomings were revealed; many of the same problems continued for decades, many others were solved.

The Peace Corps can be evaluated by various reactions to its policies, procedures, and performance. In surveying individual and group reaction, a number of achievements were revealed. On the other hand, the volunteers recognized many problems and shortcomings of the agency, and they suggested methods for improvement of its operation. The operations of the Corps had positively influenced educational institutions by increasing the teacher supply and change in teaching methods, including to improve academic diversity and discipline.

The Congress had generally supported the Peace Corps as an agency; yet, individual congressmen and congressional committees have questioned specific policies and procedures. The Corps, overall, had received favorable foreign reactions from their local counterparts.

Note: Up to this point, this book is based on the dissertation of the primary author; the next chapter is written by the second author as a summary for courses for high school and undergraduate students.

CHAPTER VI

THE NEXT TWO DECADES
OF THE PEACE CORPS

Up to this point in this book, the development, operation, problems, and evaluation of the first five years of the Peace Corps are presented from a perspective of its agency management, and oversight by Congress and WH.

The next two decades of the U.S. Peace Corps as an independent agency of the U.S. State Department represented the first generation of one of only a small few new U.S. independent government agencies to be created after WWII, and involved many innovations to structures of U.S. government that required a lot of 'tweaking'.

Notably however, the Peace Corps was to prove to be very effective in research about its internal operations in a manner that 'quickly learns from and fix its mistakes'.

After its original organization, it increasingly adopted more traditional U.S. Federal Executive Branch bureaucratic policies and procedures, which included to align with more traditional Foreign Aid, and to move increasingly away from its original roots in the local community action support and humanitarian objectives that were fundamentally responsible for its innovative creation.

251

Greater emphasis after the first five years of the U.S. Peace Corps were less focused upon peace and humanitarianism, and more focused on coordination and collection of intelligence for American economic and military interests – which was exactly what anti-American and communist sympathetic press had predicted from the very beginning of the Peace Corps under Kennedy.

This was not only to complicate and hinder many benevolent, well-intentioned efforts of the Peace Corps abroad during the Cold War, but was also to directly impact a gradual decline in enthusiasm from many original political supporters of the Peace Corps during its first five years.

During the first five years of the U.S. Peace Corps, it was overwhelmingly welcomed by the American public as an antidote to a growing worldwide image of the "Ugly American", and a way to provide an alternative symbol of friendlier America – as intent of most of U.S.A.

Yet, as the Peace Corps was increasingly to be involved in scandals and implicated to be involved as a front for clandestine activities funded by CIA and military intelligence, just as had been the warning of anti-American and pro-communist press from the very beginning; and so the image of the 'Ugly American' got even worse.

If foreign host nations had realized that Peace Corps volunteer teachers or community workers would ever become the focus for conflict and violence for social and political revolution, they very probably would have said 'No way'; even to its original creator, President Kennedy.

If the American press had at that same time reported widely both the failures and frustrations of the volunteers that were being surveyed and reported back to the U.S. government Executive branch and Congress – instead of just romantic success stories – the public might have been better prepared to understand both sides of the many complex issues involved – rather than be blind-sided by U.S. news reports about the Peace Corps that were increasingly part of the opposition to a War in Vietnam.

If the Agency for International Development and the U.S. State Department had really believed that the volunteers would become a substantial factor in both the social and economic development of underdeveloped countries, the Peace Corps' independence might have been preserved for long-term benefits of the nation.

Yet, this did not happen, and instead the U.S. Peace Corps was assimilated into much the same bureaucratic infrastructure that the Peace Corps was created to counter. This was increasingly the case during Vietnam War, and then in more dangerous Cold War years.

Declining Independence of the Peace Corps as an Agency

The freedom of the Peace Corps was protected in its first five years by Congressional confidence in its first Director Sargent Shriver. The agency was permitted to go its own way, to experiment and find itself, and to grow up with a freedom unique in the history of all previous Executive branch agency bureaucracies.

Any chaos arising from this development, was at the beginning under Kennedy and Shriver, regarded and viewed with an open mind to have been necessary for simply growing up. It was thus often necessary to honestly re-evaluate Peace Corps contributions and achievements in order to maintain the support of the American people and the Congress; but under Kennedy and Shriver, both Congress and the American people had more considerable trust and confidence in the leadership of the Peace Corps.

But after the assassination of President Kennedy and the ascension of President Johnson, that confidence by both Congress and the American people quickly eroded.

Despite the new President Johnson tried very hard to continue and build upon the base of optimism of the Kennedy administration, he was increasingly diverted away by his many very progressive and well-intentioned social and civil rights objectives, and by an increasing real and present danger to the U.S. by Cold War communism.

Despite the great respect of Johnson for Shriver to ask him to continue to head the Peace Corps, he relied on Shriver to ask him to be director of Peace Corps as well as several other new and emerging government initiatives all at the same time. After trying desperately to divide his attentions several ways, Shriver decided to step down as Dir. of the Peace Corps, and soon after resigned entirely.

A Call for Tough Decisions for the Early Peace Corps

The first five years of U.S. Peace Corps were only a beginning. The years ahead demanded reorganization and improvement of programs to help meet the needs of underdeveloped countries in a more exacting way. Yet, this was difficult without the vision and leadership that had been characterized by Pres. Kennedy and Director Shriver.

However, those first five years had laid an important foundation upon which the future Peace Corps could be built. The greatest benefit of the change in leadership at the Peace Corps was ironically that one of the first assumptions of the Peace Corps – that it would be an agency of 'short temporary service' and that returning Peace Corps volunteers would not be eligible for permanent career positions in the new agency – was in fact quickly changed after Shriver left, and instead past Peace Corps volunteers were recruited and welcomed to Federal career positions at the new Peace Corps agency.

This change was vigorously criticized even by many past Kennedy staff who had supported the original views of both Kennedy and Shriver – however, this change actually made both Congress and the American people to be more comfortable with the future direction of the Peace Corps – as it made a 'lot of common sense' that past volunteers in the field would make very good supervisors and managers for future Peace Corps field volunteers.

Thus, it was stated by one Congressman to the U.S. Press that:

"The Peace Corps has to find its context within the United States government; within American society and politics; and within the process of the development, the building of institutions, and the social revolutions in the underdeveloped world".

New leadership including Director Jack Vaughn, with his experience in the Agency for International Development and the State Department, seemed well equipped to help the Peace Corps find its best proper role.

There was a growing consensus in Congress that role should be more closely linked to AID and CIA. There was also an increasing view by Congress and U.S. State Department that the past policies regarding large numbers of Peace Corps volunteers who were paid very low compensation was a mistake, and it was better to 'hire a lesser number of more highly educated volunteers and pay higher salaries'; to achieve 'better quality with less quantity'.

This view began a change official agency policies, to have a lesser number of volunteers on projects to 'live among local people without protection', and was to instead begin a policy for Peace Corps volunteers to live primarily at embassies and consulates under protection of the U.S. military and State Department security contractors; and to travel more often with security forces of U.S. government to meet with local officials for Peace Corps projects.

The new changes in policy after Shriver stepped down were very controversial to many, including most of the early volunteers, and those who left the Peace Corps along with Shriver. But operational performance results were very impressive, since the number of the kind of early security threats, and actual harm to Peace Corps volunteers, dropped greatly after these new policies were introduced.

Requests for Peace Corps volunteers to 'live among the local people' were still considered; but only on a case-by-case basis, and only if the host nation was regarded by State Department as 'very low risk' – and also if there was high level of 'security support personnel' ready at a moment's notice from nearby secure locations.

This 'measured approach' by the Peace Corps with the oversight of AID, as well as U.S. military was actually very well to be received not only by the American public, but also was to be highly respected by local host nation leaders – who asked U.S. to approve more projects.

Early Solutions to the Peace Corps Crisis of Growth

The Peace Corps, as constituted at the end of the first five years by 1966, had a severe backlog of accepted Peace Corps applicants. Yet, the decline in acceptances by applicants diminished, just at the same time when the American government under the new President Johnson increasingly prepared for War in Vietnam. Early Peace Corps federal budget funds were increasingly diverted from humanitarian agencies and directed to the U.S. military.

Many analysts, including both academic and consultant contractors to the Peace Corps and Congress, quickly came to the same conclusion as many U.S.

journalists. Their conclusions were simply that 'since 1961 when thousands of recent college graduates first applied, by 1966 most had other jobs already – and many were even taking jobs for companies in the military-industrial complex that were funded by growth in contracts to prepare for and support growing concerns over the Vietnam War efforts'.

Meanwhile, the number of accepted Peace Corps applicants that did not respond rose to over 80%. The 200,000 college students estimated in 1962, and forecasted to increase by sixty-seven per cent by 1970 and 111 per cent by 1975, no longer seemed likely, or to have any major sustained support by 1966. In fact, GAO recommended to Congress that original estimates should be reduced 50%.

In addition, both Congressional Budget and support by the American people seemed to level off, and even to diminish, starting in 1966. Up until that time, the Peace Corps may have been living off past memories of Pres. Kennedy and its magical beginnings; but no longer.

Despite that NASA and some other new agencies created by the Kennedy administration were growing in support and excitement of the American people, the U.S. Peace Corps agency was struggling more than ever, to not only gain acceptance, but to even hold on to the its original support. The number of college applications remained stationary the first two years after President Kennedy's death, but were to drop dramatically after that.

The number of non-college applicants to the Peace Corps had fallen drastically by 90% during the same two years. This was most critical as it reflected a major reduction in support for Peace Corps by a vast majority of American voters, and was to have major implications to the make-up of the new Congress to approve future budgets.

For a Peace Corps agency that began with rapid growth, this was to create a crisis which was familiar for many other past 'grass-roots' movements and institutions. The U.S. Peace Corps was approaching a crossroads.

One approach led on toward the big vision with growth in size, scope, and effectiveness toward a Big Peace Corps. The other approach led to consolidation and a Little Peace Corps. Increasingly, reality was somewhere between.

Based on requests of host countries in 1964 – much of which may have been related to sympathy shortly after death of Kennedy – President Johnson had asked the Peace Corps to double its number of volunteers and continue to improve its quality in the next four years. But within the next two years, these requests slowly diminished – which created a big problem, as the Peace Corps had as a result recruited double what was needed in 1966.

Notably, this was to coincide with a big push by President Johnson to 'redirect at least half of Peace Corps applicants to the U.S. Job Corps, which needs them more'.

Practical Realities of Early Peace Corps Number Games

For many of the first returning Peace Corps volunteers that were interviewed and surveyed, the 1964-1966 expansions appeared to perpetuate the mistakes of the past that they saw as 'Washington political numbers games'.

For some volunteers, many of the organizational deficiencies were related to 'willy-nilly ramp-up' in numbers at a time most felt a need for more selective recruitment.

Robert McGuire, a former Peace Corps volunteer and staff evaluator, felt the need was for more professional volunteers, and that the right number of volunteers might be far fewer than 10,000 a year (which was half of what President Johnson had originally asked for in 1964). He commented that:

"Peace Corps Volunteers help to meet the critical manpower needs of host countries and promote mutual understanding. There needs to be a leveled pool of well trained volunteers more similar to the way that the U.S. military recruits, trains and deploys".

Meanwhile the Wofford study (by a Yale educated lawyer) was to observe:

"There are two keys to success in these areas. First, the volunteers relationship to the host country was not as advisers to foreign institutions but as employees of those institutions.

The second key was that the volunteers go in large numbers. By going in large numbers, they help to meet middle-level manpower needs on a substantial, not just a token scale. Thus, the pressure for an increased number of volunteers was real.

This pressure comes largely from the field in response to the needs of expanding programs in forty-six host countries where the volunteers have already gone."

This analysis was also noticed by many journalists as similar to military witnesses who spoke before Congress.

It was also observed by several journalists at the time that 'skeptical past volunteers have an important point which is that a number of foreign host governments are pressing for higher proportion of technical personnel – yet for the Peace Corps to reduce its size to increase the proportion of more highly skilled volunteers would reduce a significant part of its contribution of practical unskilled volunteers to local communities'.

This summed up a major division that was developing within Peace Corps leaders.

Early Challenges to Direction of Numbers in Peace Corps

If the early Peace Corps was to fulfill its humanitarian and democratic objectives on a broad scale beyond its first five years, it had to 'see beyond itself and present policies'. The gap between the poor and the industrially developed nations appeared to be widening, rather than receding. To many researchers, this was also a reflection that there was potentially a lot of stubborn opposition to sharing of U.S. technology, and its transfer for mutual benefit to include underdeveloped nations.

To close this gap, there needed to be more effective utilization of professional U.S. manpower in more effective ways. The U.S. Peace Corps was one of only a number of organizations asked help to achieve this goal.

The members of U.S. Congress, as a reflection of the humanitarian beliefs of the American people, seemed to desire a larger Peace Corps – as they had consistently approved larger quotas than the Corps organization had attained. Yet it had also been the continuing position of Congress that a dual approach was needed, to both support an American Peace Corps that could address both the needs of most host nation local communities – for very practical dedicated yet not as highly educated workers willing to live and work among the people – as well as more highly educated technical advisors who could live among the academics and professionals at university campuses and host government office complexes, in order to 'cross-train' and share research for technology transfer. Both were equally needed for the best possible results.

President Johnson, as previously noted, first desired a larger Peace Corps, and this was actually to be also a goal for each president for the next several decades.

Yet, each presidential administration, and each make up of Congress, for the next several decades, went back and forth between extremes to emphasize either mostly 'hands-on' skilled volunteers versus more theoretical academic professional adviser volunteer college professors.

Early Years After Departure of Director Sargent Shriver

To many, the resignation of Director Sargent Shriver from the Peace Corps, as well as eventually all his responsibilities to report directly to President Johnson, were regarded by many who had been so inspired by President Kennedy, as sadly the 'last days of Camelot'.

This was to include President Johnson, who had regarded himself, and was to tell many of his personal confidants, that he felt he was a 'humble knight of the round table of Kennedy Camelot' – and in reality, Johnson did as much as he could to make both the Peace Corps and NASA possible, by using his long experience in Congress to get the votes needed by Kennedy to create them.

After Shriver resigned, President Johnson reluctantly accepted, and realized he had asked too much of Shriver to server in multiple roles. As he told his closest friends, that happened only because of his great respect for Dir. Shriver and others from the Kennedy 'think tank'.

After Shriver left, the next in command at the Peace Corps was Director Jack Vaughn, who rose to take over the transition of the original independent agency of U.S. Peace Corps, to be a more traditional 'sub-agency' of the State Department, under the same auspices of the Agency for International Development (AID) – as was to have been originally proposed to President Kennedy by Congressional leaders that were more to lean to traditional Foreign Aid coordinated with the other agencies – but was rejected by Kennedy after Director Shriver and Johnson had proposed a plan for a more independent agency.

This was to be regarded by President Johnson as first acceptance that his own visions for Civil Rights and War on Poverty, which he had originally believed he could build upon the idealistic foundations of the remains of the 'Camelot' of President Kennedy, were no longer possible.

So from then on, President Johnson regrettably accepted the inevitable, and was in all of his memoirs and documents in his presidential library to express his sadness to back away from his priorities, and admit that there was too great of a growing threat from communism and anti-American sentiments to avoid the impending Vietnam War.

Under Director Jack Vaughn, for the duration of the Johnson administration, there was a gradual reversal of nearly all of the early operational policies of the Kennedy era Peace Corps, and became increasingly a partner of AID.

The concepts of short one or two year deployments to live among people of underdeveloped nations, focusing on single unmarried men, with no opportunities for returning volunteers to apply to serve as career Federal staff employees as the Kennedy think tank had envisioned – were gradually all replaced under Johnson administration, as Director Vaughn was to implement the very same policies that had been proposed by those who had disagreed with the original Kennedy era Peace Corps.

This was not to say that the leadership of Vaughn and Johnson by 1967 – which had very wide support among a much more conservative Congress, U.S. State Department and U.S military, as the Vietnam War was increasingly unavoidable, was in any way wrong – any more than the original idealistic Peace Corps as was to be first envisioned and implemented by Kennedy and Shriver was wrong. They were simply different times – and as many songs of 1967 noted – 'the times they are all a-changing'.

In all fairness, under the next Peace Corps Director Vaughn, there were many major improvements in the security and protections of Peace Corps volunteers related to making sure they were always closer-by to U.S. military.

There had to be much greater coordination with both strategic and tactical objectives of the United States, in order to protect Peace Corps volunteers, as well as better serve broader U.S. interests. This was to involve new policies whereby U.S. Peace Corps volunteers were based in secure American embassy and consulate locations, yet were still to meet, and coordinate, with more critical technical and management expertise for host local projects.

Complications of Nixon Years Upon the U.S. Peace Corps

Despite that Director Vaughn was to provide the basis for three effective years of transitional integration of the 'independent' Peace Corps, as was envisioned by President Kennedy and Director Shriver, into the much more traditional models of U.S. Federal Executive branch agencies – after President Johnson was replaced by Richard Nixon – the future Peace Corps became an even more complex and fluid situation.

President Nixon had never been convince the Peace Corps should ever have a place in U.S. government.

From the very beginnings of proposals of a U.S. Peace Corps by Sen. Humphrey, Sen. Kennedy and others during the 1950's, as the Vice President under President Eisenhower, Richard Nixon was always openly against the concept of a U.S. Peace Corps, and regarded it negatively.

Nixon was on many occasions as he was to campaign for president in 1960 to express to the press and American public that he believed "U.S. Peace Corps could be a perpetual future haven for many anti-Americans, Communist-sympathizers and draft dodgers".

As was pointed out by many in U.S. press and historians since, this was a revealing comment, since at the time of Nixon's initial statements to refer to Peace Corps volunteers as 'draft dodgers', there was as yet no such draft.

So from the beginning, Nixon was very strongly opposed to the entire concept of a U.S. Peace Corps, and in many of the ill-fated 'Nixon Tapes' to transcript his personal White House Oval Office conversations, he was to make many comments that reflected his own bias against the U.S. Peace Corps and his desire that it be 'neutralized'.

So after Richard Nixon was elected president, over the next 6 years until he was forced to resign, there were fully 4 Directors Nixon appointed to head up the U.S. Peace Corps. This was a period of chaos for the U.S. Peace Corps, as well as an increasingly divided nation and world.

The first U.S. Peace Corps Director under President Nixon was Joseph Blatchford, who served fully two years from 1969 to 1971. During this time the U.S. Peace Corps was essentially eliminated by putting it under the auspices of a new permanent agency that was created by President Nixon – known as ACTION.

In effect, during the Nixon years, the Peace Corps was to no longer exist, as it was re-organized as a sub-agency under ACTION, which was headed by Blatchford as Director. What was previously the Peace Corps was renamed as 'New Directions Project' (a very telling new title as all of the references to the Peace Corps were excised as completely as new Egyptian pharaohs of ancient history used to remove the names of predecessors); also all 'returning volunteers' were offered positions as 'unpaid volunteers' to ACTION (few accepted and result was a small public relation fiasco for Nixon - but he did not care).

After Dir. Blatchford was forced to retire after considerable pressure from Congress and the U.S. public (who were already increasingly concerned about the ways that the new President Nixon was to conduct himself) – the next appointee by Nixon to head the U.S. Peace Corps was Dir. Kevin O'Donnell.

Notably, this was also noticed by the press to be a very strange appointment by Nixon – because O'Donnell was very much exactly the opposite of the public views of President Nixon as well as Blatchford – who had been under direction from Nixon to eliminate the Peace Corps and make it a very small sub-agency under ACTION.

Kevin O'Donnell was not only a very successful 3-year veteran Peace Corps volunteer who served in local communities in Korea from 1969 to 1971 – he was also a very vocal advocate to return to the original model of Peace Corps – as a short 1-2 year assignment similar to military service, and receive similar GI Bill benefits; but not to support the creation of a large bureaucratic agency for career Federal civil service, such as was started by Blatchford to hire a 'select few' returning Peace Corps volunteers – who had similar political beliefs as Nixon.

So what was even more to offend O'Donnell, Congress and the U.S. public – was that other returning Peace Corps volunteers were denied the full benefits they had been promised under their contracts that they received prior to Nixon to be the president – which Nixon cancelled by what many felt was an illegal Executive Order action.

In response to returning Peace Corps volunteer 'activist' press coverage, Nixon asked Blatchford to resign, and then nominated O'Donnell as his choice for next Director of the U.S. Peace Corps – which Congress quickly approved on a bi-partisan basis (despite many from both parties in Congress expressed confusion at Nixon actions).

During this same time, as all of the personal conversations of President Nixon were routinely recorded on audio tape 'for the future posterity', Nixon was to repeatedly refer to the Peace Corps in derogatory terms, and to refer to his appointment of Kevin O'Donnell to head up the Peace Corps as 'a strategic necessity'.

Officially as Nixon faced a second presidential campaign, the White House pledged to restore the Corps to the status of a full agency under the U.S. Dept. of State as President Johnson and Director Vaughn were to have put in place, as if being respectful to the Kennedy vision. Yet at the same time, Nixon was to be quoted by his own Oval Office recordings, that 'after we win this election we should get rid of the Peace Corps agency once and for all'.

True to his word, as soon as Nixon was to win his re-election, he terminated O'Donnell without to even ask for a resignation, and asked a still confused Congress to replace him with Donald Hess. Director Hess, who again had title of full Director of the Peace Corps, was widely regarded as a 'well-meaning Federal career bureaucrat'.

Under advice from his new direct reports, as the re-elected Pres. Nixon administration increasingly directed itself to Vietnam War matters, the new Director Hess was to quickly institute several programs to train new Peace Corps volunteers in the host nation universities – rather than previous policies to train at U.S. universities with academic – rather than more 'immersive' or real world training in language and culture of assigned host nations.

This was actually a very successful new approach, and yielded substantial academic research to prove efficacy of his effective new management concepts.

Yet this was largely ignored by the troubled Nixon administration, and Hess was also replaced barely a year later. Yet, much of what was achieved under Director Hess resulted in similar immersive language technology that was eventually to be used by U.S. Dept. of State as well as the U.S. military since 1973, and became a very major success.

Within the next year, Hess was replaced by yet another Director, Nicholas Craw, who was even more to align the U.S. Peace Corps with more quantifiable and operationally manageable methods and procedures – which were to effectively combine for as a middle range between early years of U.S. Peace Corps of Kennedy and Shriver, and the pragmatic adjustments of Johnson and Vaughn.

Despite the joint accomplishments of O'Donnell, Hess and Craw were to become a normal range adjustment within a period of time when much that was increasingly abnormal in White House at the time – overall everything worked out well for best of Peace Corps and World Peace.

Redefining Peace Corps Under President Gerald Ford

After Sen. Gerald Ford was to ascend to be appointed U.S. President after Nixon resigned in disgrace, President Ford was to very often simply express to define his role as 'a return to decency'.

Despite the very many serious challenges to the United States, President Ford should be regarded as a 'common man hero', to hold together the United States at a time so many challenges faced America and the world.

For the next two years, President Ford gave new confidence and support to the best Federal career talent he could find. For the Peace Corps, he chose John Dellenback to be the next Director of the U.S. Peace Corps. New Dir. Dellenback was a very effective leader of the U.S. Peace Corps, and ultimately a great model for all future Directors.

He was able to make internal U.S. government alliances to healthcare agencies such as NIH, as well as leverage their contacts to U.N. World Health Organization – as well to create many pilot programs to recruit both advanced technical professionals, as well as potential volunteers with basic skills, to help in third-world humanitarian aid – who could be mentored by advanced technical professionals in healthcare, engineering and technology. In many ways, Dir. Dellenback was the first to provide for an all-encompassing future of the Peace Corps.

Return to Peace Corps Basics by President Jimmy Carter

Under President Jimmy Carter, all of the very practical and scientific management policies of Peace Corps Director Dellenback were largely preserved intact (after all, President Carter was also a Ph.D. scientist and was unique to respect academic success data from Dir. Dellenback, to implement international aid policies of former Pres. Ford).

Thus, the new President Carter was to build upon what he regarded as success of the former Pres. Ford and Dir. Dellenback for what was a very sincere personal mission to Jimmy Carter – a better world with Christian humanitarian goals – and recognize all good faith religions.

Under President Jimmy Carter, all of the previous organizations such as under President Ford and Director Dellenback were to remain intact, and to be built upon with his focus. His wife Rosalynn, as a First Lady, took the U.S. Peace Corps also 'under her wing' as was reported by many and in the Jimmy Carter Presidential library.

For the first time since President Kennedy, no one other than President Carter was to have such idealistic goals to fully embrace and seek to offer the humanitarian and sincere Christian hopes of America. Yet, many enemies of the United States regarded this benevolence as weakness.

In many ways there were as many, or even more, disappointments by Carter, as were previously faced by Johnson. In the harsh realities of any progressive U.S. president, and as well likely any truly proud American statesperson, from local government up to a president, great personal sacrifices are known only to their families. Just as the sacrifices of Returning Peace Corp Volunteers.

The U.S. Peace Corps was built on sacrifices of many people, which were to be cherished and valued in varying degrees by both Peace Corps volunteers and presidents. But enemies of freedom hate humanitarianism.

During the Carter years, not only were the original and practical aspects of the U.S. Peace Corps preserved – but under President Carter there were two new innovations (which were reportedly proposed first by his wife, one of the many great First Ladies of all American history).

What was to be first confirmed from the administration of the previous U.S. president as a good and fair foundation for a U.S. Peace Corps – by the most proudly Christian presidents of U.S history was most of all humanitarian. Notably, there had never been any American president who was personally to involve in his own life greater commitment to the basic goals of the Peace Corps.

It had been widely reported from many sources that soon after President Carter was to take office, his wife Rosalynn and other family, including with his mother present, discussed at a first WH dinner their admiration for humanitarian achievements of the U.S. Peace Corps.

Yet, there were reportedly comments at that dinner that 'despite Peace Corps accomplishes so much, could it not do more with influence of more women rather than mostly men?'. This was to greatly influence Carter.

Soon after, when the new President Carter was to appoint a new Director of the Peace Corps, it was yet another milestone – as both the first female and the first black Director of the Peace Corps, Carolyn Payton.

Director Carolyn Payton was to encourage both the diversity of race and gender into all agencies, and historically even beyond only the Peace Corps itself.

What was most important about the tenure of Director Payton was that she championed new opportunity for women and minorities in the Peace Corps like never before. She was to implement Affirmative Action policies for women and all minorities in a manner that was to be implemented first in the U.S. Peace Corps, but then to later be the model for similar policies in all U.S. government agencies and eventually a model for such policies to all of American society, including many major U.S. corporations.

Director Payton was also a very well respected professional psychologist, and was to move on to other positions soon after she first implemented her new ground breaking policies within the Peace Corps, to a series of positions for leadership in the American Psychological Association (APA) unexpectedly the very next year.

When she was replaced by Richard Celeste to serve until the end of the President Carter administration, she was often asked about her association with the Carter era Peace Corps; and she was always positive in her responses, as she was rightly proud of her lasting influences.

Director Payton's replacement, the new Peace Corps Director Richard Celeste, was to largely continue her policies, especially to hire and deploy an unprecedented number of women, minorities and naturalized U.S. citizens born in third world nations, as both volunteers and even more were hired into senior roles in Peace Corps administrations – working out of Washington D.C. in offices adjacent to the U.S. State Department, or working out of U.S. embassies and consulates around the world.

Under directives from President Carter, the visibility of the Peace Corps was stepped up as a major initiative to create positive public relations for the United States, with the goal to reverse past negative stereotypes such as the "Ugly American"; yet enemies of U.S. persisted.

The Peace Corps under Director Celeste achieved to build much closer alignments to work in cooperation with the humanitarian agencies of the United Nations, and both U.N. and Peace Corps administrators began to meet together effectively on a more and more regular basis, both at U.N. headquarters in New York City, but also at U.S. consulates and embassies in many of the world's most dangerous and turbulent political and volatile 'hot spots'.

This was to both threaten and elevate tensions with communist nations, and most especially the Soviet Union; however, this was also to even more to result in the emergence of a new complication – radical Islamic extremists, who were to beginning increasingly violent protests and even terrorist activities. This was originally directed specifically toward open U.S. support of Israel – but were also to spill over from perceived U.S. support of several dictators that were to emerge in nations that were primarily Islamic – which was in some cases largely true; but in others was exaggerated by anti-American pro-Communist agitators in Islamic nations around the world.

As a result, it was soon to be regrettably the case that President Carter was increasingly otherwise to be involved in seriously dangerous national security issues, culminating with the as Iran embassy hostage crisis.

Because of growing U.S. public awareness of risks to send innocent and largely un-protectable U.S. citizens such as Peace Corps and other nonmilitary humanitarian aid workers into dangerous circumstances – after inability of U.S. military to protect even U.S. citizen civil service workers at an embassy from Islamic extremist terrorists, the role of U.S. Peace Corps was forever changed by the brutality reported on television that impacted most Americans during humanitarian President Carter years – as much or more than the assassination of Pres. Kennedy.

As a former U.S. Navy officer, President Carter had great confidence in ability of Navy Seals to rescue the Americans who were taken hostage at the U.S. Embassy in Iran by Islamic extremists. Several missions were to be approved by President Carter; which all regrettably failed.

Meanwhile, the mission of the U.S. Peace Corps under the Director Celeste was to increasingly limit the physical deployment of all Peace Corps volunteers, and instead to focus on assignments of Peace Corps volunteers to work with the State Department for studies of 'potential risk' to deploy Peace Corps volunteers – to U.S. embassies and consulates, let alone to live among local host communities, as in the original model for the Peace Corps under Kennedy and Shriver.

This was an entirely new set of circumstances, as the U.S. was not only faced with threats from anti-American communist influences – but increasingly also extremist Islamic religious fanatic terrorists as well.

Yet another new wrinkle was to in effect change in the previous simple dynamic of East-vs-West that had existed up until the time of the end of Vietnam War. The new wrinkle was that both America and Russia were by then equally under attack by extremist Islamic terrorists.

Thus, the old adage that 'the enemy of my enemy was my friend' was soon after to play out at the end the Cold War, as surely as America and Russia were to be allies against Hitler in WWII. The time was ripe for a new leadership by United States that would be more respected by Russia, and to show enemies that U.S. could change quickly when America offers a hand of friendship and are attacked in return – to both Russia and Islamic nations.

Fate of the U.S. Peace Corps Under the Reagan Presidency

Despite the good early but troubled progress of the U.S. Peace Corps from President Kennedy to President Carter – to build seminal foundations of the U.S. Peace Corps as a 'middle ground' to bridge from commitments of early Christian missionaries – as well as the 'Thomasites' as U.S. Army veterans to live among and teach Philippine natives English after the Spanish-American War fully eight decades previous to the new administration of President Reagan – none of those accomplishments seemed relevant or useful as the two super-powers of America and Russia were on the edge of a Cold War that could end humanity.

Due to the stalemate of the Embassy hostages in Iran, which was to go over a year with daily focus of the press on nothing else; no progress was made to rescue Iran Embassy hostages, either by diplomacy or military action.

After a year of no success, as was repeatedly to be reported daily by the press to an American people who felt they had been promised safety by Pres. Carter in speeches and press releases with the year before the next presidential election; the American people (and especially young people) seemed to give up on such limited special forces solutions, and were ready to accept more drastic measures.

In the final months and weeks before the 1980 presidential election, Ronald Reagan began to increasingly refer to the 'Mutual Assured Destruction' (MAD) policy that was proposed by Kissinger under President Nixon.

Reagan announced in no uncertain terms that if he was elected President, he would not hesitate to make immediate pre-emptive strikes against Tehran, or even

Moscow, if the Iran Embassy hostages were not returned unharmed. This was to result in many protests by Soviets, to no avail (and actually to build wider support for Reagan).

Since Reagan was only a presidential candidate, his PR team was before the election to say to the world press that 'Russia better stand down or they might be next – USSR has no business to interfere with the recovery of citizens of United States under international law'. In reality, the only real consequence was more headaches for Carter.

Yet the message resonated resoundingly with the American people, and in overwhelming numbers, Ronald Reagan was elected next U.S. President, to replace Jimmy Carter. Within barely 24 hours after the election, Iran immediately announced release of all their U.S. hostages.

The Reagan Administration was fairly unique among past transitions to new presidency, as they had planned in precise detail for over a year what was to be done as soon as Reagan was to be declared the next president. They were not surprised that Iran would release all hostages the day after the election results were announced, and were already to issue detailed instructions for Peace Corps as well as every other U.S. agency.

Within the first few days after Ronald Reagan was declared to be the next president, a long list of pending appointments were announced in the press, including Mrs. Loret Miller Ruppe as the new Dir. of the Peace Corps.

In addition, an 'Executive Branch Transition Document' of several hundred pages was circulated to all U.S. government administration officials and members of Congress, which described in great detail hundreds of changes to be implemented by temporary executive orders – similar to the same way Kennedy had first created the Peace Corps – also with detailed outlines of a long list of

Bills to be introduced to Congress by the new Reagan administration, including budgets for each Federal agency.

In most new U.S. administrations, presidential appointments are usually announced in a piece-meal manner; as meanwhile, the previous top-level agency administrators are interviewed by the new president and White House staff – in order to consider some of the previous administration to be continued – even if they were highly connected to the party that is no longer in power.

But in the case of the new Reagan administration, there was none of this 'adaptive transition'. Under Reagan, nearly all Executive Branch directors and senior administrators were to be made aware of the names of their effective replacements, some with different titles. But it was clear that all previous appointees under Carter were to be summarily replaced, and would have no input into the changes in both the detailed re-organization and budget request plans from the new Reagan White House.

It was an unprecedented document, which went far beyond what was common as a 'National Platform Document' by either major political party; and was clear by its scope and detail the Reagan campaign had been working on the plans months. It was in effect a 'pre-emptive strike'.

It included a great many new initiatives and changes in policy and procedures for every government agency, including the Peace Corps, which had not been previously to have been emphasized in Reagan campaign speeches; which were instead to have focused pragmatically on issues with greater interest in latest political polls.

Of course the Democrats and their supporters in the press cried 'foul'; yet the Republicans and their supporters were to mostly casually note that 'all Democrat presidents including Carter did the same and announced the new changes of their administration over time – Pres. Reagan is just faster'. In other words, 'politics as usual'.

This was hard for the Carter administration to counter; and all their attempts to do so were regarded by the American press and majority of public as 'sour grapes'.

So immediately the same week after his election, more than two months before his inauguration in 1980, President-Elect Reagan began to make speeches to explain and sell his sweeping changes to the American public.

Reagan was a 'Great Communicator', and able to sway even the most entrenched Carter supporters to his own base – as easily as Kennedy was able to sway Nixon supporters back in 1960. The new President Reagan began his term of office with the highest approval ratings of any previous president, despite America was in a bad recession.

Many of the major initiatives of the new Reagan administration were to include a long list intended to radically change the entire Federal bureaucracy, such as: the 'Paperwork Reduction Act' (which was to require to replace all long documents and forms to a single page and to test that they could be easily understood by average citizens rather than legalese); elimination of tax loopholes and reduction of administrative action powers of IRS, EPA and other agencies; as well as major shift of Federal powers (as well as title block funding) back to control of State legislatures: and to reduce Federal bureaucracy of all kinds.

This was in addition to not only continue the Carter era 'Zero Base Budget' directives (simply put, 'no budget increases'), and a 100% freeze on the Federal hiring at most agencies – but Reagan also proposed 'Active Base' budget cuts for all agencies of between 10% to 50%, with detailed requests to Congress that left no discretion to Federal agency leaders who had long tenure, and instead were very specific down to each sub-level department within all agencies, many of which were to be given new objectives as well as re-organization goals for funding cuts.

Notably, the Peace Corps was impacted greatly – but overall, Peace Corps agency changes were less extreme than to most of the other government agencies.

The American press was effectively overwhelmed to report and analyze the many changes during the first years of Reagan Administration. This was to include the Peace Corps – but as there were not as many radical changes as to most other Federal agencies, it took more than a year for the Peace Corps changes to get a wider focus of attention by the American Press.

At first, the appointment of Director Ruppe to head the Peace Corps was analyzed by many in the press as first intended to be a way to 'bury' the Peace Corps by the new Reagan administration – as yet another 'slap in the face' to previous President Jimmy Carter.

Despite she was the second woman to head the Peace Corps, there was little that was known about her, except that: she was the wife of Republican Congressman from Michigan, on many humanitarian nonprofit boards including United Way and charities such as St. Joseph Hospital; and who was heiress as grand-daughter of the founder of the Miller Beer empire – but probably most important, she was manager for presidential campaign of George Bush against Ronald Reagan, and part of the negotiations at Republican National Convention to secure George Bush as V.P. running mate to Ronald Reagan.

There was wide speculation that George Bush had first advocated Ruppe to the short list for next Director of the Peace Corps but there was also speculation that Ruppe had impressed Nancy Reagan during the negotiations for Georg Bush to be offered the slot as Vice Presidential candidate. In reality, it was probably a combination of both.

To a degree, it was just 'politics as usual' when a new party was to get a new president into the White House, and it was no different under Carter than Reagan. All new presidents were expected to 'clean house', and they usually always pick a 'rising star' from within their own party to fill positions in potentially politically critical agencies.

Both Loret Miller Ruppe and her husband, Congressman Philip Ruppe were clearly 'rising stars' within the Republican party. In the past (and mostly since), the first appointees of a new president to head up any critical Federal agencies were most often selected in order to be un-opinionated, docile and tactful not to offend anyone of either party – which was usually necessary in order to get Congressional confirmation – but in the case of the new Reagan administration, his ability to communicate directly to the American people, and his high approval ratings, it was uniquely possible for Reagan to get pretty much whatever he asked for from Congress at that time.

In this case, Director Ruppe was not the kind of person to be manipulated easily; and she was to prove herself to engage most of the power structure of both sides in friendly and respectful intelligent debate.

This was to impress all she talked to – including members of Congress and press. So she was easily confirmed, despite the Peace Corps was one of the few agencies not listed in Reagan "Transition Plans" for any major changes. As such, Reagan was open to any options for his own personal reshaping of the U.S. Peace Corps.

So for whatever reason – but very likely because of her ability to make intelligent and insightful comments to Congress and the Press – Ruppe was to become the longest lasting Director of U.S. Peace Corps ever (over 8 years, which was a very incredible real accomplishment in all history of such high level bureaucratic service).

Both President Reagan and his wife Nancy liked Rupp, and were convinced she could head an agency of the stature of the Peace Corps in a way that that could help demonstrate the Good Will of Reagan Presidency, after they got to know her personally as part of negotiations with the campaign management of George Bush. Yet there were other influences that were reported by many in the press.

There were several anonymous reports in the U.S. press from insiders in the Reagan administration that Nancy Reagan – who was widely known to be an advocate and believer in astrology – had requested many astrological reports of alignment of her own and Pres. Reagan's natal horoscopes to a select few in new Reagan administration.

It was reported that Loret Ruppe and her husband Philip were among those that Nancy Reagan sought to have horoscopes drawn up as part of a portfolio that the First Lady collected. It was rumored that Nancy Reagan was to feel comfortable enough with the results to share with Loret Ruppe, and that Nancy was to trust Loret and support Director Ruppe to head Peace Corps for 8 years as a result. This was at the time a very unprecedented tenure.

This was never fully confirmed by anyone, but for whatever reason, Director Ruppe was to become the longest Peace Corps Director, and also one of longest Directors of any U.S. government agencies in U.S. history.

In total, Director Ruppe was to be a very successful bureaucratic appointee leader, and was to very effective to maneuver the ins and outs of leadership of a large agency as Peace Corps – and to actually double its size and budget over the decade of her leadership.

This was at the same time Pres. Ronald Reagan was also to overcome great domestic and international diplomacy as well as world peace challenges, to end a Cold War – which were so amazing that many people were to suspect that rumors of some kind of special connections behind Nancy Reagan and Loret Ruppe influences.

However, on a more practical and provable level, Vice President Bush was to openly asking to lead the initiatives of a new 'Kinder and gentler' Peace Corps and State Department (both of which he had special knowledge and insights into as former Director of the CIA – and often was to report that he felt strongly that the U.S. Peace Corps could be a unique and powerful instrument to counter world stereotypes of the 'Ugly Americans').

Bush was reported to arrange to invite Director Ruppe not only to many state dinners with foreign leaders, but also to give her the opportunity to speak to impress both Reagan and the foreign leaders – and was thus instrumental in many situations to build foundations for critical trade and military alliance agreements that effectively 'blind-sided' the communist anti-American diplomatic regimes, and thus helped to end the 'Cold War'.

There were many such projects and influences that were to begin from the early Reagan years forward. There was strong support by many in the Reagan White House that Peace Corps should be 'broken up', and to split its staff to report under two smaller programs, both ACTION (the volunteer domestic movement created by President Nixon), and VISTA (which was even more unfunded, as an essentially volunteer action organization).

Vice President Bush said he was 'torn', as he was a big believer in volunteerism (and was already to talk of his concept of a 'Thousand Points of Light'); yet he strongly believed personally as a former Director of CIA in the State Department that the Peace Corps could have a much more powerful role if it was to be re-organized more like it was under Kennedy and Johnson – to be an independent, or at least at least a semi-independent, agency with direct and coordinated reporting to the highest levels of the U.S. State Department (which despite all opposition from 'hard-liners' in Reagan administration, Bush and Ruppe made a strong case for direct White House reporting that was eventually to be supported fully by President Reagan – and by Nancy).

In a political coup that was also largely unprecedented in American history, Director Ruppe and Vice President Bush went directly to Secretary of State Alexander Haig – in order to help build the case to place the Peace Corps under the direct accountability of the U.S. State Department – rather than to be a lower sub-level organization split between ACTION and VISTA.

After a heated meeting at the White House that was organized by Vice President Bush and Director Ruppe to give Secretary Haig opportunity to request Peace Corps to report directed to him – President Reagan agreed and backed up with Executive Orders – but with one condition.

Secretary Haig the next day announced that the Peace Corps was to report directly to Dept. of State, with oversight by Vice President George Bush – and with the absolute directive that the Peace Corps "will never to be used to collect information for any intelligence agency, and will be involved exclusively in humanitarian projects, to help friendly nations in need of technical and public health assistance around the world".

Of course, anti-American and pro-communist press around the world were horrified and blind-sided, and began to charge yet again their old mantra that U.S. would be 'using Peace Corps to spy on foreign nations and organize pretend projects to claim to be humanitarian but are not'.

But the world free press were unimpressed with such hollow accusations, and were instead to ask for more Peace Corps projects and volunteers that were based on the hybrid models of Johnson era, which were to fund and manage humanitarian projects (which coordinated primarily with AID, but with active support and protection of U.S. military and contractor security forces – for mutual safety).

This was the beginning of a new more effective era for the Peace Corps, which became a 'Public Relations Gold Mine' for worldwide pro-American freedom press.

Among the many important accomplishments of the U.S. Peace Corps under Director Ruppe were to include: despite proposed 20% reductions in budget of the Peace Corps, she was able to convince Secretary Haig to ask for less severe cuts due to redirection and changes in assumptions for the value of Peace Corps; and although she knew budget increase was impossible, was able to limit cuts in a way to expand Peace Corps services; was unprecedented to ask President Reagan to bring back 20 top Peace Corps appointees under Carter, which Reagan as well as the U.S. Congress approved; deployed over 1,200 Peace Corps volunteers to local farming projects in Latin America, even after many local nation anti-American press were to claim to U.N. that they were not doing their jobs.

Ruppe was also to quickly re-assign half of over 600 farming projects in Latin America to Africa; set up new structure for teams of 5 to 10 volunteers to support up to 20 local farm projects with rotating weekly site visits, which was to be proven as an enormously successful innovation to past Peace Corp models of management; set up organizations to establish 'food banks' and local farmers markets, as well as other community advisory guidance, which were to have been pioneered by many of the returning Carter appointees; set up fast-track programs to send African-Americans with interest to work for humanitarian personal goals to African; or Latin-Americans to work with local communities where they had 'Roots'; and set up programs for American Women with interest to help the women of underdeveloped nations to get education, women's healthcare, and to raise the cultural status of women in all nations – among all the many awesome accomplishments under Dir. Russe leadership.

Thus the 8-year Peace Corps tenure of Director Russe was to effectively culminate in selective application of all the best ideas and pilot projects of all previous Peace Corps Directors and presidential administrations – in a manner that was to efficiently implement, deploy, monitor and continuous improve – than has rarely been seen in any New U.S. government agency. It has been suggested by many historians and political scientists as not only a 'golden age' for the Peace Corps, but also to suggest that the very effective administration of Peace Corps Director Russe, who was reported to have attended most White House Security briefings, was in fact a big factor in the end of the Cold War, and pro-communist opposition to the Corps. As a result the Peace Corps was to 'come of age' under Reagan era; and the end of the First Generation of the Peace Corps that began with Kennedy and Johnson.

So the story continues toward a 'Next Generation' for the Peace Corps; but that is another book, to be written in the history of that generation – if they are also inspired and to learn from early years of the Peace Corps, to apply them to new challenges for progressive humanitarian achievement for Good Will, democracy and freedom – using new technologies to re-affirm the same goals that led to original creation of U.S. Peace Corps. As we are more than ever before in a dangerous time for world peace, freedom, and democracy both domestic and abroad, it is a time for 'all good people to come to aid' of good nations, and good people everywhere. Hopefully, organizations such as the U.S. Peace Corps can help in that, by uniting with other organizations to preserve freedom with security.

BIBLIOGRAPHY

Adams,Velma. The Peace Corps in Action. IL: Follett Publishing Company, 1964.

Alam, Assadollah. "Peace Corps in the Past and in the Future". Peace Corps Volunteer, Vol. 4 (March, 1966).

Arabgo, John. "A New Self-Image for the Future". Peace Corps Volunteer, Vol. 4 (March, 1966).

Bean, Maurice. "The Philippine Emphasis on Education". Peace Corps Volunteer, Vol. 3 (October, 1965).

Bowles, Chester. "Wanted: Professional Technicians for Amateur Volunteers." Peace Corps Volunteer, Vol. 4 (March, 1966).

Brenneman, William. "Senior Status for Peace Corps Volunteers". Peace Corps Volunteer, Vol. 3 (March, 1965).

Calvert, Robert. "Opportunities for Returning Peace Corps Volunteers". Career Information, Vol. 11 (October, 1964)

Carp, Al. "A Response to the Past". Peace Corps Volunteer, Vol. 3 (October, 1965).

Childs, Marquis. "The Peace Corps and Its Veterans", Washington Post, April 16, 1965.

Duhl, Leonard. "A Medical Health Program for the Peace Corps". Human Organization, Vol. 23 (Summer, 1964).

Frankel, Stanley. "View of a One-Eyed King". Peace Corps Volunteer, Vol. 4 (March, 1966).

Goldwin, Robert. Why Foreign Aid? IL: McNally, 1963.

Hayes, Samuel. An International Peace Corps. DC: Public Affairs Institute, 1961.

Hoops, Roy. The Complete Peace Corps Guide. NY: Dial Press, 1961

Howard, Naomi. "Peace Corps: The Modern Hull House or a Threat to Professionalism?". Vol. 8, Social Work (October, 1963).

Howitzer, Julius. "The Peace Corpsman Returns to the Darkest America". New York Times (October 14, 1965).

Hunter, Marjorie. "Peace Corps Wins Scientists Praise", New York Times, January 7, 1966.

Iverson, Robert. "Peace Corps Training: Lessons of First Year". Peace Corps Volunteer, Vol. 19 (January, 1963).

Jungman, Dean. "Pay May Be Too High". Peace Corps Volunteer, Vol. 4 (March, 1966).

Kauffman, Joseph. "A Report on the Peace Corps Training for Overseas Services". Journal of Higher Education, Vol. 33 (October, 1962).

Kennedy, J.F. "Message to Congress for Establishment of Peace Corps". Dept. of State Bulletin, (3/61), pp. 400-403.

Madow, Pauline. Peace Corps. NY: Wilson Press, 1964.

McNamara, Robert. "Draft Alternative Posed". Peace Corps Volunteer, Vol. 4 (July, 1966).

Middleton, Drew. "Peace Corps Role in Africa Shifting", New York Times. (March 31, 1966).

Millikan, Max. Memorandum On An International Youth Service. MA: MIT Press, 1961.

Mirel, Larry. "On Exporting American Values". Peace Corps Volunteer, Vol. 4 (April, 1966).

Morgan, Lloyd. "Does Training Promote Only the Bland?". Peace Corps Volunteer, Vol. 3 (October, 1965).

Ottenand, Thomas. "The Peace Corps Wins Its Way". Vol. 26, The Progressive (August, 1962).

Ottinger, Richard. "Hey Peace Corps! Take the Lead!". Peace Corps Volunteer, Vol. 4 (March, 1966).

Reuss, Henry. "A Point Four Corps". Vol. 72, The Commonweal (May, 1960).

Reuss, Henry. "Youth for Peace". Vol. 25, The Progressive (Feb., 1961).

Robinson, James. "Why Remain A Slave to an Idea?". Peace Corps Volunteer, Vol. 4 (March, 1966).

Samuels, Gertrude. "Peace Corps Trains in New York", New York Times, October 21, 1962.

Severeid, Eric. "The Problems of Re-Entry". Peace Corps Volunteer, Vol. 3 (April, 1965).

Solanders, Ian. "The Peace Corps: Nursery for Diplomats". The Nation, Vol. 89 (March, 1966).

Sullivan, George. The Story of the Peace Corps. NY: Fleet Publishing, 1964.

Smith, Brewster. "Peace Corp Teachers in Ghana" (Final Report of US Contract PC-W-55). Berkeley, CA: Institute of Human Development, 1964.

Stein, Morris. "A Study of Young Adult Performance in A Service Program (Unpublished thesis, US Contract PC-W-54). NY: NYU Dept. of Psychology, 1964.

Stolley, Richard. "The Re-Entry Crisis". Life Magazine (March 19, 1965).

White, Jean. "Peace Corpsman Speed Peruvian Tasks", Washington Post, January 7, 1966.

AFTERWORD

This book is based largely upon edits of the original 1967 doctoral dissertation by my father Charles C. Jones, Ph.D., combined with additional unpublished material and interviews conveyed two decades later by him to me, several months before he died of terminal illness in 1983.

Thus, this book was enhanced by both discussion of his Ph.D. dissertation, but was to also to explain additional materials not included in the dissertation, as well as his personal discussions about events and between the time of its publication, and up to nearly 20 years after that, in 1983; with additional commentary in retrospect fully 30 years later in this book (and as such was a mostly new material).

Yet, this new book publication is primarily based on doctoral dissertation of Charles Clyde Jones, Ph.D., from 1967 by West Virginia University, first published by Univ. Microfilms (67-11,789). It also includes both additional material and edits of personal notes and interviews not included in the original work, from the estate of father Charles Jones to son Keith Jones in 1983, for publication and derivative copyrights to accrue to their heirs.

There is a long tradition of republishing of personal historical documents and commentary based on private talks between a father and son. One of the earliest and most famous was the first such book by the son of Christopher Columbus to provide additional details about the travels of Columbus beyond the earlier verbatim publication of his ship Captain Logs from the early Spanish explorations of the American continent.

This is a much humbler historical document, and it is more about a common modern person who was given the rare opportunity to personally interview the first U.S. Peace Corps Director Sargent Shriver, and received copies of research studies that were not widely circulated. Shriver was at the time in a stressful situation of having served the U.S. in 'double-duty' for both Peace Corps and other agencies, at direct request of President Johnson.

After Shriver resigned, my father was still able to contact Shriver several times for advice and guidance about how to present the information in his doctoral dissertation. Each time, Shriver simply told my father to cite his interviews and sources using academic research standards; and that Shriver 'preferred that academia would preserve such personal background information in dissertations' – along with the more official documents preserved by presidential libraries of Kennedy and Johnson – and also was to advise my father to use his 'professional responsibility' to history; which he did. As a popular history publication, a short bibliography is provided at the end of this book – but detailed academic citations can be found in the 1967 WVU dissertation published by Univ. Microfilms.

Charles Clyde Jones was a decorated veteran of WWII who was drafted at the age of 18 immediately after graduating from high school in 1942, and was previously to receive many W.V. state awards including champion of state Debate Clubs and FFA ribbons. He was trained in U.S. Army and sent as a reinforcement as a tank gunner under Patton for Battle of the Bulge, and after WWII, GI Bill allowed him to go to college and get his Ph.D.; and was later to serve over a decade as Dean of Liberal Arts at Arkansas State University to teach U.S. Constitutional Law History, and to have a direct influence on many talented law students, including future President Bill Clinton, as well as witness at Congressional hearings to represent the Brookings Institute, and published in the U.S. Federal Register, and was always a supporter of World Peace. If he had lived longer, he might have been a U.S. Congressman.

Although he was like so many WWII veterans to be an avid supporter of President Eisenhower after serving under him as his general in WWII, he was always independent and non-partisan, and told his students to "vote for the person, not the party". So he was open minded like so many in the 1960 election to lean toward to vote to continue the stability of the 'I like Ike' years, with support for Richard Nixon; yet I remember watching my father as a child when Nixon debated Kennedy, and how I saw my father's eyes get big as he listened to the inspirational words of Sen. John F. Kennedy.

Even as a child of 6, I was not surprised that Sen. John Kennedy was elected as the next president, or my father was so inspired to be an early advocate of the Peace Corps. I was also just as inspired, like so many young boys of those days, to work for NASA to help America reach the moon. So as a boy of 9, I was as shocked as all Americans, to see over a Thanksgiving holiday the assassination of President Kennedy on television. My father was more dedicated than ever to help the U.S. Peace Corps; but as married men were not allowed then to volunteer, he wanted to support the Peace Corps movement by becoming one of its many academic researchers.

Only a few months later, the new President Lyndon Johnson came to W.Va. to announce his 'War on Poverty'. My parents took me to the airport to greet and cheer on our new President Johnson. I did not know much about the new President except he was from Texas, so I was determined to wear my best Roy Roger's cowboy hat and cap pistols to go to greet him. We were at a chain link fence cheering for him at the airport, but nobody else was wearing a cowboy hat, let alone toy cap pistols. So out of all the crowd, President Johnson saw me, and walked with Secret Service up to me and put out his hand, saying with a wink: "Howdy There, Partner!". It was my first time to shake hands with a U.S. President, but not my last. My father used to say he was 'more proud to have a son to shake hands with a President' than if he did; and that pretty much summed up my father as my own hero role model.

My father was determined to get his Ph.D. with a dissertation for an analysis of the emerging U.S. Peace Corps, as a way to help diminish the many challenges that faced Freedom and Democracy around the world in the mid-1960's. One lone professor had given him a harsh ultimatum that 'if you cannot get an interview with Shriver, then I will stop your graduation'. So my father got on a bus from WVU to Washington D.C., and went to offices of Dir. Shriver, armed only with a personal letter of introduction from Sen. Byrd of W.Va., which had been obtained with the help of a kinder professor. He was told by the secretary to take a seat and 'if there were any openings', he might get a 'few minutes' to interview Director Shriver. My father sat and waited patiently for 4 long days, watching many important people come and go. He was very discouraged; but on late Thursday, he was told by the secretary that he was to have one hour to meet with Sargent Shriver, the man that had inspired him and so many others like my father, same as President Kennedy.

But the visit was bitter sweet. Dir. Shriver and his secretary were in the process of 'clearing his desk'. Shriver gave my father a stack of folders that were all related to exactly the same research that my father was seeking, some review notes on articles, yet mostly were public documents.

As Shriver was clearing his desk, the documents that he chose to give my father were to reflect what Shriver was to be most proud of to a doctoral student in Political Science as what he wished to be his legacy and Kennedy's.

This was near the end of the time when Dir. Shriver was serving 'double duty' – to lead the Peace Corps part time, and overworked across several Johnson special projects. My father got to interview Shriver for one hour, at a very critical point in history for the U.S. Peace Corps.

Shriver asked only that my father give him the 'courtesy' to review my father's dissertation draft; which my father was to eagerly agree. Both knew approval by Shriver would assure approval by the W.V.U. professors; and it did. So my father did not get to shake hands with a president, yet arranged that honor for me. But my father got to interview and shake hands with first Peace Corps Dir. Shriver – who was a critical member of Kennedy Camelot.

Barely ten years later, I got to shake hands with yet another inspired by JFK – who became another U.S. president – and was known to both my parents and family. But that is another story. This is my father's book – about Peace Corps early years, and those he admired to create it.

Since then, many presidents from both parties of Democrat and Republicans worked together, yet we have now many challenges after a time of division, to all seek to reach out to other Americans to make a better America in order to work together for a better World – to Achieve Peace using our best technology – as Blessings From God.

As U.S. and World face so many serious challenges today, we seem to need good leaders like Kennedy, Shriver and Johnson, who truly made choices for good of both the American people and the World. So this book is also to hopefully be to re-dedicate such ideals to work within the U.S. government system to find a way – with both New Technology and Good Will – to better Serve Humankind. But also to help our Children have a Better World of Peace.

Keith Allan Jones, Ph.D. (2014)

INDEX

ABOUT THE PRIMARY AUTHOR

Charles Clyde Jones, Ph.D., was born in 1926 and died in 1983. He married Frances E. Jones, Ph.D., and has 3 grand-daughters, Andrea F. Jones, Alana R. Jones, and Emelena V. Jones. He was drafted at age of 18 to U.S. Army and assigned as a reinforcement tank gunner into combat under Gen. Patton forces at Battle of the Bulge to the final months of WWII. He was to return home to U.S. with awards including Bronze Star and French medals, as documented in many books and movies such as <u>Band of Brothers</u> and <u>Fury</u>. He was with help of the G.I. Bill to achieve academic degrees including U.S. History and Economics, and then a Ph.D. in Political Science. Later, as a Dean at Arkansas State University, he was to influence many students to include a future president, Bill Clinton. He was known as "a peaceful thoughtful good smart man".

ABOUT THE SECONDARY AUTHOR

Keith Allan Jones, Ph.D., born 1953, was from an early age inspired by both Pres. Kennedy and Johnson. Later, he served as Congressional Aide to Minority Whip Alexander during Pres. Ford years; and was to know Pres. Clinton also, in a time when bi-partisan negotiations were to benefit most American citizens, as well as all Freedom loving people for common good. As his father was to say to him: "Have faith in the Good of All Good People – and trust in God for a Better World". So after a long career as a psychologist, computer scientist, and principal data scientist consultant for NASA, EPA, FDA, DoD, DofEd, Medicare, Social Security, American Airlines and others, he continues to consult, edit and publish books for STEM secondary and higher education for courses in science and humanities.

www.ingramcontent.com/pod-product-compliance
Lightning Source LLC
Chambersburg PA
CBHW070629290526
45790CB00001B/53